TREKKING
PERU

A TRAVELER'S GUIDE

"No suelten el camino." ("Don't let go of the trail.")
—Julián Gamarra (Huaccollo outside Phinaya, Cuzco)

TREKKING
PERU

A TRAVELER'S GUIDE

ROBERT AND
DAISY KUNSTAETTER

MOUNTAINEERS
BOOKS

Mountaineers Books is the publishing division of The Mountaineers, an organization founded in 1906 and dedicated to the exploration, preservation, and enjoyment of outdoor and wilderness areas.

MOUNTAINEERS BOOKS

1001 SW Klickitat Way, Suite 201, Seattle, WA 98134
800.553.4453, www.mountaineersbooks.org

Printed in China
Distributed in the United Kingdom by Cordee, www.cordee.co.uk

First edition, 2017

Copy Editor: Jane Crosen
Design: Jen Grable
Additional Design and Layout: McKenzie Long
Cartographer: Robert Kunstaetter
Front cover photograph: *Toritos de Pucará, see Bulls on the Roof, Chapter 12* (photo by Anna Stowe Travel/Alamy)
Back cover photograph: *Escalerayoc, the monumental Inca "Stairway to Heaven" (Trek 13)*
Frontispiece: *The nearly vertical terraces on the east side of Choquequirao (Trek 22)*
All photographs by the authors unless otherwise indicated

Library of Congress Cataloging-in-Publication Data
Names: Kunstaetter, Robert, author. | Kunstaetter, Daisy, author.
Title: Trekking Peru / by Robert and Daisy Kunstaetter.
Description: First edition. | Seattle, WA : Mountaineers Books, [2017] |
    Includes index.
Identifiers: LCCN 2016039894 (print) | LCCN 2016047398 (ebook) | ISBN
    9781594858727 (trade paper) | ISBN 9781594858734 (ebook) | ISBN
    9781594858734
Subjects: LCSH: Walking—Peru—Guidebooks. | Hiking—Peru—Guidebooks |
    Peru—Description and travel. | Peru—History. | Peru—Guidebooks.
Classification: LCC GV199.44.P42 K86 2017 (print) | LCC GV199.44.P42 (ebook)
    | DDC 796.510985—dc23
LC record available at https://lccn.loc.gov/2016039894

Mountaineers Books titles may be purchased for corporate, educational, or other promotional sales, and our authors are available for a wide range of events. For information on special discounts or booking an author, contact our customer service at 800-553-4453 or mbooks@mountaineersbooks.org.

ISBN (paperback): 978-1-59485-872-7
ISBN (ebook): 978-1-59485-873-4

CONTENTS

SECTION II THE TREKS

MAP LEGEND

Contour
Glacier contour
Summit or spot elevation
(elevations in meters)

Quebrada, waterfall

Lake, river, or stream

Underground river or dry stream

Huaraz   City

Huari   Town

Acopalca   Village or hamlet

Airport

Main road (paved)

Secondary road (paved or unpaved)

Vehicle track (rough dirt)

Railroad

Pre-Hispanic road

Trail

Cross-country route

)(5250   Pass (elevation in meters)

Bog

Hotel, inn, or lodge

Community accomodations, hostel, or *tambo*

Rustic shelter

Site suitable for camping

Archaeological site

Thermal baths or hot springs

□ ●   Point of interest

Ranger station

S E   Start and end of trek

T1   Trek number

COLOMBIA

ECUADOR

PERU

BRAZIL

Tumbes

Iquitos

Piura

Moyobamba

Chiclayo

Chachapoyas

Cajamarca

Trujillo

Pucallpa

Huaraz

Huánuco

Cerro de Pasco

Lima

Huancayo

*Pacific
Ocean*

Huancavelica

Ayacucho

Puerto
Maldonado

Cuzco

Abancay

Ica

*Lake
Titicaca*

Puno

Arequipa

N

BOLIVIA

0   100   200 Km

Moquegua

Tacna

0   100   200 Miles

Scale = 1:12,000,000

CHILE

Chapters
7 Chachapoyas
8 Cordillera Blanca
9 Central Highlands
10 Cuzco
11 Arequipa
12 Lake Titicaca and Cordillera Carabaya

TREKS AT A GLANCE

TREK	CHAPTER	DISTANCE (KM)	ELEVATION (M)	DAYS
EASY				
1 GOCTA	Chachapoyas	14.5	1700–2325	1–2
15 LUICHUMARKA MAQUETTE	Central Highlands	7	3319–3534	½
17 CACHICCATA	Cuzco	14	2830–3545	1
27 PUENTE JIPATA TO MOHO	Lake Titicaca and Cordillera Carabaya	30	3850–4190	2–3
MODERATELY DIFFICULT				
2 RÍO ATUEN CIRCUIT	Chachapoyas	88	2218–3973	7–9
3 WILLKAWAIN TO AGUAK COCHA	Cordillera Blanca	11.5	3430–4590	1
4 ISHINCA TO AKILPO	Cordillera Blanca	40	3010–5075	3–4
5 LAGUNA TISHUGYOC*	Cordillera Blanca	27	3200–4795	4–5
6 HUARI TO CHACAS	Cordillera Blanca	37	3070–4530	3–4
7 CHACAS TO HUARI VIA YAUYA	Cordillera Blanca	86	2940–4385	3–9
8 MARCAJIRCA	Cordillera Blanca	11.5	2830–3800	1
10 POMABAMBA TO CHACAS	Cordillera Blanca	60	2875–4385	5–7
11 CARAZ TO YUNGAY	Cordillera Blanca	22	2250–3625	1
12 HUASQUI TO LAGUNA PACA	Central Highlands	50	3400–4222	3–4
14 PUZAPAQCHA WATERFALL	Central Highlands	15	3470–3800	1

*moderate to very difficult

TREK	CHAPTER	DISTANCE (KM)	ELEVATION (M)	DAYS
16 SONDONDO CIRCUIT	Central Highlands	48–65	2980–4205	3–8
18 HUCHUY CUZCO	Cuzco	42	3700–4472	2–3
19 Q'ESWACHACA	Cuzco	45	3650–4270	3–4
20 QOYLLUR RIT'I	Cuzco	40	3826–5020	3–4
23 HUANCACALLE TO MACHU PICCHU	Cuzco	56	1573–4567	5–6
24 COTAHUASI CANYON	Arequipa	61	1520–3435	3–4
28 MOHO TO TILALI	Lake Titicaca and Cordillera Carabaya	32	3860–4355	3

DIFFICULT

9 ALPAMAYO	Cordillera Blanca	57	3130–4868	6–10
13 LLOCLLAPAMPA TO HUAROCHIRI	Central Highlands	102	2710–4829	9–11
22 CHOQUEQUIRAO TO HUANCACALLE	Cuzco	84	1500–4600	8–12
25 COTAHUASI TO VALLEY OF THE VOLCANOES	Arequipa	52	3475–4943	3–4
29 ALLIN CAPAC LAKES	Lake Titicaca and Cordillera Carabaya	27	4300–5080	3–4

VERY DIFFICULT

21 VILCANOTA TO CARABAYA	Cuzco	135	3800–5250	14
26 VALLEY OF THE VOLCANOES TO COLCA	Arequipa	79	2065–5171	6–8
30 CARABAYA TRAVERSE	Lake Titicaca and Cordillera Carabaya	103	2680–5075	12–14

FOREWORD

Those of us who trek know, deep down, that we can never arrive at our journey's end . . .

A young Italian friend (a confirmed city-dweller) once said to me, as we were trekking along the stony and inhospitable desert coast of Peru: "How stunning the Earth must have been before humans reshaped it!" Until then I had never considered how many areas of the planet had been totally redesigned and, through human activity, had lost their authenticity.

It was that very desert that had attracted me as a child. Dozing against the window of the car as we travelled along the Panamerican Highway, I dreamed of walking toward the mountains and never stopping. It is still my dream.

It would, however, be foolish to depict Peru as an untainted paradise. Peru does have much untouched, virgin land to inspire dreams and invite exploration. But it also has many landscapes that have been transformed with less-than-harmonious results.

In this country opposite extremes are more obvious than anywhere else. Lima offers all the beauty and ugliness of a crowded metropolis; aggressive, chaotic, and stubbornly claiming to be modern. Yet not far away, you can breathe in the tranquillity of a mountain village still unaware that the 17th century ended a long time ago.

The heavy machinery that builds roads here, there, and everywhere has to stop once in a while to give way to a shepherd and his flock, while nearby an indigenous matron shouts stridently, in Quechua, into her smart phone. On every city corner, the traffic light, trapped like a dragonfly in a web of indecipherable cables, glows red with rage, powerless, because none of the mototaxi drivers pays it the slightest heed. Technology has burst into Peru with no respect for an ancient world, setting in motion an unending chain of clashes.

There is however the other Peru. Boundless, timeless, alien to the present, and eternal. The country of the driest desert, the richest sea with an abundance of fish and birds, the highest snowcapped peaks in the tropics, the idyllic countryside where people still work communal land with song and laughter, and the endless jungle that teems with life reverberating in every tree, every leaf, and every drop of water.

This is the Peru that Robert and Daisy know so well, better than anyone, I would say. Their perseverance in accumulating a treasure-trove of knowledge step by step, through years of first-hand experience, research, and discovery, has given them an unmatched insight into this land. They haven't simply travelled around the country; with their footsteps they have woven a vast carpet that, in these pages, they depict faithfully sharing all they have learned.

And with what results! In addition to their knack for tracking down what really matters, they have an exceptional capacity for conveying it, giving detailed instructions for how to enjoy what they have experienced and relive it as if for the first time.

I have had the good fortune and special privilege of trekking with them on several occasions, both on long difficult stretches and on easier walks of only a few hours. It is a pleasure to see how they complement and understand each other in all the tasks that outdoor adventure demands and it is even more remarkable when you realize that they have been doing this for a lifetime together! For an old grouch like me, who would rather be seen as the terrifying Yeti that no one dares approach, this is doubly admirable.

Only those who love what they do have the patience and dedication to crisscross continents and record everything that they find along the way. And this, I believe, is what all of us who trek share. Who would take the time to paint a landscape when they could photograph it so much more easily? Only someone who loves to paint and wants to add something of him or herself to their creation. Trekkers likewise interpret the landscape with their feet, their eyes, and all their senses, in ways that a camera or motor vehicle can never do.

Besides, as Aristotle rightly said, walking with obstacles in one's path is far more rewarding than walking across flat land, and it's far less tiring! I recall a trek of several months through the coastal desert of Peru in which I was forced to stick to the highway for long periods because huge cliffs didn't allow any alternative. How difficult and depressing it was! In contrast, after struggling (almost crawling) up gigantic sand dunes that swallowed my every step, I leapt about like a goat, rejoicing and reinvigorated by the sight of the new scenery that lay before me when I at last reached the crest.

This is another trait shared by trekkers: we nourish and fortify ourselves by contemplating nature, that natural beauty greater than ourselves, that we cannot duplicate nor at times understand, and that, regardless of how many elements comprise it, is always in harmony. Such vast beauty often has the effect of making us feel very small, and feeling small is the first step toward seeing things as they are.

Ay! How I cringe to see people strutting on treadmills in the gym, staring at a video screen. With Robert and Daisy you won't embark on a disciplined exercise regime or strive for athletic goals, you'll be riding on the shoulders of two dreamers, albeit dreamers with their feet firmly on the ground, who will lead you down paths and into corners from which the world can be better appreciated.

As I said at the outset, it's a question of experiencing the journey, of passage not arrival.

I have learned so much in the company of this remarkable pair of trekkers. Their frugality and their generosity, their good judgment, their gentle yet indomitable spirit, their noble hearts. Their respect for their fellow human beings no matter what their condition and their capacity to retain a curious child's delight at all the surprises with which each new route presents them. They are a couple worth emulating.

I am honoured and very happy that they have allowed me to write to their readers and express my admiration.

—*Ricardo Espinosa*
translated by Ben Box

PRÓLOGO

Los que caminamos sabemos -en el fondo- que no llegaremos nunca a ninguna parte . . . Recuerdo lo que me dijo una vez con asombro una joven amiga italiana, citadina a ultranza, cuando paseábamos por la árida, pedregosa e inhóspita costa peruana: ¡Así de espectacular debe haber sido la Tierra antes de que el hombre la transformara! Jamás había pensado hasta entonces que había zonas del planeta que habían sido totalmente rediseñadas y, humanizadas, habían perdido su originalidad.

Fue ese mismo desierto el que me había atraído desde niño, cuando viajaba adormecido, apoyado contra la ventana del auto en la carretera Panamericana, y me había hecho soñar repetidamente con caminar hacia las montañas y no detenerme jamás. Todavía sueño con ello.

Pero sería imprudente pintar un paraíso. El Perú tiene mucho de tierra no tocada, virginal, que te incita a soñar y te invita a seguir y seguir, sin parar; pero también tiene muchos paisajes transformados, y no exactamente de manera armónica.

En este país se dan cita los polos opuestos más que en ningún otro lugar. Uno no acaba de salir de una ciudad como Lima, con toda la belleza y la fealdad de una populosa urbe que pretende ser moderna, aunque agresiva y caótica, y ya está respirando la quietud de un pueblito serrano al que nadie le avisó que el siglo XVII terminó hace mucho.

La maquinaria pesada que construye carreteras por doquier se detiene cada tanto para dejar que pase un pastor y sus animales, mientras cerca una mamacha le grita con voz aguda, en quechua, desde el interior de una combi, a su teléfono inteligente. El semáforo, rojo de impotencia porque no hay chofer de mototaxi que lo tome en cuenta, luce como una libélula atrapada en una telaraña de cables imposible de descifrar, en cada esquina. La tecnología se introdujo con velocidad irrespetuosa en un mundo anciano, ocasionando un choque en cadena que no termina de producirse.

Sin embargo, hay otro Perú. El más grande, sin tiempo, ajeno al presente, y eterno. El país del desierto más seco, del mar más productivo, repleto de peces y aves, de las montañas nevadas tropicales más altas, de las campiñas de ensueño donde la gente aún trabaja la tierra de todos cantando y riendo, y de la jungla interminable infestada de vida bullendo en cada árbol, en cada hoja, en cada gota de agua.

Y ese otro Perú lo conocen muy bien Robert y Daisy; mejor que nadie, diría yo. Su sorprendente perseverancia para sumar paso a paso, años de búsqueda y descubrimiento, los ha hecho dueños de un caudal de conocimiento sobre esta tierra que es un tesoro único y valiosísimo. Ellos no solo recorren el país; lo que hacen es dibujar y tejer una gran alfombra con sus andares, retratando de manera fiel y al mismo tiempo muy propia, todo lo que en él se encuentra.

¡Y qué resultado! A las habilidades para rastrear lo que realmente vale la pena conocer le suman una capacidad excepcional para relatarlo, dando las pautas precisas para disfrutarlo tanto como ellos y repetir su experiencia de manera integral.

He tenido la suerte de caminar con ellos en algunas oportunidades, tanto en tramos largos y difíciles como en paseos de unas horas, y lo considero un regalo muy especial. Es un placer ver cómo se compenetran y complementan en las tareas propias del excursionismo y es aún más notable cuando te das cuenta de que ¡llevan toda una vida haciéndolo juntos! Para un viejo cascarrabias como yo, que prefiere ser temido como al "yeti" para que nadie se acerque, esto es doblemente admirable.

La paciencia y la dedicación con la que recorren el continente (y el planeta) y registran todo lo encontrado, solo la tienen quienes aman lo que hacen. Y eso, creo, lo compartimos todos los que caminamos.

¿Quién se pondría a pintar un paisaje si puede fotografiarlo tan fácilmente? pues el que ama pintar y conoce las satisfacciones que produce, además de la posibilidad de agregarle algo de uno mismo y recrear lo que ve. Eso es caminar, a diferencia de trasladarse a algún lugar en cualquier vehículo, lo que uno hace es interpretar el paisaje con sus pies, con sus ojos y con todos los sentidos, viviendo cada detalle y cada momento como en una obra de arte.

Además, debemos confesarlo junto con Aristóteles, el caminar con obstáculos es mucho más agradable que caminar sobre terreno plano, ¡y cansa menos! Recuerdo que en una caminata de varios meses por el desierto costero peruano estuve obligado en tramos largos a continuar por la carretera pues los enormes precipicios no dejaban otra opción. ¡Qué duro y deprimente fue! En cambio, trepando cuesta arriba, casi a rastras, por gigantescas dunas que se tragaban mis pasos, llegaba a la cima y empezaba a saltar como una cabra, feliz, con energías renovadas por la visión de los nuevos paisajes que me esperaban adelante.

Esa es otra característica de los caminantes: nos alimentamos y recibimos nuestra fuerza principalmente de la contemplación de la naturaleza, de esa belleza natural que nos sobrepasa, que no podemos repetir y a veces ni entender, que no importando cuántos elementos tenga, siempre es armónica. Esa belleza gigantesca que suele tener el efecto de hacernos sentir muy pequeños, y sentirse pequeño es el primer paso para ver las cosas tal como son.

¡Ay! cuando veo gente caminando sobre fajas sin fin mientras ven una pantalla... se me encogen las tripas. Con Robert y Daisy no se montarán en un tren de ejercicios disciplinados ni de metas atléticas, se subirán a los hombros de dos soñadores -con ambos pies bien puestos en la tierra- que los llevarán por senderos y rincones desde donde el mundo se ve mejor.

Como decía al principio, lo nuestro es pasar, no llegar.

Es mucho lo que he aprendido de mi cercanía a esta dupla de caminantes tan singular. Su austeridad y su generosidad, su buen juicio, su espíritu manso pero indomable, su gran corazón. Su respeto por el prójimo sin importar su condición y su capacidad para seguir gozando como niños curiosos de las sorpresas que depara toda nueva ruta. Una pareja digna de imitar.

Que hoy me hayan permitido escribirle a sus lectores y mostrarles mi admiración, es un gran honor que me ha hecho muy feliz.

—*Ricardo Espinosa*

ACKNOWLEDGMENTS

A well-known form of acknowledgment is to say that one has stood on the shoulders of giants. We have had the privilege of following their large strides and sure footsteps. Ricardo Espinosa provided endless valuable advice regarding trekking routes, reviewed various chapters, wrote the foreword, and always guided us with his enthusiasm and his example. Ben Box's example as a professional guidebook writer, a true gentleman, and a scholar has likewise been guiding us for many years. Ben skillfully translated Ricardo's foreword into English. Also exemplary are our adoptive parents, Baruch and Aviva Aziza, enthusiastic campers into their eighties who watched over us and vicariously lived all our adventures in Peru. The example of soft-spoken kindness and generosity set by our very own gentle giant, the late Craig Kolthoff, will always be with us.

We are grateful to the following specialists, who either contributed information or reviewed sections in their respective areas of expertise: César Abad (cartography and Sondondo), José Bareda (cartography), Chris Benway (Cordillera Blanca), Stephen Bezruchka (medicine), Richar Cáceres (Carabaya), Alberto and Aidé Cafferata (Cordillera Blanca and Sondondo), Paul Cripps (Cuzco), Rob Dover (Chachapoyas), Leo Duncan (Cuzco), Peter Frost (Cuzco), John Gorfinkel (medicine), Alex Guttman (medicine), Klaus Hartl (Arequipa), José Mestas (Puno), Justo Motta (Cotahuasi), Gustavo Reeves (Conchucos), Gustavo Rondón (Arequipa), Mark Smith (Cuzco), and Hernando Tavera (seismology).

For their hospitality on and off the trail, we thank Nilda Aldoradín (Cabana), David and Alicia Aliaga (Isca Jaa), Eladio and Victoria Asencios (Sharco), Florencio and Edubiges Ayma (Perccaro), Roberto and Adelaida Barzola (Tingo), Ladislao and Hilda Bellota (Andahuaylillas), Wilson Benítez (Jacabamba), María Bolaños (Junuta), Catalina Borda (Cotahuasi), Otto Brun (Orurillo), José Cahuana (Siani), Wilgen and Norma Cajamarca, Efraín and Evelina Carrión (Yanatile), Isidro and Juana Ccanccapa (Chaccone), Santos Ccoa (Chaupicocha), Revelino Chávez (Hualcayán), Miguel Chayguaque (Cullicocha), Flavio and Yolanda Cobos (Huancacalle), Julián Cutipa (Aymaña), Raymundo Cuyo (Ccotaña), Saida Espinoza (Santa Rosa Baja), Orel and Zenayda Fernández (Otutupampa), Hilario and Hermelinda Figueroa (Huecroncocha), Pascual and Rosalvina Flores (Andamarca), Julián Gamarra (Huaccollo), Mario Hacho (Pacaje), Ciriaco Huamán (Racachaca), Epifania Huamán (Yanama), Nelson and Nelly Huamán (Cochabamba), Wilmer Huamán (Chuquibamba), Apolonio Jara (Morocancha), Aníbal and Elizabet Jiménez (Yanacancha), Valentín and Victoria Laucata (Hanccoyo), Irene Mallma (Sondondo), Rosa Mamani (Huancané Apacheta), Filomeno and Dina Medina (Soro), Ignacio and Claviana Mendoza (Ragrajpamba), Freddy Mollo (Chachas), Roberto Moncada (Cabanaconde), Máximo Pérez (Maucallacta), Hermenejildo and Viviana Pitanzo (Taucca), Juan and Epifanía Ramos (Hampatura), Valentín and Tomasa Saca (Maizal), Marcelino Santana (Yanaututo), Teófila Tantavilca (Tambo Real), César Totocayo (Puyca), René Urquizo (Chaupo),

Neira Valladares (Acochaca), Juan Velázquez (Maucallacta), Manuel Zaumar (Atuén), Cristina Zinni (Vilcabamba), Teresa Zorrilla (Huaritambo), Alí and Marlene (Andagua), Ramiro and Janeth (Quechualla), Julio César and Virginia (Rosariopampa), Mechi and Jorge (Tarmatambo), Edwin, Hildebrant, and Filomena (Incapatacuna), Simeón and Martín (Upis), and Gavino, Roxana, and David (Chillca).

Our special thanks to Kirsten Colton, Jane Crosen, Jen Grable, Lynn Greisz, McKenzie Long, Mary Metz, Kate Rogers, and the entire team at Mountaineers Books; it is a pleasure to work with such skilled professionals.

Others who helped in many different ways include Giraldo and Juana Aguirre, Manolo Alegría, Alex and Adán Ancalle, Dimitry Balberin, Carola Behrendt, Henry Blanco, Jean Brown, Carlos and Charo Burga, Gina Cáceres, Jorge and Wanda Cobos, Mariluz Covarrubias, Cayetano Crispín, Jean-Jacques Decoster, Rigoberto Delgado, Felipe Díaz, Yahira Echarri, Nora Espinosa, Pedro and Lidia Flores, Wilfredo Flores, Grupos GEA Andagua y Cotahuasi, Evaristo Hancco, Kieron Heath, Michel Hediger, Jonathan Hollander, Rainer Hostnig, José and Lucía Hualca, Sixto Huamani, Leonidas Huisocayna, Emiliano Huizacayma, Bebel and Margarita Ibarra, Ernesto Jancco, Lou Jost, Henry Lares, Valentín and Victoria Laucata, Padre Lino, Pedro Lizarzaburu, Héctor López, Yonny López, Felipe Mayoría, Honorato Menéndez, Nenny Menéndez and family, Benita Merma, Juan and Dionisia Merma, Diana Morris, Marcelo and Grace Naranjo, Jesús Nolberto, Ali O'Neal, Vicente Paloma, Eudosia and Raul Peña, Juan Pérez, Walter Pérez, Gerardo Pinto, Michel Portier, Jesús Quispe, Ariel Ramírez, Froilan Ramos, William Reyes, Clímaco Romero, Francisco Romero, Boudewijn de Roover, Raúl Rosas, Pablo and Carolina Saavedra, Janeth Saliz, Ronal Salvador, Percy and Analía Sánchez, Marcos Sánchez, Waldo and Fabiola Sánchez, Cecilia de Sarfaty, Ella Smyth, Noemí Soto, Felipe Varela, Sandro Vilcape, Carlos Zárate, Teresa Zorrillo, Celso and Braulia, Felix and Petita, Fernando, and Gregoriana.

SECTION I

INTRODUCTION

1

TREKKING IN PERU

WHAT IS TREKKING?

Two days before leaving for Peru to begin researching this book, we attended a family gathering and could not resist regaling our relatives with enthusiastic plans for the project. To our surprise, a worldly and well-traveled cousin, Daniel, asked, somewhat naively, "What exactly is trekking?" We did not have the opportunity to offer him a thoughtful reply at the time, but the subsequent three years and 1500 km on the trail gave us ample opportunity to ponder the question. If you are reading this book, then chances are that you already have your own ideas about trekking. We briefly offer ours to give a better sense of who we are and what you might expect from us in the following pages.

To us, trekking is more than just a form of tourism, sport, or leisure; it is our passion. Independence appeals to us. We like carrying everything we need on our own backs, relying on our own abilities to safely enjoy a long journey, and immersing ourselves in solitude and the rhythm of life on the trail. We are curious, always seeking out new routes, new experiences, and new forms of cross-cultural interaction. We love all aspects of nature. For some people,

spirituality is a quest for supernatural experiences; for us it is inspired by the boundless wonders of the natural world. We enjoy challenges: climbing a higher pass, photographing a tiny flower or an elusive bird, making a better map, and the challenge of adapting to the unexpected. Above all, we are grateful for the privilege of exploring and trekking together.

We warmly invite you to share our passion and our interests in a land that is ideally suited to them.

WHY PERU?

Peru has everything for the trekker. No other country in South America combines the variety of world-class natural, archaeological, and living cultural attractions that Peru does, making them all part of an exceptionally rich and diverse trekking experience.

The nation's heritage includes an ancestral tradition of long-distance foot travel. Horses were introduced only in the 16th century by the conquering Spaniards. Centuries earlier the Inca Empire had consolidated, improved, and extended tens of thousands of kilometers of *runa ñan* (people's roads) built by previous civilizations, to create one of the greatest road networks of the world.

Peru boasts 190 protected natural areas, covering 17 percent of the country's surface area and home to 84 of the 117 life-zones on Earth. They include glaciated mountain ranges dropping through cloud forests and fertile green valleys to the Amazon jungle. These national parks and reserves offer outstanding trekking venues. Other superb routes simply run from village to village, or one archaeological site to another; sheer remoteness being their best protection.

Peru receives around three million visitors a year, but many have only heard about the country's most famous attraction: Machu Picchu. For all its fame and glory, this "lost city of the Incas" and the fragment of Inca road leading to it are just tips of the proverbial iceberg. For those seeking a more authentic and affordable trekking experience, Peru offers a grand array of outstanding alternatives spread over vast and seldom-visited territory.

Tourism infrastructure is good, and getting to and around Peru can be quite easy and comfortable. Agencies offer all-inclusive treks in the more popular areas, such as Cuzco and the Cordillera Blanca, where there are also ample opportunities for independent trekkers to rent gear, obtain supplies, and hire guides, porters, or muleteers. Farther afield, trekkers must be self-sufficient, but the extra effort is richly rewarded by a genuinely independent trek through uncharted territory.

Peru's climate is reasonably predictable, with a well-defined trekking season from May through September. Acclimatization to altitude is an important consideration in highland areas, but elevations are nonetheless substantially lower than in the Himalaya, and there are also lower-elevation valley routes.

EXPLORERS AND TREKKERS

Peruvians have trekked since time immemorial to reach their crops, tend their flocks, trade with neighboring regions, and create empires. Foreign trekkers in Peru are also not an invention of the 21st century. For over five hundred years the country has attracted rogues, adventurers, and explorers who traveled its many roads and trails in search of elusive goals. The following is but a small and eclectic sample; references to their works and exploits are given in Appendix A.

From 1549 to 1550, conquistador and chronicler **Pedro Cieza de León** traveled extensively in early Peru to gather material for his book El Señorío de los Incas. Unlike others of his generation, he "trekked" to observe and record, rather than merely plunder.

From 1570 to 1575, **Francisco de Toledo**, the fifth Viceroy of Peru, had himself carried in a litter along Inca roads throughout the territory he had been sent to rule. That's hardly trekking, but it is an early attempt to come to grips with the immensity of Peru (which at the time included large parts of Bolivia and Argentina) rather than simply taking up residence in Pizarro's Palace in Lima. Toledo later became infamous for ordering the execution of the last Inca, Tupac Amaru (see Toledo's biography by Arthur F. Zimmerman).

In 1802 German **Baron Alexander von Humboldt** traveled in Peru as part of a much larger Latin American scientific expedition, described in Cosmos—an enormous treatise written over the rest of his

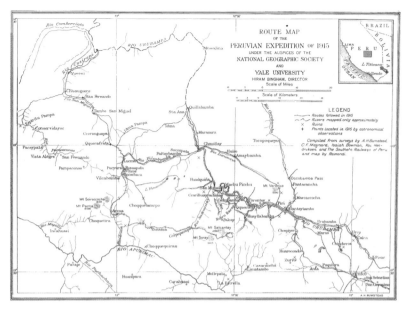

Map of Hiram Bingham's 1915 Peru expedition (by A. H. Bumstead, National Geographic, *May 1916)*

life. Among his many achievements was the discovery of the cold ocean current that bears his name. It bathes the coast of Peru and regulates much of the country's climate.

Sir Clements Markham, the British explorer and later president of the Royal Geographical Society, traveled to Peru in 1852 in a successful search for the bark of the chinchona tree, from which quinine was extracted to treat malaria. He tells his own story in *Travels in Peru*, while a comprehensive historical review is found in Mark Honigsbaum's *The Fever Trail*.

Antonio Raimondi was an Italian professor and true renaissance man who traveled and explored throughout Peru during three decades starting in 1850. His discoveries span the disciplines of geography, archaeology, geology, and botany and are detailed in *El Perú*. Among the most emblematic is the *Puya raimondii* plant (see Queen of the Andes, Chapter 2).

George Squier arrived in Peru in 1863 as representative of the United States government. Following the completion of his duties he traveled throughout the country investigating and sketching archaeological sites. His published work, *Peru Illustrated*, provides a valuable record of many ancient structures, like the rope suspension bridge over the Río Apurímac, which have since been lost.

August Weberbauer, a German naturalist, explored Peru in the early 20th century in search of new plant species. Numerous publications between 1905 and 1942, including *Flora of Peru*, record his findings. A genus of cactus and various plant species bear his name.

Yale University history professor **Hiram Bingham III** traveled to Peru in 1911 and found Machu Picchu, Vitcos, and Vilcabamba. He returned in 1912, 1914, and 1915, with the support of Yale and the National Geographic Society.

His discovery of Machu Picchu has been disputed, but his work unquestionably brought the site to the forefront of world attention, as told in *Lost City of the Incas* and two extensive *National Geographic* articles.

During 1953-54, **Victor von Hagen**, under the auspices of the American Geographical Society, traveled throughout Peru to explore, describe, photograph, and film the Inca road system, as described in his book *Highway of the Sun*.

During the 1960s and 1980s, **Gene Savoy** made several journeys of exploration from the United States to Peru. He was a controversial, larger-than-life figure but is unequivocally credited with identifying the location of the last stronghold of the Incas at Vilcabamba (as told in his book *Antisuyo*), as well as later discoveries in the Chachapoyas area.

Canadian archaeologist and writer **Ronald Wright** traveled the Peruvian highlands in the late 1970s. In an entertaining and informative book (*Cut Stones and Crossroads*), he shares his knowledge of ancient Peru and contemporary Peru of the time. Although somewhat dated, his work is very insightful.

In the early 1980s, American archaeologist **John Hyslop** undertook a detailed scientific study of Inca roads in Peru and Ecuador. His book *The Inka Road System* remains a landmark work in the field.

Starting in 1982, American architect **Vincent Lee** led various expeditions to Vilcabamba. He has published a comprehensive history of the site, entitled *Forgotten Vilcabamba*, including a detailed set of technical drawings.

British-born writer, photographer, and independent scholar **Peter Frost** traveled throughout Peru in the 1970s, circum-ambulating Lake Titicaca. A National Geographic expeditions grantee in 2001, he specializes in investigation of the Incas. His latest guidebook is *Exploring Cuzco*.

Limeño **Ricardo Espinosa** (known as "El Caminante") walked the entire desert coast of Peru in 1995-96 to write *El Perú a Toda Costa*. In 1999 he trekked 2000 km of diverse Andean terrain, mostly along the Capac Ñan (Great Inca Road), from Quito, Ecuador, across Peru, to La Paz, Bolivia. His experiences, maps, and photographs are published in a bilingual book faithful to the grandeur of the road it describes (*La Gran Ruta Inca*). His subsequent work includes a compendium of the country's national parks and reserves (*Areas Naturales Protegidas*).

Felipe Varela ("El Chaski") is a tireless Peruvian promoter of the living cultural importance of the Inca road system. Having walked thousands of miles since 2000, he is known along the length and breadth of the *runa ñan* he fiercely defends. See Appendix A for his blog's address.

As a trekker you will be following in these large footsteps. Please do so humbly and responsibly (see Chapter 3), being sensitive to the fragility of the natural and cultural environments. And expect the unexpected—for, to this day, trekking in Peru is all about exploration.

THE WORLD'S GREATEST ROAD

[A]nd they built a road, the most haughty seen in the world, the longest, because it left Cuzco and arrived in Quito and it joined the one going to Chile. Its greatness is unmatched in all human history, carved along deep valleys and high sierras, over snow-capped mountains and quagmires, alongside

*raging torrents, hewn out of the living
rock. Through these places it went,
level and cobbled, with foundations
along the slopes, well cut into the mountains, carved into the cliffs, with retaining walls along the rivers, with steps and
landings in the snow; everywhere clean
and swept. Along the way it was full of
lodges, storehouses laden with treasure,
temples of the sun, posthouses. Oh!
What grandeur can we ascribe to Alexander the Great, or any of the mighty
kings that ruled the world, that they
should build such a road? Neither the
great Roman road that passed through
Spain, nor others we read about, can
compare to this road.*

—Pedro Cieza de León, 1553
El Señorío de los Incas

In the Old World all roads once led to Rome.
In the Andes of South America they led to
Cuzco. Considered by the Incas to be the
navel of the universe, Cuzco was capital of

*Escalerayoc, the monumental Inca "stairway
to heaven" (Trek 13)*

the empire they called Tawantinsuyo, mean-
ing "union of the cardinal points." Cuzco
was connected to the far-flung reaches
of this vast empire by an extraordinary
30,000-kilometer road network, designated
a UNESCO World Heritage Site in 2014.

Two parallel trunks of the Capac
Ñan (Qhapaq Ñan) or Great Road ran
north–south from Colombia all the way
to central Chile and Argentina, one
along the spine of the Andes, the other
on the Pacific coast. These were linked
by east–west roads joining the coast and
the mountains like rungs of a ladder,
with extensions farther east toward the
Amazon basin. *Suyo* means direction, district, province, or region, and the roads
went north to Chinchaysuyo, today
northern Peru, Ecuador, and Colombia;
south to Collasuyo, now Bolivia,
Argentina, and Chile; east to Antisuyo,
eastern Peru, and parts of Bolivia; and
west to Contisuyo, by Arequipa and the
Peruvian coast. Off the Collasuyo road,
a branch went southeast to Omasuyo,
around Lake Titicaca.

The impressive extent of the road network was rivaled only by the quality and
audacity of its construction. Climbing
to 5000 m above sea level, roads usually
ranged from 3 to 10 m in width, but
reached an amazing 30 m in some places.
Many had smooth cobbled surfaces, while
steeper portions climbed to passes and
summits on immense stone stairways.
On many sheer slopes the roads were
supported by retaining walls. In wet areas
they were drained by culverts and carried
over swamps on raised causeways. In populated areas, roads were lined by adobe
walls to prevent travelers, and the llamas
used as pack animals, from invading
neighboring homes and fields.

Many swift rivers rush down the slopes of the Andes, and the Capac Ñan used various ingenious strategies to cross them. These ranged from simple low wood and stone bridges to spectacular suspension bridges built of rope cables supported by massive stone columns. In a few places travelers crossed rivers on ferries or in *oroyas*, baskets hung from ropes, a sort of ancient cable car. The Río Desaguadero, outflow of Lake Titicaca, was spanned by a unique pontoon bridge supported by *totora* reed boats.

The grandeur of the Capac Ñan often exceeded the transportation needs of the areas it served. It was as much a monumental work, like the pyramids of Egypt, as a purely utilitarian one. The Great Road was the umbilical cord that emanated from Cuzco, navel of the universe, carrying wealth to the capital of Tawantinsuyo as well as imprinting its sovereignty on the landscape of distant dominions.

Not just anyone was allowed to travel the Capac Ñan; it was reserved for those on official state business. Privileged travelers included the Inca emperor and his court, generals with their troops, government bureaucrats, llama caravans bearing goods to Cuzco, and, in one of the Inca's major sociopolitical innovations, the *mitmaq* or *mitmacuna*. These were entire communities subjugated by the Inca Empire and sent as a group to live thousands of miles from their original homes. This effectively quelled rebellion among newly conquered peoples and distributed a diversity of skills and crafts throughout the empire. Even today, the influence of the Cañari people of the southern highlands of Ecuador, who were taken south as *mitmaq* by the Incas, can be

Inca suspension bridge (from chronicles of Felipe Guamán Poma, 1613)

felt in Cajamarca, Peru, and even distant Bolivia.

The swiftest feet to tread the stones of the Capac Ñan were those of the *chaskis*, messengers who ran a tag-team relay race that enabled them to move verbal messages (the Incas had no written language) and *kipus*, knotted strings used to record accounting, 250 km a day. This meant news could travel from Cuzco to Quito (today Ecuador, then the northern capital of Tawantinsuyo) in about a week, and seafood could be brought from the ocean to the royal table in Cuzco in less than two days.

The Great Road was lined by various facilities for travelers. There were thousands of *tambos*, post-houses of various sizes, one about every 25 km, which corresponds to roughly a day's travel. The larger *tambos* had travelers' accommodations called *kallankas*, corrals for llamas, and storehouses for merchandise. The road was also lined by fortresses or guard posts called *pucarás*, and by *apachetas*, large mounds of stones used to mark intersections and mountain passes as well as for ceremonial and religious purposes.

Maintenance of the road and its associated infrastructure was the responsibility of local communities, as a form of *mit'a*, tax or tribute to the Inca rulers. Following the Spanish conquest, many parts of the road fell into disrepair because of the collapse of this system and also because of the introduction of horses. The Incas had not invented the wheel, largely unnecessary in their geographic environment, nor did they have horses or donkeys. The Capac Ñan was designed for human feet and the delicate hooves of llamas and alpacas.

The segments of ancient road that best survived the colonial period were those that were too steep for travel by horse and were therefore not damaged by iron-shod hooves. Sadly, some of the surviving roads later fell victim to contemporary road construction. The Inca roads were so well built that, over five hundred years after they had been abandoned, engineers continued to use them as foundations for paved streets and roads. Today this practice is, in principle, prohibited, but modern roads are often built sufficiently near the Capac Ñan that the latter is buried by construction debris.

Fortunately many sections still survive intact, some over 100 km long. The best ones are in Peru, and they are among the country's most spectacular trekking routes. Except for the small fragment of Inca road that today carries five hundred visitors a day to Machu Picchu, they are seldom visited by outsiders. Perhaps responsible trekking can play its part in protecting the road by raising awareness of its importance and by bringing sustainable economic benefits to the remote communities through which it passes.

The authors trekked 400 km along the Capac Ñan in 2007, and that extraordinary experience has been one of the inspirations for this book. Segments of Inca and pre-Inca roads are included in Treks 2, 7, 12, 13, 17, 18, 22, 23, 27, 28, and 30. They are likely included in others as well, albeit without our knowledge. Who really understands the origins of all the winding paths along which we travel?

2

PERU AND ITS PEOPLE

For sources of additional background information, see Appendix A.

GEOGRAPHY AND GEOLOGY

Peru, located along the Pacific coast of South America, is larger than many people realize. At 1,285,216 sq km, it is the third-largest country on the continent. The Andes are the principal topographic feature, a massive mountainous spine that defines three regions: coast, highlands, and Amazon basin. The magnificent scenery we see today has been forged by geologic events over millions of years, most significantly the uplifting of the Andes. Growth of these colossal mountains is the result of subduction of the Nazca tectonic plate under the South American plate. The Amazon River, which some twenty-five million years ago flowed to the Pacific, found its route blocked by the rising Andes and eventually made its way to the Atlantic. The Amazon and coastal plains were both formed by alluvial sediments arising from the Andes. Volcanic activity and earth tremors, both related to the shift of the tectonic plates, as well as water, wind, and glacial erosion, are all forces that constantly mold the Andean slopes and their surroundings.

Coast

This densely populated region, *La Costa*, is a narrow strip of land 2424 km long, 12 percent of Peru's surface area. In the far north are some forests, but most of the Peruvian coast is desert where rivers originating in the Andes create fertile oases. Mangoes, grapes, citrus, olives, asparagus, and cotton are among the most important crops, some of which are exported.

Highlands

The Andean highlands represent 28 percent of Peru's territory. Steep mountain ranges incised by deep rivers (including the deepest canyons in the world) rise dramatically to the east of the coast and make up *La Sierra*. Several massive ranges run parallel to the coastline from northwest to southeast, 250 km wide in the north, 400 km wide in the south where they surround high plateaus. Thirty-two mountains exceed 6000 m; the highest is Huascarán (6768 m) in the Cordillera Blanca. Peru has the highest concentration of glaciers in the tropics, receding rapidly with climate change. In the southern highlands are several volcanoes, some of them active. Lakes dot the highland scenery, including the large Lago

Titicaca (3810 m) and Lago Junín (4080 m). Cities and towns are found in river valleys, on plateaus, or perched on mountain slopes, many of them between 3000 m and 4000 m. Most highland valleys are cultivated or used for grazing. The best trekking opportunities in Peru are in the highlands, and this region is the focus of this book.

Amazon Basin

To the east of the Andes lies *La Selva*, the jungle, Peru's largest (60 percent of surface area) and least populated region. Countless rivers drain the eastern slopes of the mountains to form six main tributaries of the Amazon. Here Peru is at its widest and has borders with Brazil and Colombia. Rainfall in the jungle is very high, in contrast to other regions of the country.

Administrative Divisions

Peru is administratively divided into twenty-five *regiónes*, formerly called *departamentos*, a term still in use. Each *región* is divided into *provincias*, which are in turn divided into *distritos*.

CLIMATE

In Peru, the terms *verano* (summer) and *invierno* (winter) are ambiguous and best avoided. In principle, they refer to the seasons of the Southern Hemisphere where Peru is located, but in the highlands they may denote the dry and wet seasons, respectively, which is exactly the reverse. Climate information is available from the Peruvian meteorological service, SENAMHI; see Appendix A. Climate charts for the trekking areas in this book are found on www.trekkingperu.org.

Coast

Average annual temperatures are 24°C in the north, 18°C on the central and southern coast. The cold Humboldt ocean current arising in Antarctica runs north along the Peruvian coast. Prevailing winds pick up so little moisture over the cold water that there is hardly any precipitation, hence the coastal desert. During May to November, humidity in the tradewinds cools over the water and condenses, forming a layer of mist known as *garúa*, up to an altitude of 1000 m; and temperatures are cool, around 13°C. From December to April skies are clear, it is hot, and the air is dry.

Highlands

Temperature is determined mostly by elevation. The wet season is November to March, with an average daytime temperature of 18°C, and nights only a little cooler. During the dry season, May to September, there are great daily temperature fluctuations: mornings and afternoons are cool, it gets hot at midday, and nights are very cold, often below freezing. April and October are transition months and less predictable but can be good for trekking. Trekking in the valleys is possible at any time of year, although during the wet season there may be snow at higher elevations, trails are very muddy, and some roads become impassable. The dry season sees most visitors.

Amazon Basin

The jungle has a hot and humid climate with very high precipitation. There can be rain at any time of the year. The wet season is November to April, the drier season May to October.

Peru's spectacular biodiversity comes in all shapes and sizes.

El Niño

This global climatic phenomenon is associated with a periodic warming of the equatorial Pacific Ocean. During an El Niño year the coast of Peru may experience unusually high temperatures, heavy rains, high tides, and flooding, while drier-than-usual conditions may occur in the highlands and jungle. Historically El Niño occurred about every five years; however, this pattern has changed in the 21st century. For current information, see the El Niño website, Appendix A.

FLORA AND FAUNA

Peru is among the ten most biodiverse countries on Earth. It has two marine and nine land ecological regions, and over 17,000 species of trees. Peruvian fauna is very rich with some 462 species of mammals, 1822 species of birds, 379 amphibians, and 383 reptiles. Only a few emblematic species are mentioned below, especially highland mammals and birds the trekker is likely to see. Many animals are found in more than one geographical region. The largest number of all species is found in the Amazon basin. Links to additional information about flora and fauna in Peru are given in Appendix A. Additional photos of flora and fauna along our trekking routes are found in www.trekkingperu.org. Local names for plants and animals often vary from region to region.

Coast

The Peruvian Pacific Ocean is very rich in life and supports a great number and diversity of birds. On land, the greatest diversity on the coast is found in the far north, where there are mangrove forests, Pacific tropical forest, and dry equatorial forest. Farther south are some of the driest deserts on Earth and vegetation is limited to river valleys, where agriculture has replaced the native flora. On the Andean foothills are a few *lomas* (fog oases) that trap the humidity found in *garúa* and come to life from June to November.

Highlands

The complex topography of the Andes has many habitats. The western Andean

Corn is one of the most important subsistence crops of the highlands.

slopes are dry with cacti and shrubs. Farther east, nestled between mountain ranges are populated river valleys long given over to agriculture. Ancient civilizations terraced and irrigated even the steepest slopes for cultivation. The vegetation varies greatly with altitude and humidity. Higher, more easterly, and more northerly areas are all better watered.

The deep western canyon slopes at elevations below 2500 m have spiny bushes, a variety of cacti, some puyas, and a few trees like the *p'ati*, a kapok, and *molle* (Peruvian pepper, *Schinus molle*). Most agriculture is at elevations between 2500 and 3800 m. Crops include corn, *habas* (broad beans), *tarwi* (*chochos*, lupin), potato, and other native tubers like *oka*, *olluco*, *isaña*, and *maca*; the latter grows above 4000 m. Among the cereals are the native *quinua* (quinoa), *kiwicha* (amaranth), and *cañihua* (similar to *kiwicha* but smaller), as well as wheat, barley, and oats.

With the exception of polylepis (see below), the tree line is between 3200 m and 3600 m. Trees include alder and the introduced eucalyptus, cypress, and, at the lower end of the mid-elevation range, fruit trees like *pacay* (ice cream bean), *palta* (avocado), *chirimoya* (custard apple), and *lúcuma* (eggfruit). Native forest remnants survive in sheltered lower valleys or on inaccessible slopes, including *pisonay* or *basul* (*Erythrina* spp) with orange-red clusters of flowers. Higher are *quishuar* (*Buddleja* spp) with large leaves with a silver underside, and *arrayán* (*Myrtus communis*), a myrtle. If you trek early in the dry season, you will find a delightful array of colorful wildflowers, many of them in the daisy family.

Above 3800 m is the *puna*, a region of plateaus, glacial valleys, lakes, and bogs. Vegetation here is adapted to cold temperatures and a lack of precipitation during the dry season. It includes endemic grasses, bushes like the *chinchircuma* (*Mutisia acuminata*) with bright orange flowers, cacti, and *queñua* (polylepis) forests up to 4500 m (see A Tree of Many Skins, Trek 5). *Bofedales* are Andean peatlands, boggy areas fed by glacial meltwater, which in addition to grasses have cushion plants. Look carefully and you will also see tiny colorful flowers. Around Lake Titicaca are important wetlands with endemic vegetation.

The richest highland ecosystems are cloud forests of the slopes that face the Amazon basin. This area is also the source of many fast-flowing rivers. When hot, humid jungle air hits the steep Andean slopes, it rises, cools, and condenses, forming a blanket of mist that waters dense forests, rich in ferns and epiphytes like bromeliads and orchids. Downslope, the eastern flank of the Andes gets heavy rain. Here are a variety of palms and vines. Podocarpus species, the only native conifers in Peru, thrive at intermediate and higher altitudes.

Amazon Basin

Below 800 m is the lush Amazon jungle, with large meandering rivers. This is the largest, wettest, and most biodiverse region of Peru, beyond the scope of this book.

Birds

Seeing an Andean condor (*Vultur gryphus*) flying overhead is a special treat while trekking. Among the raptors, the *huamán* (variable hawk, *Geranoaetus polyosoma*) and *alqamari* (mountain caracara, *Phalcoboenus megalopterus*) are both com-

QUEEN OF THE ANDES

Of Peru's countless spectacular plants, the Queen of the Andes (*Puya raimondii*) is perhaps the most unusual. Largest member of the Bromeliad family, which includes the pineapple, the plant is an immense porcupine of spherically arranged spiny leaves reaching 3 m in height. Once, at the end of its eighty-year life, it produces a flower spike up to 10 m high. The puya's longevity has earned it the nickname of "century plant." A single mature individual can produce up to 12 million wind-dispersed seeds of which a very few, if any, will be lucky enough to germinate in the harsh conditions where it grows, between 3000 and 4800 m.

The Queen of the Andes is endangered and exists only in Peru and neighboring Bolivia. Shepherds burn it to protect their animals from the sharp curved spines or to provide fodder for them. Although protected by Peruvian law, there is no enforcement in most of the remote locations where the puyas are found. *Puya raimondii* can be seen in the Cordillera Negra (Chapter 8), Central Highlands (Chapter 9), and, to a lesser extent, the Lake Titicaca basin (Chapter 12). Specific locations are given in Treks 13, 16, and 27.

mon. Birds easily seen around *bofedales*, lakes, and rivers include *huallata* (*huachua*, Andean goose, *Chloephaga melanoptera*), almost always seen in pairs; *liqlish* (*leqecho*, *lique lique*, Andean lapwing, *Vanellus resplendens*); *qellwa* (Andean gull, *Chroicocephallus serranus*); the black *yanavico* (puna ibis, *Plegadis ridgwayi*), in large flocks; and tan *bandurria* (Andean ibis, *Theristicus branickii*), in smaller groups. Several species of ducks, teals, grebes, coots, and gallinules thrive on the lakes. Unmistakable are Chilean flamingos (*Phoenicoparrus chilensis*), found at high altitudes, and torrent ducks (*Merganetta armata*), in fast-moving streams. A common bird is the *pito* or *carpintero andino* (Andean flicker, *Colaptes rupicola*,) which nests in holes in riverbanks and adobe walls. Among the many hummingbirds, the Andean hillstar (*Oreotrochilus estella*) can be seen in the *puna*, the sparkling violetear (*Colibri coruscans*) has a wide distribution throughout the highlands, and the giant hummingbird (*Patagona gigas*) is widespread in dry habitats and polylepis forests. The cloud forest has many birds including motmots, trogons, quetzals, and a great variety of tanagers, as well as the emblematic *gallito de las rocas* (Andean cock-of-the-rock, *Rupicola peruvianus*), often considered the national bird.

Giant hummingbird (*Patagona gigas*)

Mammals

The best-known mammals are camelids: domestic llamas and alpacas, as well as wild vicuñas and guanacos (see South American Camelids, Trek 29). The large and elusive *taruca* (Andean deer, *Hippocamelus antisensis*) is also found at high elevations in remote areas. *Luichu* (white-tailed deer, *Odocoileus peruvianus*) and *venado enano* (dwarf deer, *Mazama*

chunyii) live at lower elevations. A native mammal you are likely to see while trekking is the rabbit-like *vizcacha* (see Hopping Stones, opposite). Among the carnivores, the puma (*Puma concolor*), *atocc* (Andean fox, *Lycalopex culpaeus*), and *titi* (Andean mountain cat, *Leopardus jacobitus*) are present in several regions but difficult to see. *Oso andino* (spectacled bear, *Tremarctus ornatus*), the only South American bear, inhabits mostly eastern cloud forests and *páramo* which it shares with the *pinchaque*, (Andean tapir, *Tapirus pinchaque*), a large endangered herbivore. The *viringo* (Peruvian hairless dog) is found mainly on the coast.

CONSERVATION

Although lip service is paid to traditional respect for *Pachamama* (Mother Earth), environmental conservation is not a priority for most urban or rural Peruvians. Their concept of progress includes expansion of agricultural and grazing lands, more roads and motor vehicles, and an increasingly consumption-oriented society. Roads have proliferated in formerly isolated areas, resulting in a degradation of their natural environment. Forests, which cover about 60 percent of the land, are being lost to logging and slash-and-burn clearing at an alarming rate of 113,000 hectares per year. Soil erosion is a serious problem on steep deforested slopes. Widespread industrial and small-scale mining are responsible for water and air pollution, as is petroleum extraction in the Amazon basin. Industrial and automotive air pollution, as well as widespread noise and visual pollution, are all rife in big cities.

Despite this grim picture, there is hope. Peru created fourteen new state-protected areas between 2010 and 2015, and eighty new private reserves were established from 2010 to 2016. Community-based environmental protection and ecotourism projects, sponsored by local and international NGOs, are also increasing. For more information, see Appendix A.

ABORIGINAL CULTURES, ARCHAEOLOGY, AND HISTORY

It is difficult to hike in Peru without stumbling on something ancient. The country has the most extensive collection of

HOPPING STONES

If you think a stone hopped, pay close attention and spot the vizcacha, much like a rabbit with a long bushy tail, long drooping whiskers, and furry ears. It is common in rocky areas throughout the highlands. Vizcachas can move fast, but when they feel threatened, they usually remain motionless and blend in perfectly with the rocks. They are herbivorous rodents in the chinchilla family and live in colonies. Cats are their main predators, and they are also hunted for their meat and soft fur.

Five species of vizcacha have been described from southern Ecuador to Chile; two of these are found in Peru. The northern vizcacha (*Lagidium peruanum*) is native to central and southern Peru and northern Chile. It has a wide altitude range, from 300 m to 5000 m, but is most common above tree line. The southern or mountain vizcacha (*Lagidium viscacia*) has long hind legs and short front legs. It is found in southern Peru and mountainous areas in Bolivia, Argentina, and Chile, at elevations between 2500 m and 5100 m.

The Chanca ruins of Kaniche (Trek 16)

archaeological sites in South America and an exceptionally rich pre-Hispanic history. Only a few fragments are mentioned below, and interested readers are referred to Appendix A. Some archaeological sites have been cleared or restored, but many, many, more remain untouched.

Earliest Cultures

Rock art dating suggests hunters and gatherers were present in Peru as early as 9000 BC. Settlements followed, at first on the coast and later along the river valleys and up into the highlands. The first cultures with widespread influence were Chavín (1500-300 BC) in the northern highlands (Trek 5), allied with Sechín (1800-900 BC) on the coast.

On the southern coast, the Paracas (800 BC–AD 200) and Nazca (AD 100-600) are best known for their fine textiles and the Nazca lines (monumental figures engraved on the desert sands). On the northern coast, the Moche (AD 100-800) built an important empire with roads and irrigation canals. The Wari-Tiawanako (Huari-Tiahuanacu, AD 600-1100), of the Titicaca basin and central highlands, respectively, spread their influence through most of Peru and beyond. A period of local kingdoms followed their decline, and among these were the Chachapoya (AD 0-1500) in the northern highlands, who built Kuelap (Chapter 7). The Chimú (AD 1100-1450) dominated the

northern coast and built Chan Chán, a 20-sq-km adobe city, the largest of its kind in the world.

Inca Empire

Legend has it that from the waters of Lake Titicaca emerged Manco Capac and Mama Ocllo, children of the creator-god Viracocha, destined to found Cuzco and the Inca Empire. In a period of 300 years starting around AD 1200, the Incas transformed their small kingdom around Cuzco into Tawantinsuyo, the largest empire ever seen in the Americas. Efficient and prosperous, it included what is today southern Colombia, the coast and highlands of Ecuador and Peru, western Bolivia, northwest Argentina, and half of Chile.

The Incas were strategists who conquered by building alliances. Local chieftains were invited to become part of the Inca elite, and war was a last resource. This resource was used effectively, however, for example against the fierce Chancas across the Río Apurimac. Following this milestone victory in the 15th century, Inca expansion grew rapidly under the rule of Pachacutec and his successors: Tupac (Topa) Inca and Huayna Capac.

Mit'a was a form of taxation by which every conquered community provided labor for the empire. With it they built or improved existing roads (see The World's Greatest Road, Chapter 1), agricultural terraces, storehouses, temples, and administrative centers. Each community also had to assign a percentage of arable land to the state and work it, so the Inca *colcas*, or storehouses, were well supplied. Collective labor lives on in the form of *minka*, whereby rural communities join forces to build or maintain infrastructure, including trails. If you happen on a *minka*, you are welcome to participate and experience firsthand how the Incas got things done.

Following the death of Huayna Capac in 1527, a five-year civil war broke out between his heirs: Huáscar who ruled the southern half of the empire from Cuzco and Atahualpa, ruler of the north in Quito. Atahualpa emerged victorious and subsequently ordered the execution of his half-brother.

Spanish Conquest and Colonial Rule

Huayna Capac's death took place during a massive epidemic as European diseases introduced to Mexico and Central America surged southward. In their wake, in 1532 Francisco Pizarro landed on the north coast of what is today Peru. That same year the conquistadores ambushed and captured Atahualpa at Cajamarca. He was held captive while an immense ransom of gold and silver was gathered, and then he was killed. The empire collapsed, and the Spanish marched into Cuzco. In 1536, Manco Inca, half-brother of Atahualpa, almost succeeded in expelling the Spaniards but was forced to flee and ruled for a time from Vitcos (Trek 23) and later from Vilcabamba. Vilcabamba was invaded and destroyed in 1572, and the last Inca, Tupac Amaru, was publicly executed in the main plaza of Cuzco.

The first decades of Spanish rule were chaos, taken up with founding new cities, looking for treasure, fighting among conquistadores, and crushing

remaining Inca resistance. Francisco de Toledo, the fifth viceroy (1569–1581; see Explorers and Trekkers, Chapter 1), was the first to consolidate colonial rule. The indigenous population was enslaved in mines and workshops, and their culture repressed. This system would be maintained over the next two centuries. In 1780, José Gabriel Condorcanqui, of Inca lineage, who adopted the name Tupac Amaru II, led an indigenous rebellion that, although it was quelled, became a spark of the independence movement. Between 1814 and 1815, another unsuccessful revolt in southern Peru was led by Mateo Pumahuaca.

Independence and the Republic

By the early 19th century discontent ran high throughout the Spanish colonies of South America. In 1816 Argentina declared its independence and José de San Martín led an Argentine army across the Andes to assist Chilean rebels. In 1820 they landed on the southern coast of Peru and advanced to Lima. On July 28, 1821, San Martín proclaimed Peruvian independence, although most of the country was still under Spanish control. From the north, following victories in Venezuela, Colombia, and Ecuador, Simón Bolívar and Antonio José de Sucre led their rebel army into Peru. In 1824 they definitively defeated the Spanish at Junín and later Ayacucho.

Independence brought little change for most Peruvians. A small elite of landowners continued to dominate the political and economic scene well into the 20th century. Political instability and military rule corresponding to times of economic hardship alternated with interludes of calm during periodic export booms. With each boom

TWO DECADES OF TERROR

Sendero Luminoso (Shining Path), a Maoist insurgent movement, and the Movimiento Revolucionario Tupac Amaru (MRTA), a smaller Marxist group, arose around 1980 with the goal of radically changing the established order in Peru. They ushered in a twenty-year period of fear, hardship, instability, and death. Although bombings and attacks on infrastructure also hurt the urban population, people in rural areas were most severely affected. If they collaborated with insurgents out of conviction or fear, they were severely punished by the military, who committed many human rights abuses. If they collaborated with the military, they faced cruel retaliation from insurgents. Many people left everything and fled to the capital, swelling the shantytowns of Lima.

The introduction of *rondas campesinas* during the Fujimori era helped ease the rural situation. These community patrols continue to operate in some areas, and you might meet them while trekking. In 1992 leaders of both guerrilla movements were arrested, and by 1995 many insurgents had given up their arms in exchange for amnesty. A 2003 Truth and Reconciliation Commission confirmed that atrocities had been committed by insurgents and government forces alike, and it estimated that the violence had taken seventy thousand lives. This tragic era is eloquently commemorated at the Museo de la Memoria in Ayacucho (Chapter 9).

Since 2000, only a very few small insurgent groups remain active in jungle areas, usually in collaboration with drug runners. At the time of publication, they did not represent a threat along the trekking routes described in this book.

and bust, however, the gap between the elite and rural poor grew wider. Between 1855 and 1875, following the abolition of Afro-Peruvian slavery, one hundred thousand Chinese indentured laborers were imported for manpower, and their descendants remain an important part of the demographic makeup of the coast. Political opposition to the elite arose in the 1920s with the founding of movements like the Socialist Party and the Alianza Popular Revolucionaria Americana (APRA). In 1968, General Juan Velasco Alvarado seized power and finally implemented land reform, an event still fondly remembered by older rural Peruvians, but by 1975 a conservative government was back in power.

From 1980 to 2000, Peru endured some of its darkest years (see Two Decades of Terror, above). Recovery, during the controversial presidency of Alberto Fujimori (1990–2000), was slow and painful but subsequently gained momentum on the heels of the latest boom—mining. Tourism also grew rapidly and is an important industry. Some of the growing national revenue was eventually applied to social programs, and old scars began to heal. Since 2000, Peru has been a stable and increasingly prosperous

Neny Menéndez and her children outside Aymaña, Carabaya, Puno

constitutional democracy, but an open question remains: What will happen when the current boom goes bust?

POPULATION

In 2015 Peru had an estimated thirty-one million inhabitants (twenty-four per square km, 76 percent urban), an increase of 20 percent since 2000 and a threefold increase since 1960. Lima is the largest city with almost ten million people, followed by Arequipa and Trujillo with close to one million each. Despite its large size, Peru is a very centralized country. Political and economic power are concentrated in the capital, and many Peruvians from all regions and all walks of life have ties there. The population of Peru is young; 37 percent are under twenty and 70 percent under forty. The literacy rate among adults was 94 percent in 2012.

Spanish is the main language, spoken in all regions. Based on mother tongue, about 30 percent of the population is indigenous, much reduced from 75 percent in the colonial period. The largest indigenous group speaks Quechua, the language that unified many nations during or even before Inca times. Different dialects of Quechua are spoken in different highland areas:

Ancash (Cordillera Blanca), Cajamarca, the Central Highlands, Cuzco, and Puno. The second-largest group speaks Aymara and lives mostly around Lake Titicaca. An additional thirteen linguistic families have been identified in the Amazon basin.

The coast is the most densely populated region with 56 percent of Peruvians; about 30 percent live in the highlands. Many *serranos* (highlanders) live in rural areas and are bilingual, speaking Spanish and either Quechua or Aymara, sometimes all three languages. Rural dwellers are known as *comuneros* or *campesinos* (peasants, neither term is pejorative), and their lives revolve around the agricultural calendar. In Peru, the terms *indígena* and *indio* (Indian) are considered derogatory and not used. The Amazon basin is the least populated region, with 14 percent of the population, and has the greatest diversity of ethnic groups.

(Also see Protecting the Cultural Environment, Chapter 3).

RELIGION AND FIESTAS

Most of Peru's population is Roman Catholic, although other Christian and non-Christian religions are also present. Religion in Peru is closely related to the festival calendar. *Día de fiesta* is not an easy concept to translate. It is at once a festival, a feast, a party, a holiday, and a holy day. It is a day to be looked forward to and prepared for. It can be a time to be very happy, like Carnival; or very solemn, like Holy Week; or very patriotic, like Fiestas Patrias (Independence Day, July 28). It is a day when the restraints of social hierarchy may be temporarily relaxed, when rich and poor can celebrate together.

There is not a hamlet too small to have its own special *fiesta*, usually held to honor a patron saint. This is generally celebrated with a solemn mass, a parade with floats and folk dancing, exhibits, bullfights, live music, dancing, fireworks, traditional foods, and much drinking. If your trek happens to take you through a village during its fiesta, take advantage of this special opportunity. You may be invited to dance, have something to eat, and, even more likely, you will be offered *chicha* (a fermented corn beverage) or beer. People will be offended if you do not accept; take some, but also find a polite way to say no when you have had enough.

Note that if you were planning to get transport, a local guide, or pack animals, you might have to wait until the fiesta ends and the town sobers up before these are available. Transport to a village is crowded before and after festivities, hotels fill, and prices rise. The government tourism agency posts a monthly Peruvian fiesta calendar (see Appendix A).

Syncretism

Peruvian customs and beliefs seamlessly combine (syncretize) Roman Catholic and aboriginal elements. The latter are often based on the worship of deities from nature, such as Pachamama and the *apus* (mountain gods). In every celebration, it is traditional to spill on the ground the first drop of liquor to honor Pachamama. Tributes to her are also placed in front of ornately decorated crosses, especially on May 3, the Catholic day of the cross. You will see many such crosses while trekking, atop hills and at gateways to towns. *Pago a la tierra*, also called *challa* in Aymara communities, is a ceremonial tribute to

Mother Earth presided over by a *paq'o* (Andean priest or shaman) in which alcohol, coca leaves, sweets, and incense are burnt as offerings.

Perhaps the finest example of syncretism in all the Andes is Qoyllur Rit'i (Trek 20). It precedes Inti Raymi, in which the June solstice is celebrated alongside Saint John the Baptist. Syncretism is likewise evident in the Fiesta de Santiago in the Central Highlands (Chapter 9). Three cultures—Amerindian, Catholic, and African—combine in celebrations to honor Señor de los Milagros in Lima, a much-venerated image of Christ painted by a slave of Angolan descent. The admixture of traditions, old and new, continues. Todos Santos (All Saints Day, November 1) celebrations combine the Catholic commemoration, native traditions to honor departed relatives by offering them *tanta wawas* (bread baked in the shape of babies or animals), and, in cities, all the consumerist paraphernalia of Halloween.

Syncretism takes many forms and can catch you off guard. Just before we reached the village of Siani, along the north shore of Lake Titicaca (Trek 28), we noticed a large stone resembling a bull and decorated with streamers. We later learned it was called Taurani or Turuni, from the Spanish *taurino* (relating to bulls) with the Aymara suffix "-ni." During the May festival in honor of San Isidro, patron saint of agriculture, people decorate and bring offerings to Taurani, asking for a good year in which their herds of cattle multiply. (Also see Bulls on the Roof, Chapter 12.)

Pre-Hispanic values also prevail in other ways. Three Inca commandments—*ama quella* (don't be lazy), *ama llulla* (don't lie), and *ama sua* (don't steal)—are the motto of the Peruvian National Police.

3

WHAT TO EXPECT

Several factors will determine when and how you trek in Peru: time, money, language skills, experience, and personal preference. The best time to trek is the dry season, May to September. May is particularly nice, green after the rains and not too crowded in the popular areas. (See also Climate in Chapter 2.) High season for international tourists is June to August, although Cuzco is busy all year. Peruvians take holidays in January through February, as well as for Carnival (February or March), Semana Santa (Easter, March, or April), Fiestas Patrias (one or two weeks following July 28), and Todos Santos (November 1). These are good times to be out on the trail and avoid crowds in cities and towns.

The Peruvian government tourist office, iPerú (see Appendix A), is very good and has offices in the main cities. Municipal tourist offices found in many smaller towns vary in quality.

INDEPENDENT VS. ORGANIZED TREKKING

There are several different ways to go trekking in Peru: on your own, with a company or guide, and with or without pack animals.

Trekking with an International Company

Many companies from all over the world offer trekking trips in Cuzco (Chapter 10) and the Cordillera Blanca (Chapter 8). This is the easiest and most expensive option. Everything will be arranged for you, and your guide and companions will speak your language. The drawbacks are lack of flexibility regarding routes, reduced exposure to local culture, and of course the price.

Trekking with a Peruvian Company

Trekking with a local company has the advantage of lower cost, greater flexibility, and perhaps the opportunity for more local interaction. Prices vary considerably with location and with high versus low seasons. The range at present starts around US$50 per person per day in a group, everything included, US$100 per person per day for a private tailor-made trek. Fierce competition forces some operators to compromise on quality, safety, working conditions of their employees, and environmental responsibility. Although a higher price will not guarantee a better experience, the

Independent and organized group trekking are two different experiences.

cheapest option is seldom the best. Arrangements can be made on-site at the last minute or in advance from abroad. Many Peruvian trekking operators speak English and sometimes other languages.

A number of very reputable Peruvian agencies run excellent trekking tours. Operators based in the region where you will trek know their area best and offer a greater variety of routes but will not necessarily know all the treks described in this book. If you do not speak Spanish, make sure you are assigned a guide who speaks your language. Some companies have lodges and run lodge-to-lodge trekking tours.

Independent Trekking

This is the most economical option and offers the greatest flexibility and challenge. You plan your hike, choose the route and pace that best suit you, make your own preparations, and rely exclusively on your own abilities to get in and out safely. To trek independently you should have a flexible itinerary, adequate experience, clothing and equipment, and

a more-than-basic knowledge of Spanish. If you meet these requirements and are so inclined, then independent trekking is by far the most satisfying option. It will give you an opportunity to explore the many wonders of highland Peru on its own terms, beyond the grasp of mass tourism. This book is written with independent trekkers in mind.

Note, however, that it is not safe for one person to trek alone. If you were to get into any trouble, even something as minor as a sprained ankle, nobody would be there to assist or seek help. A trekking party of two to four people is ideal; more than six is too many. If you are traveling alone, it is easy to find trekking partners; post a notice in hotels and restaurants frequented by travelers.

Hiring a Local Guide

Even if you are trekking independently, there are still circumstances in which you might wish to hire a local guide, such as where navigation is particularly difficult. You will need additional time to find a guide and make arrangements. There may or may not be someone willing to guide you or help you carry gear in the village near the trailhead. In the most popular areas, organizations keep lists of recommended guides (*guías*), muleteers (*arrieros*), and porters (*porteadores*): Casa de Guías in Huaraz, for treks in the Cordillera Blanca (see Chapter 8) and AGOTUR in Cuzco (Chapter 10). There are also associations of guides and muleteers in other cities near trekking destinations; the tourist information office can help contact them. Choose carefully, as the quality of the guide will in large measure determine the quality of your experience. Prices vary greatly, about US$30-100 per day for a local guide. You must also provide food (ask what to get; local dietary preferences might be very different from your own), usually a tent, and sometimes a backpack or waterproof clothing for your guide. Note that all the above (except price) also applies to muleteers and porters (see below).

Pack Animals and Porters

There is nothing quite as simple and satisfying as carrying everything you need on your own back. If you wish to lighten your load, however, some routes are suitable for pack animals which may be hired near the trailhead or arranged in larger centers. A worthwhile option is to hire pack animals for the first day of treks that start with a long climb (when your pack is heaviest), allowing enough time for the muleteer to return the same day. Take a day pack in which you carry everything you may need during the day (valuables, maps, navigation instruments, camera, a warm jacket, raingear, water, snacks, sunscreen, and so on) while your main pack rides the horse, donkey, or llama. The cost is about US$12-18 per day for the muleteer, who can usually handle up to five animals, plus US$8-12 per animal per day.

Porters are common along the Classic Inca Trail and other routes in Cuzco where pack animals are prohibited, but they are less frequent elsewhere. Unlike pack animals, porters can travel on any trail you can. Porters charge US$15-40 per day.

RESPONSIBLE TREKKING

The benefits of trekking and travel, such as financial gain for the host or the opportunity to have an enriching personal

Waste processing facility outside Machu Picchu

experience for both the host and trekker, may be obvious. The downside is less evident but equally important, and care must be taken to minimize impact on both the natural and cultural environments. Many treks go through remote areas that are most vulnerable; in a few places you might be among the first tourists to visit these sites and should be especially careful not to spoil them.

Natural Environment

In Peru, as elsewhere, the elemental standards of trekking conduct apply: "Pack it in, pack it out," "Take nothing but photos, leave nothing but footprints." Stay on existing trails whenever possible. If walking cross-country (off trail), be careful to do as little damage as you can; the wetland vegetation of *bofedales* is particularly fragile.

When camping, always keep impact to a minimum: disturb as few plants as possible, do not dig gutters, do not build a fire unless indispensable, and avoid staying at the same site for several days. Your goal should be to leave the spot where you camped just as you found it.

Many Peruvians do not discard trash properly, and parts of the countryside show it. You can help by setting a good example and by insisting that guides and companions pack out all refuse. Toilet paper and sanitary napkins represent a particular eyesore, as anyone who has come across the last trekker's latrine in the middle of the trail can testify. Do your business well away from water sources, trails, and campsites. Bury or at least cover the evidence, and pack out sanitary napkins, tampons, and toilet paper used after urinating; these "white flowers" do not enhance the trail.

Water sources must be protected. Although oats are organic, the scraps of your porridge don't belong on the shore of that pristine stream. Wash your dishes, clothes, and self well away from water sources, and avoid using soap.

You can help protect endangered species of plants and animals by being selective in the purchase of souvenirs.

Protecting the Cultural Environment

The impact of our interaction with local people is not easily measured, but the negative consequences of tourism can be seen in areas that receive large numbers of visitors. Communication is the first step toward a positive cultural exchange. The more Spanish you speak, the more meaningful your experience will be. A

Sarita Mendoza and her piglet in Ragrajpampa, San Luis, Ancash.

Walking together is a great way to break the ice.

few words of Quechua and Aymara are also an asset in remote areas, and a smile always goes a long way.

As a polite guest in Peru, learn about Peruvians and respect them. Most trekking routes go through sparsely populated highland areas. The reception you get will vary from one place to another. In areas frequented by tourists, a trekker might be seen as a potential customer for services or crafts, and people will generally understand why you are there. In seldom-visited areas, locals might wonder what you are up to, and you might be regarded with suspicion.

Andean people are shy and stoic. An initial wariness of outsiders is ingrained in their culture, and for good historical reasons (see Chapter 2). This does not mean they are hostile; they can be very

friendly, but it takes time to break the ice. Many of the people you will meet along the trail are shepherds grazing their flocks. They will probably see you long before you notice them. On occasion children, women, or even adult men might hide as you approach. In a very few areas, where a community is fighting the entry of mining companies or cattle rustling is a problem, outsiders are simply not welcome. If you encounter such a situation, excuse yourself and move along.

Some communities have *rondas campesinas* (see Two Decades of Terror, Chapter 2). If you meet one of their members, you might be asked for ID (always carry some) and to explain what you are doing. Minor officials like to feel important, and local authorities have considerable prestige in small communities. If you arrive in a village and inquire about a place to stay, you will likely be directed to the *presidente de la comunidad, alcalde, regidor,* or *varayoc.* After an audience, he will usually authorize you to spend the night in the village and direct someone to show you where.

Reciprocity is deeply rooted in Andean culture. Along the trail, you may be the recipient of hospitality and food. Don't forget to reciprocate, even if this means giving away one of your last cookies or carrying token gifts from home, such as postcards or flag lapel pins. If you were invited to stay in someone's home or given substantial assistance along the trail, always offer to pay. Ask "*¿Cuánto le debo?*" (How much do I owe you?) Most of the time the response will be "*Su voluntad*" (It's up to you, the amount being left to your discretion). Guide yourself by the cost of a basic hostel and meal in a town in the area. Giving too much will create an unfair expectation of the next trekker.

"Point and shoot" is the most common cultural indiscretion committed by tourists and trekkers in Peru. Folks in colorful indigenous outfits or cute local children may get seriously offended if the first thing you do is aim a camera at them. Introduce yourself, get to know them a little, and always ask for permission before taking someone's picture. Then show them the photo. Offering to send a copy is a small courtesy that is always appreciated. Some shepherds have smartphones and email addresses; many others have homes or relatives in towns to which prints can be sent. Never offer, or agree to give, money for taking photographs.

Begging is a particularly difficult issue. Peru has some genuinely destitute people to whom a contribution can make a big difference. Others, especially in tourist areas, have acquired the habit of asking any foreigner for money. If you decide to give something, consider food rather than cash. Do not give anything to children. On the trail, well-meaning trekkers' gratuitous gifts to children of money, candies, or pens lead to future begging. Instead, contribute to the local school or a community development project.

Peruvian highlanders are often bundled up, as suits the climate, and they consider scanty dress on the part of trekkers to be offensive. Nude bathing in public is out of the question, and even men should not go bare chested.

TREKKING INFRASTRUCTURE

Peru's trekking infrastructure is concentrated in the most popular destinations: Cordillera Blanca, Cuzco, and to a lesser extent Arequipa. Away from these areas, trekking is an independent adventurous activity, and the trekker must be self-sufficient in all respects.

Protected Natural Areas

Some of the treks described in this book go through national parks and reserves, while others follow public paths through the countryside, and some go through both protected and unprotected areas. Servicio Nacional de Áreas Naturales Protegidas por el Estado (SERNANP, see Appendix A, Chapter 2, Flora and Fauna) is in charge of national protected areas, of which there are seventy-seven. There are also seventeen regional and ninety-six private reserves. Over twenty-two million hectares have some protected status. Some are exclusively for conservation or scientific purposes and have no infrastructure for visitors; others have insufficient rangers for the size of the reserve,

El camino te lleva. *The trail will show you the way.*

few shelters, and few marked trails. The most-visited parks have better infrastructure, although it might not match that found in other parts of the world.

Permits and Fees

Entry fees to protected areas vary from one park to another. For some areas, these are payable in advance at the park headquarters, and tickets must be presented at entry points or shown to rangers. Visitor fees are also charged by some regional authorities, such as those in the Colca Canyon. The permits and fees applicable to each trek are given in Section II.

Trails and Ancient Roads

"El camino te lleva." ("The trail will show you the way.")

—*Anonymous*

Peru has an extensive network of often rocky trails. *Caminos de herradura* are horse trails, and *caminos* are foot trails. Both connect villages, *estancias* (small ranches), fields, and grazing areas. Many trails might date to Inca times or earlier, it's hard to say. Surviving cobbled sections, retaining walls, stairways, causeways, and stone bridge foundations are all suggestive, but more prosaic trails may also have ancient origins, evidence of which has long since been lost. This is especially common along segments used by horses and cattle. Walking along even a clearly ancient road does not necessarily mean it will all look just as it did hundreds of years ago; there are some well-preserved fragments, while others have been all but obliterated. In remote areas where villages have no road access, these various types of

trails remain the mainstay of transportation. *Carreteras* (vehicle roads) are increasing rapidly, in many cases built over trails, in others leaving them to deteriorate for lack of use. *Pista* is the Peruvian term for a paved road.

The treks described in this book follow a combination of trails, ancient roads, vehicle tracks, larger contemporary roads, and cross-country routes (walking over open highland terrain without following a trail). There are many intersections, and the larger branch is not necessarily the one to follow. Even major trails seem to vanish in flat areas where there might be numerous animal tracks, so keep your general direction of travel in mind. Many passes are marked by *apachetas*, stone cairns of varying sizes built up by generations of travelers adding a stone every time they pass. Some trails have gates to control the movement of animals; always leave gates just as you found them. In the rainy season, especially in the north, trails can be muddy.

Campsites, Homes, and Shelters

Camping amid the Andean peaks is a delight. A great many spots to camp are not merely suitable but splendid, though few of these are marked "campground." The more popular commercial trekking routes have designated camping areas or shelters, where trash may be a serious problem. Beware latrine holes dug for groups; they are not always covered properly.

Always carry a tent and sleeping bag when trekking independently. Even if there are towns en route, you might need to camp between them. The sites suitable for camping that are described in this book generally have reasonably flat

Campsites are often gorgeous but have few, if any, amenities.

There are few shelters specifically for trekkers along the routes described in this book. Where they exist, some are no more than a roof without walls, providing no protection from the wind. Others are very basic or have been vandalized but at least keep out the elements. There are also a few large comfortable shelters on or near our routes in the Cordillera Blanca, which better fit the description of a mountain lodge.

Community Accommodations

Some villages have a municipal guest house (*hospedaje municipal*) with dormitory accommodations. Quality varies from very basic to simple. Some towns might also have basic private lodgings. Where this is not available and camping seems inappropriate, ask about spending the night in the local school.

Community tourism programs (*turismo comunitario, turismo vivencial*), available in some villages along our trekking routes, include homestays with families in rooms or cabins set up for this purpose. Meals are also available, usually with advance notice. Ask about prices beforehand. Many Peruvian highlanders are short; taller trekkers must crouch and constantly watch their head.

During Inca times, *tambos* were posthouses along main roads, about one day's walk apart. Today, Peru has a system of *tambos* set up by the government in remote locations for the use of public servants who visit to provide services in these isolated communities. They have dorm accommodations, bathrooms with hot showers (sometimes working), a kitchen, and office facilities including Internet access, and are usually open to trekkers for a nominal fee. In 2016 there were

ground on which to pitch a tent, some shelter from the wind, and a water source nearby. They usually have nothing else. If possible, look for a spot with eastern exposure for morning sun.

It is not advisable to camp in populated rural areas without asking permission to do so. You might be invited to sleep in a dwelling or offered a camping spot in a yard or corral. If you are invited to eat, try to accept some food even if it does not appeal to you, so as not to offend. Meals often consist of soup and boiled potatoes or other root crops, which are generally safe and nutritious. Always try to reciprocate with some of your own food and offer to pay as well (see Protecting the Cultural Environment earlier in this chapter). In remote areas you might not meet anyone for days. Even where there are houses, these might be only seasonally occupied or abandoned, as many *campesinos* have migrated to cities.

238 *tambos* throughout the hinterlands of Peru, with more under construction (see Appendix A). Those along our trekking routes are mentioned in Section II.

MAPS AND NAVIGATION

"A trekker with one map is always oriented. A trekker with two is never sure."

—Anonymous

All our trekking routes present some navigational challenge, and finding your way is part of the fun. The ability to read a topographic map and to navigate with a compass and altimeter are essential for independent trekking in Peru. A GPS is also recommended, but you should not rely on it exclusively. All electronic devices can be lost, damaged, or fail when you most need them.

Tall trekkers should watch their head.

Maps

Larger maps of the treks in this book, map files for upload to GPS smartphones, and links to download ESCALE maps (see below) are all available on www.trekkingperu.org.

Topographical maps for Peru are produced by the Instituto Geográfico Nacional (IGN). Their 1:100,000 scale series, with a contour interval of 50 m, is the most useful for trekking. GPS users should note that older IGN sheets use the PSAD-1956 datum for Peru; newer ones use WGS-1984. Topos are most reliably purchased at the IGN in Lima (for IGN contact information and that of other map providers listed below, see Appendix A). They are very difficult to obtain elsewhere, except Cuzco, where Maratón sells southern Peru quadrants, and at Librerías San Francisco in Arequipa, where a few regional topos may be available. When purchasing a topo map, specify both its name and grid coordinates. Note that the Spanish alphabet has the extra letter Ñ, between N and O; this letter is used in the IGN's map grid, which also omits the letter W. IGN maps have generally accurate topography and hydrography, but they are old and many features have changed. Glaciers have receded, for example, and trails shown may have become vehicle roads or may be totally overgrown. Toponyms are also a problem (see below).

Lima 2000 produces *Mapa Vial del Perú*, a recommended road map of the country, as well as city maps and tourist maps for popular destinations. These are available in bookstores in larger cities, but most reliably in the capital. The Ministry of Education's ESCALE website has good regional orientation maps for free download. They include some trails and precise locations of schools in remote areas, which can be useful landmarks. The

Österreichischer Alpenverein (Austrian Alpine Club) has good topo maps of the Cordillera Blanca and Huayhuash, but not without a few errors and many discrepancies with IGN topos. They show popular trekking routes and are generally available in Huaraz and Caraz. A good orientation map for the Cordillera Blanca area, widely available locally, is produced by Felipe Díaz.

Toponyms are an important source of confusion. Many have indigenous roots, and the sound of vowels O and U, and E and I, are identical in Quechua, with many possible transliterations of names to Spanish. Substantially different versions appear on different maps or in different features on the same map. Furthermore, names shown on maps may be different from local usage. Common examples of alternate spellings include *capac, capaq, q'apaq, qhapaq, kapak,* and *ccapaq;* Cuzco, Cusco, and Qosqo; Huari and Wari; Sinakara and Cinajara; and Tinki, Tinqui, and Tinque. In our trek descriptions, alternate names and spellings are shown in parentheses. Also note that many rivers change names along their course, taking on the name of towns or villages as they flow by them.

Navigation

Many GPS-enabled electronic devices are available to trekkers. In our experience a smartphone is especially versatile, providing both navigation and communication (see Chapter 4). In addition to geo-referencing your photos, a camera with GPS provides backup in case your main GPS fails. Put the GPS and camera in your sleeping bag overnight to keep batteries warm.

Your maps, instruments, intuition, and the trek descriptions in this book are all important elements of navigation. None should be relied on in isolation; rather, they must be brought together. Check your position at regular intervals and consult local people whenever possible, with the following caveats.

Understanding Spanish does not guarantee you will understand the directions of a Peruvian *campesino,* nor should you assume that locals are familiar with a map and compass. *Campesinos* always move faster than trekkers; as a rule of thumb double the walking times given by them. Always ask for as many specific details and landmarks as possible. General inquiries usually elicit the following reply: "*Siga recto,*" continue straight. Without fail, there is a confusing fork up ahead. Not all forks can be mentioned in our trek descriptions or shown on the maps. Keep an eye on the general direction of travel; if after some time you are diverging from the route, head back to the intersection.

By definition, explorers spend a good deal of their time being lost. If you get lost, consider it an opportunity to discover new routes. Take a break, consult your map and instruments, and think over the situation calmly. With a little patience and perseverance, you will make it safely to your destination or somewhere even more interesting.

4
PREPARATIONS

There is not enough space in this book to provide all the information you need to travel in Peru. Many excellent guidebooks have been published about the country (see Appendix A) and are a recommended companion to this volume.

GETTING YOURSELF READY

Since the finest trekking opportunities in Peru are in the highlands, where walking up and down steep mountain slopes, often at altitudes above 4000 m is the rule, being in good physical condition is especially important. Even if you are in great shape, you will need a period of acclimatization when you arrive at high altitude. Acclimatization, immunizations, and other health preparations are discussed in Chapter 5.

Your stay in Peru will also be easier and more meaningful if you can communicate with its people. Although some Peruvians in the main tourist centers speak English or other foreign languages, the vast majority do not. Throughout the coast and in the larger cities of the highlands, Spanish is the main language. In smaller highland towns and rural areas, the majority of people speak Quechua, or Aymara around Lake Titicaca, with Spanish as a second language. A few older people speak little or no Spanish. Appendix B is a basic glossary but is not sufficient for your travels. Learn some Spanish ahead of your trip or begin your trip by learning Spanish. Lima, Arequipa, and Cuzco, among other cities, all have Spanish schools. Several dialects of Quechua are spoken in different regions of the highlands, so it is impractical to learn them all, but it is worth mastering a few phrases.

Passport and Visas

A passport, valid for at least six months, is required to enter Peru. If you are arriving by plane, you may also be required to present a return or onward ticket. Citizens of North and South America, most of the Caribbean, most of the European Union, Australia, New Zealand, South Africa, and Israel do not need a visa. Others should inquire in advance with a Peruvian embassy or consulate, or check the Ministerio de Relaciones Exteriores' list of countries that require a visa to enter Peru (see Appendix A). A free tourist card (*Tarjeta Andina*), valid for up to 183 days and not renewable, must be filled out on

GEAR CHECKLIST

Items marked with an asterisk (*) are easily available in Peru.

BASIC ITEMS

backpack and rain cover
day pack (for day walks or if your
  main pack will be carried for you)
stuff sacks (waterproof or lined with
  plastic bags)
*sturdy plastic bags (various sizes)
three-season tent
*plastic sheet cut to footprint of
  tent
three-season sleeping bag
insulating mat or pad
camping stove
fuel bottle
*matches and lighters
*pot, bowl, and spoon
pocketknife with can opener and
  tweezers
water bottle
*container to fetch water (e.g.,
  an empty plastic mineral water
  bottle)
water filter and/or purification
  supplies (Chapter 5)
first-aid kit (Chapter 5)
sewing kit and gear repair kit
thin, light cord
handkerchief or bandanna
*wide-brimmed sun hat with neck
  protection
*sunscreen for skin and lips
sunglasses
*insect repellent

lightweight washcloth and towel
headlamp
maps
compass
altimeter
cell phone/GPS with extra batteries
camera with extra batteries and
  memory cards
water-resistant watch
*notebook, pen, and pencil
breathable waterproof jacket and
  pants
warm jacket and pants
down vest or jacket
*wool hat (*chullo*)
*warm gloves or mitts
neck warmer (neck gaiter)
*light sweater
moisture-wicking, short-sleeved
  T-shirt
light cotton or poly-cotton pants
long-sleeved shirt
underwear
moisture-wicking long underwear
  (for pajamas, top and bottom)
wool socks
boots

OPTIONAL ITEMS

solar battery charger
binoculars
walking stick(s)
rope

arrival. Keep this with your passport; it must be handed in on departure. Since there are no extensions, be sure to request the full number of days to cover your visit, plus a little extra. The amount of time granted is at the discretion of border officials, but tourists seldom experience any difficulties. You will be charged a fine of US$1 per day if you exceed your authorized stay.

ID is required when reserving plane or bus tickets or checking into a hotel. You are required to keep your passport on you at all times. Store it safely in a waterproof pouch. In a separate location, keep a photocopy of your passport, including the entry stamp and a copy of the tourist card.

Insurance

Travel insurance, including medical and baggage coverage, should be purchased by all visitors to Peru. Read the fine print before you travel, to confirm what is and is not covered. Trekking might be considered a dangerous activity and therefore not covered by some policies. Search, rescue, and air ambulance flights might or might not be covered. Familiarize yourself with claims procedures, and bring the necessary contact information with you. Foreign insurance companies will generally not pay directly for medical expenses in Peru, but there are a few exceptions. You will usually have to pay out-of-pocket and then request reimbursement. If you incur a loss or medical expense, notify your insurer at once. Keep all receipts and, in the event of theft, always obtain a police report. There are tourist police in the main destinations such as Lima, Arequipa, Cuzco, and Huaraz.

Clothing and Equipment

Some trekking gear can be purchased or rented in the larger cities and major destinations like Cuzco and Huaraz. Consider bringing as much of your own clothing and equipment as possible, so you know what you have and can rely on it. Furthermore, because of customs regulations, it is expensive and time-consuming to have anything sent to you once you are in Peru. If you buy or rent equipment, check it thoroughly before you head out on the trail. Think light and compact in order to make trekking less strenuous and to extend your range. Our suggested gear checklist in

this chapter is just that—a suggestion—and experienced trekkers will have their own variations. A few items, however, merit additional comment.

You must be prepared for all weather conditions, including snow, even in the dry season. Since daytime temperatures can be high and nights very cold, layering works well. Lightweight alpaca and other wool sweaters, *chullos* (warm hats with ear flaps), gloves, and mitts are available throughout the Peruvian highlands. Cold temperatures, at times combined with strong wind, rain, or snow, call for adequate warm clothing to prevent hypothermia. A set of separate light, but warm, sleeping clothes, which can be kept dry in a waterproof stuff sack during the day, is likewise required.

Boots and good socks are obviously fundamental for trekking. Many trails in Peru are rocky, so bring a sturdy pair of boots. New footwear of any kind should always be tried first on day walks; your boots and feet need time to get used to each other.

A reliable camping stove is very important; most treks are above tree line, and elsewhere forests should not be turned into firewood. Screw-on gas canisters are the most commonly available form of camping fuel in Peru, but such stoves do not perform well in the cold or at high altitude. In our experience, liquid-fueled stoves are efficient and reliable. White gas, known as *bencina*, is available at hardware stores in cities and larger towns. Gasoline (*gasolina*) can usually be used where *bencina* is not available, but that sold in small towns is likely to be leaded and dirty. All fuel must be drained from stoves and bottles before air travel, but even so they may not be allowed on international or domestic flights if they have been used and smell like fuel. It is safest to start with a brand-new stove and fuel bottle, and, if taking flights within Peru, send these items ahead by bus parcel service to your next trekking area. If your stove fails, learn from the locals who cook with dry cow or llama dung.

TRAVEL IN PERU

Getting to and around Peru is easy but it's worth keeping a few hints in mind.

Getting to Peru

International flights arrive in Lima with the exception of one regional flight from La Paz in Bolivia to Cuzco. The main air travel gateway from North America is Miami. There are also nonstop flights from Atlanta, Dallas, Houston, Los Angeles, Mexico City, New York, Toronto, and Washington, DC. From Europe, Madrid is the main gateway; other flights originate in Amsterdam, London, and Paris. There are also flights to Peru from most other South American capitals as well as Panama and Costa Rica. For those traveling from neighboring countries, there are land borders with Ecuador, Bolivia, Chile, Brazil, and Colombia.

Money and Prices

The currency of Peru is the sol (S/), formerly called nuevo sol. In December 2016, US$1 = S/3.38, €1 = S/3.58, £1 = S/4.26. *Casas de cambio* (exchange houses), major banks, and some smaller regional banks change US dollars to soles. *Casas de cambio* in larger cities also change other currencies, especially euros. Elsewhere, only US dollars can be changed. Nobody will accept dollar bills that are torn, taped, or

dirty; bring only crisp clean notes, and do not accept damaged dollars as change.

You generally get a better exchange rate at a *casa de cambio* than at a bank. Street changers might offer a slightly higher rate than *cambios*, but, for safety, changing in the street is not recommended. At some borders, street changers might be the only choice; beware of tricks and scams. There are counterfeit dollar and sol notes, even coins, in circulation. Information on what to look for on legitimate sol notes is found on the Banco Central de Reserva del Perú (BCRP, Peruvian Central Bank) website; see Appendix A.

Some upmarket hotels and tour operators quote prices in dollars. Dollars may also be accepted for other services in major tourist destinations such as Lima and Cuzco. Large supermarkets usually accept payment in dollars, often at reasonable rates. Before heading for small towns and the countryside, be sure to get enough soles in small denominations (S/20 and S/10); change is scarce, and even hotels might not accept a S/100 note. Also carry some small denominations of dollars in case you need to exchange a small amount at a poor rate.

ATMs (bank machines) are common in medium to large cities but not in small towns. Visa, Plus, MasterCard, Maestro, and Cirrus cards are all accepted, but not all machines take all cards. For safety, use ATMs inside banks and during banking hours. You can specify whether you want dollars or soles (at the bank's exchange rate). Some ATMs charge a transaction fee in addition to what your home bank charges, and all have limits (as low as US$200) on daily transactions. International prepaid currency cards can also be used in Peruvian ATMs. Any card may sometimes be retained by an ATM for no good reason, and the card will not be returned to you by the Peruvian bank; you must request a new card from home.

Visa is the most widely accepted credit card in Peru. MasterCard, American Express, and Diners Club are also accepted. A credit card sign displayed in an establishment does not necessarily mean they accept that credit card. Cash advances in soles on Visa cards are available from BCP bank and on MasterCard from Scotiabank.

Outside Lima and Cuzco, travel in Peru is economical by international standards. If you are on a tight budget, you can save by traveling by bus instead of flying. Everybody has their own definition of the following budget terms, but a basic travel budget is currently about US$20 per person, per day, based on two persons traveling together. For around US$50 a day you can find much more comfort, and above US$100 a day is getting into the first-class range, but luxury travel can be much more expensive. Prices under US$10 are usually not specified in our trek descriptions.

Accommodation in Yauya (Trek 7)

Accommodations and Meals

Being a popular travel destination, Peru offers a vast array of places to stay and eat. These range from opulent and expensive (US$200 per person per night in a luxury hotel, US$60 for an upmarket meal) to basic and very cheap (US$7 per person per night, US$2 a meal). The widest variety is found in Lima and departmental capitals. In small towns along trekking routes, you may find only very basic rooms with a squat toilet outside and very simple eateries. Even in very cold areas, hot water may not be available. Some places along the treks described in this book are so small that they have no hotels at all, but you can often arrange for other forms of accommodation (see Community Accommodations in Chapter 3).

Communication

The Internet is very well developed in Peru and is the mainstay of communication for travelers. Even simple hotels in the cities have free wi-fi. Cyber-cafés are economical; they are everywhere in the cities, and small towns are likely to have one or two. Skype, WhatsApp, and similar services on wi-fi–enabled devices are the most economical form of international communication from Peru. There are phone offices (*locutorios*) and coin-operated pay phones in larger cities, but cell phones are the most common form of telecommunication. SIM cards (called *chips*) for either of the two main mobile carriers, Claro and Movistar, are economical and easily purchased (you must show your passport). These SIMs work with many foreign mobile phones, but

FOOD SHOPPING LIST

Items marked with an asterisk (*) may only be available in larger cities.

BREAKFAST

milk powder	*leche en polvo*
oats	*avena*
cream of wheat	*sémola*
*granola	*granola*
malted barley or other toasted flours	*machca, punki, cañihua, maca, api, harina tostada*
*popped quinoa or amaranth	*pop quinua, pop kiwicha*
sugar	*azúcar*
*bran	*salvado de trigo*
flax seed	*linaza*
*raisins	*pasas*
*dried fruit (prunes, peaches, apples, apricots)	*fruta seca (guindones, duraznos, manzanas, damascos)*
cinnamon sticks	*canela*
jam in packet	*mermelada en sachet o sobre*
coffee, tea, herbal tea, anise, cocoa, milo	*café, té, mate, anís, chocolate en polvo, milo*
butter, margarine	*mantequilla, margarina*

LUNCH

bread	*pan*
crackers	*galletas de sal*

inquire about your unit before purchasing. Mobile phone shops are everywhere; beware of overcharging at airports. You can get a Peruvian cell phone number and can purchase credit (*recarga*) anywhere, for any amount you like. Coverage is good in the cities and some rural areas, but remote locations may have coverage by only one carrier or none at all. You can purchase SIMs for both carriers to extend your coverage. Satellite phones, which work almost everywhere, can be rented in Huaraz from some tour operators and Casa de Guias (see Chapter 8 introduc-

tion) for about US$15 per day, plus US$2 per minute of outgoing air time.

Provisions

Shopping in Peru is fun. With many colorful markets (*mercados*) and old-fashioned general stores (*tiendas* or *bodegas*) to choose from, you can take in the local atmosphere while you stock up on provisions. There are also modern supermarkets in major cities, which offer the largest variety of products, including imported items. Check the expiration date on perishable goods, especially in small

*hard cheese	*queso maduro*
white cheese	*queso*
tuna or other canned fish	*atún*
*salami	*salami*
*canned chicken	*pollo enlatado*
mayonnaise in packet	*mayonesa en sachet o sobre*
ketchup, tomato paste,	*salsa de tomate, pasta de tomate,*
mustard, all in packets	*mostaza*
roast corn, roast beans	*cancha, numia*
*salty snacks, chips (plantain,	*chifles, camotes, habas*
sweet potato, broad beans)	
*nuts (peanuts, walnuts,	*nueces (maní, nueces, pecanas, almen-*
pecans, almonds, Brazil nuts)	*dras, castañas)*
chocolate	*chocolate*
candy	*caramelos*
sweet popped corn and	*maná*
related snacks	

SUPPER

ramen or angel hair noodles	*fideos Ajinomén o cabello de ángel*
*instant mashed potatoes	*puré de papas*
broadbean flour, pea flour	*harina de habas, harina de arvejas*
*dry soy protein	*carne de soya*
*soup mixes	*sopa en sobre*
stock cubes	*cubitos Maggi*
salt, spices	*sal, especies*
cookies	*galletas dulces*
spreadable toffee in packet	*manjar blanco en sachet*

towns. In the smallest villages, shops may stock only very basic items, if that.

Our preference is for local Peruvian foods, and many nutritious, lightweight, and nonperishable foods, ideal for trekking, can be obtained locally. Larger markets have a selection of dried fruits, nuts, and toasted flours (various cereals, peas, broad beans). The latter make soups and warm breakfast cereals heartier and more nutritious; mix a small amount in cold water, then add it to the pot. Imported dehydrated meals might be available from a few tour operators in major trekking centers such as Huaraz and Caraz, and a few dehydrated Peruvian dishes are found in large supermarkets.

Cancha, toasted corn, a Peruvian highland staple, is ideal for trekking. You might find it in shops, but more likely you will have to buy dry corn and ask someone to toast it for you (try a restaurant where you have just eaten). Canned fish is very common. Although people might call it *atún*, it is not always tuna; check the label. *Caballa* (mackerel) and sardines are also common. *Lomitos* and *filete* are the highest quality, *graté* is the lowest.

A sample shopping list of local foods is provided in this chapter. Choose according to the length of your trek, altitude, climate, taste, and of course appetite. For treks at high altitude (including most treks in this book), choose fast-cooking ingredients such as angel hair noodles and instant mashed potatoes. At altitude, water boils at a lower temperature than at sea level, hence things like rice and lentils take forever to cook.

GETTING TO THE TRAILHEAD

Most departmental capitals (except Chachapoyas—see Chapter 7) have air service with Avianca, LATAM, Peruvian Airlines, or Star Perú. Smaller cities, such as Huaraz, Ayacucho, and Jauja, are served by LC Peru. Airline websites are given in Appendix A. Prices vary, so it is worth shopping around and purchasing ahead. LATAM charges higher prices for non-Peruvians. With few exceptions, most flights in Peru either originate or terminate in Lima, and it is difficult to travel from one region to another without making a connection in the capital.

Bus service reaches almost all cities and towns in Peru. As with air travel,

Bus service of some kind reaches almost all cities and towns in Peru.

Lima is the national hub, but there are more interregional bus services than flights. Along the main coastal highway (Panamericana), from Lima to the highlands (Huaraz, Ayacucho, Arequipa, and Cuzco) and between Cuzco, Arequipa, and Puno, bus service is generally very good. There are different levels of service, and it is worth paying more for a comfortable, reliable bus. Inquire which are the best bus companies for your destination. Cruz del Sur, Ormeño, Móvil Tours, and Oltursa are all large operators; see websites in Appendix A. You can purchase tickets online and sometimes obtain advance discounts. A growing number of large cities in Peru have bus terminals; in others, each bus company has one or more private stations. Bus stations are obvious places for thieves to find tourists with all their valuables; always keep a close eye on your gear.

Airfares and bus prices increase substantially before and during public holidays, when seats may be scarce and advance booking is required.

Vans, called *minibuses, minivans,* or *combis,* are the main form of local and regional transport. In most cases, these run frequently and depart as they fill. For more remote destinations, there are only one or two vans per day with fixed departures, and it is important to purchase a ticket the day before. Shared taxis, called *colectivos, autos,* or *carros,* also provide regional transport. They are more expensive and faster than vans, often too fast. In some cases, a very remote trailhead cannot be reached by public transport. Maybe a truck runs once a week, or you might need to hire a taxi or walk from the nearest town.

5

AN OUNCE OF PREVENTION

In Peru an ounce of prevention is worth *ten* pounds of cure. Safe and healthy trekking and travel are the rule here but must not be taken for granted. Simple routine precautions will suffice to ensure a wonderful experience for most visitors, yet the consequences of carelessness can be severe.

This chapter attempts to summarize a vast and complex literature as well as the authors' experience regarding major health and safety issues. For additional sources of information, see Appendix A and check for updates because things change. Ultimately, most of the safety decisions we take while trekking, traveling, or doing anything else are personal judgment calls. You are responsible for your own welfare in Peru; nobody else will keep you out of trouble.

PUBLIC SAFETY

The trekking routes of Peru are among the safest places in the country. People in the countryside are generally helpful and honest but also poor, so you should not leave your campsite unattended or your valuables strewn about.

The big cities, especially Lima, call for greater caution and a street-smart attitude.

The roads of Peru can be riskier than any of its hiking trails.

Do not display your valuables. Use a money belt for cash and passport, and choose your hotel carefully. Avoid crowds, deserted streets, and dangerous areas of town, usually in the periphery. Be wary of con tricks, and generally stay alert to your surroundings, especially at bus stations. Request local advice before going out late at night.

The greatest hazard for travelers in Peru is road accidents. Inform yourself about which are the better bus companies, and don't be shy about asking a reckless driver to slow down. The speed is displayed in the passenger compartment of most buses. Highway robbery is also an issue in some areas; travel by day whenever possible, which also allows you to enjoy the splendid views.

Armed groups in league with drug traffickers operate in a very few remote areas of Peru, including the upper Huallaga and Ene valleys. Throughout Peru, involvement with the drug scene could lead to prolonged imprisonment or worse. The treks in this book have been selected with public safety in mind, and potentially hazardous areas have been omitted. Conditions can change, so inquire locally before heading into an unfamiliar area.

TREKKING SAFETY

The first step to safe trekking is to know your own abilities and limits, and choose treks compatible with them. Never trek alone, and keep in mind the limitations of your companions, as well as your own. Clear thinking and good communication among fellow trekkers are the best ways to avoid most hazards and prevent accidents. Some hazards are mentioned below, and those for specific treks are given in Section II.

Altitude Sickness

Some people may be affected by acute mountain sickness (AMS, *mal de altura*, *soroche*). It is unpredictable, and good physical condition does not make you immune. The key is to give your body sufficient time to gradually adapt to a change in elevation. Those arriving from sea level should take it easy for the first day or two. Avoid too much exertion, alcohol, and

tobacco. Eat light, high-calorie meals and keep hydrated. Then you can continue to acclimatize on day walks, gradually increasing the elevation. The treks in this book range from 1500 to 5250 m; most are between 3000 and 4500 m.

The symptoms of *soroche* include fatigue, shortness of breath and a pounding heartbeat on mild exertion, headache, decreased appetite, difficulty sleeping, and nausea. If these occur while trekking, stop and rest; don't take a headache higher. If it continues after one day, the only reliable remedy is to descend. *Mate de coca*, an infusion of coca leaves, can sometimes help diminish mild symptoms. The drug acetazolamide has been used to prevent *soroche* but should only be taken as directed by a physician.

Judgment may also be impaired at altitude. If you continue climbing with *soroche*, there is a risk of developing a more severe and potentially fatal form of AMS, which can include pulmonary edema (fluid in the lungs) and cerebral edema (swelling of the brain). Symptoms include severe headache, confusion, loss of coordination, severe shortness of breath, rapid resting pulse, severe cough, pink sputum, severe vomiting, low urine output, and extreme fatigue. If these symptoms occur, descend at once below the level where the symptoms first appeared; do not wait for morning. Even at more modest elevations, special precautions may be required if you have had AMS in the past.

Sun Protection

The high-altitude sun is fierce, and sunburn can be very serious. Wear a long-sleeved shirt (or other top), long pants, a wide-brimmed hat with neck protection, sunscreen for skin and lips, and good-quality sunglasses. Remember that overcast conditions do not necessarily protect you from severe sunburn.

Hypothermia

Hypothermia is a serious hazard for trekkers. The most common cause in Peru during the dry season is a combination of extreme cold and wind; wet conditions are uncommon but increase the risk of hypothermia. Thinner and older people are at higher risk. Adequate clothing is the best form of prevention (see Clothing and Equipment, Chapter 4). You lose a significant amount of heat through your head and neck, so remember to wear a wool hat and neck warmer in cold weather. Also important are sufficient high-calorie foods. Severe shivering and pale skin, the first symptoms of hypothermia, should be dealt with right away. Make camp in a wind-sheltered spot, remove the affected person's clothes if they are wet, and put him or her in a sleeping bag with a warm trekker.

Dehydration

Dehydration is also a hazard, not only on very hot treks but also on cold ones. While trekking in the cold, you lose moisture through sweat and breathing but do not necessarily feel thirsty. It can be difficult to drink very cold water. Prevent this problem by preparing generous amounts of warm drinks with breakfast, which will see you through the first part of the day. The caffeine in coffee, tea, and hot chocolate is a mild diuretic, however; too much of these can make you lose water. You can roughly gauge your state of hydration by paying attention to your urine. If you are not urinating or it is dark yellow or orange, then you need to drink more.

A generous warm drink with breakfast will see you through the first part of the day.

During the trekking season, Peru is generally dry; many streams are seasonal. It is important to drink and fill your water bottle whenever the opportunity arises. Always carry at least a liter of water when heading for ridges, passes, or other areas where you expect it to be scarce.

Hazardous Animals and Plants

Most of the treks in this book are at altitudes where the snakes and insects listed below are currently uncommon, but this could vary with climate change.

Snakes are often shy, and many are harmless. The majority of Peru's three hundred snakes are found in the Amazon basin and the eastern cloud forests. The Peru slender snake (*cola corta del norte*, *Tachymenis peruviana*) is a venomous nocturnal species, found between 2600 and 3000 m, rarely at higher elevations. It hides during the day under vegetation or between rocks on stony slopes. Additional species are found at lower elevations. Be alert when walking and camping in the lower valleys and canyons. Never walk barefoot or in sandals, and do not grope under rocks or vegetation. If you see a

Watch your step!

snake, do not panic or disturb it; retreat quietly until it slithers away.

Mosquitoes (*zancudos*) are hazardous because of the diseases they transmit. *Anopheles* mosquitoes, found below 2000 m in the Peruvian Amazon and parts of the department of Amazonas (Chapter 7), Cajamarca, and Piura, can transmit malaria. Present in the same regions at elevations below 2300 m, *Aedes aegyptii* mosquitoes can transmit yellow fever (for which there is a vaccine), dengue fever, chicungunya, and zika. Mosquitoes at higher altitudes, horseflies (*tábanos*), blackflies (*mosquitos*), and most sandflies (*jejenes*) are annoying but generally not dangerous.

Phlebotomy flies (*manta blanca, titira, Lutzomyia* spp.) are small, light-colored hairy sandflies, active in the evening and night. They are vectors of bartonellosis (Peruvian wart, *verruga peruana*), a rare endemic disease found on western slopes and inter-Andean valleys between 1100 and 3200 m; cutaneous leishmaniasis (*uta*), present at similar elevations in circumscribed areas of the highlands and the Amazon basin; and mucocutaneous leishmaniasis (*espundia*) in the Amazon.

To avoid being bitten by insects, wear long sleeves and long pants, use repellent, and make sure your tent has a good mosquito net. If you are allergic to bee or wasp stings, always carry adrenaline (epinephrine). Where there are ants, some might sting; watch where you sit and where you put your hands.

Dogs are ubiquitous; see Pastora the Shepherdess in Trek 2. In the unlikely event that you are bitten by a dog or any other mammal, clean the wound at once by washing it with soap and rinsing it with large amounts of water, and seek medical help without delay. Rabies is present in Peru; consider getting vaccinated before you travel. Treatment will be simpler if you have been vaccinated but may still be required. Public hospitals and health centers (*postas de salud*) generally stock rabies vaccine. They also keep records of local pets that have been vaccinated.

Cattle are frequently left to graze in large unfenced areas, and you will regularly meet them while trekking. Most are curious creatures who may take interest in you, thinking you are bringing them salt. Wave your walking stick to keep them at a safe distance. Fighting bulls are generally raised at high altitudes (so they will be stronger when brought down to the bull rings) and call for greater precautions. Local lore has it that a group of such bulls is usually not aggressive, but a lone *toro* should be avoided. Keep a wary eye on him from afar, and he will most likely do likewise.

Cacti are very common in Peru, even at high altitudes. Watch your step and what you brush against. Some are obvious, others are covered in fuzz, and there are tiny ones at ground level that you will be sure to notice if you sit on one. Tweezers are handy for removing spines, but some have barbs and are hard to extract. There are also spiny trees and shrubs, especially in dry valleys at lower elevations. Nettles, some with lovely orange flowers (*Loasa grandiflora*, known as *ortiga macho*, *shinua*, *puka quisa*), grow at the base of rocks between 3900 and 4700 m. Their sting goes away in a few minutes if you do not scratch. Other noxious plants are uncommon along our treks.

Fording Rivers

Caution and proper timing are required to safely ford a river. Glacial rivers that are shallow early in the morning may become impassable in the afternoon, especially on warm sunny days. Flash flooding can occur in drainages with large watersheds upstream. Never camp right at the water's edge, and keep an eye on weather conditions upriver. Do not take chances fording a flooded river; wait it out instead. Do not assume a flimsy bridge is safe to cross; fording the river may be a better option if the water is not too high.

Unstable Slopes and Ledges

Trails on steep slopes, old landslides, scree, talus, and boulder fields are generally worn into the slope and stable. After prolonged rain or where there is a new landslide, the slope can be unstable. Whenever crossing, do not lean into the slope; keep your weight over your feet and do not linger. Look for a track where people or animals might have walked. If you are not comfortable, then retreat to a secure location; there might be a better place to cross above the slide, or you might have to turn back. Some trails go along narrow ledges. Make your pack as streamlined as possible, without things hanging off the side. Stay calm,

Stay calm, do not look down, and keep moving.

do not look down, and proceed steadily without lingering.

Losing Your Way

Getting seriously lost can be hazardous because it causes some people to panic and do dangerous things. Keep your cool, and see Maps and Navigation in Chapter 3. To prevent getting lost, check your position at regular intervals and, when in doubt, go back to a known landmark. Remember that ridges are often natural routes, generally preferable to river valleys, which can become impassable canyons. Never go down a drop you will not be able to climb back up. If necessary, discontinue your planned trek and return along the route you came.

STAYING HEALTHY

Trekking in Peru makes you feel good—strong and healthy.

Before You Travel

A pretravel medical checkup is advised if you have an ongoing health problem or are unsure whether or not you are fit for your journey. Be sure to obtain adequate amounts of any medications you take on a regular basis, as these may not be available in Peru. If you wear eyeglasses, get a clearly written prescription to bring with you in case yours are lost or broken. Contact lenses may not be appropriate in the cold, dry, windy conditions of highland Peru. Always bring a pair of glasses, in addition to your contacts.

Arrange for immunizations well in advance of traveling. In consultation with your physician or a travel clinic, consider receiving or updating the following: polio, diphtheria-tetanus, typhoid fever, hepatitis A and B, and rabies. Yellow fever vaccine and malaria prophylaxis are advised if you plan to visit jungle areas.

Prepare a first-aid kit; a basic one is suggested in this chapter. Well-stocked pharmacies are plentiful in Peruvian cities and larger towns, and prescriptions are only required for drugs of addiction. Except for generics (genéricos), which you should specifically request if you want them, medications are generally expensive. Be sure to pack your first-aid kit in several layers of plastic bags to keep it dry.

While You Are in Peru

Although most trekkers experience no serious illness, minor digestive and respiratory disorders do occur. Some can be prevented as outlined below. Treat minor ailments as suggested and with patience and a positive attitude. They are part and parcel of the experience.

Drinking Water

Untreated water must not be consumed anywhere in Peru. Do not drink directly from taps, lakes, streams, springs, or wells. All water must be purified. Boiling for 1 minute at sea level is most reliable, but considerably more time is required at higher altitudes. This would mean carrying a lot of extra weight in fuel and is not practical for longer treks. None of the other methods of purification described below eliminates all waterborne pathogens. In our experience, use of a high-quality ceramic filter, followed by boiling only when the water source is particularly dirty, is an effective practical compromise. Water from obviously contaminated sources, such as mines or rivers draining larger towns, should not be used for purification.

Iodine, chlorine, potassium permanganate, and other chemicals can be used to purify water. Micropur is a chemical purification brand available in Peru, but read the instructions carefully; some tablets are for use with 1 liter of water, others for much larger volumes. Some chemical purification should always be carried for emergencies, even if you have a filter, but it is not suitable for long-term use because of potential toxicity and unpalatable taste. There are a number of portable water filters on the market. Lighter, cheaper models have a limited life

FIRST-AID KIT CHECKLIST

If you are allergic to any of the following medications, ask a physician for a substitute. Items marked with an asterisk (*) are difficult to obtain in Peru. Check all expiration dates before purchasing.

SUPPLIES
*first-aid guide
*adhesive suture strips (Steri-Strips)
*alcohol swabs
oral rehydration salts *(sales de rehidratación oral)*
water purification tablets *(tabletas para purificar el agua,* e.g., Micropur)
small bar of soap *(jaboncillo)*
elastic bandage *(venda elástica)*
gauze *(gaza)*
adhesive tape *(esparadrapo)*
adhesive strips *(curitas)*
scissors *(tijeras)*
tweezers *(pinzas)*
safety pins *(imperdibles)*
latex gloves *(guantes)*

MEDICATIONS
*all your usual medications
*acetaminophen-codeine, for more severe pain (a prescription drug in Peru)
acetaminophen 500 mg *(acetaminofén)*, for fever
ibuprofen 400 mg *(ibuprofeno)*, antinflammatory for sore joints
ciprofloxacin 500 mg *(cipofloxacina)*, broad-spectrum antibiotic
azithromycin 500 mg *(azitromicina)*, broad-spectrum antibiotic
metronidazole 500 mg *(metronidazol)*, for amoebas and giardia
an antihistamine *(antihistamínico)*, for minor allergic reactions
*epinephrine 1 mg/ml *(epinefrina)* with syringe *(jeringuilla)*, if you have had
 a severe allergic reaction, for example, to bee stings

CREAMS AND OINTMENTS
moisturizing cream *(crema hidratante)*
petroleum jelly *(vaselina)*
bacitracin-neomycin *(crema antibiótica bacitracina-neomicina)*, antibiotic
 for cuts and scrapes
isoconazole *(crema antimicótica isoconazol)*, antifungal
betamethasone *(crema betametasona)*, steroid for minor skin rashes

EYE DROPS
ciprofloxacin *(ciprofloxacino oftálmico)*, broad-spectrum antibiotic

Street food can be tasty but is not recommended.

span, and their filter elements (unavailable in Peru) may have to be replaced frequently. Higher-quality models, which contain long-lasting cleanable ceramic filters, are heavier and more expensive but very reliable. Compact ultraviolet-light devices do not remove particles.

A wide variety of bottled beverages are sold in Peru, including purified or mineral water (*agua*), beer (*cerveza*), and soft drinks (*gaseosas*). All are safe but not practical to carry on anything longer than a day hike. In cities, please purchase large bottles of water (rather than many small ones) to minimize the amount of plastic waste. Hot beverages such as coffee or tea and the very popular *mates* (herbal teas), which are prepared using boiled water, are safe.

Food

When trekking independently, you prepare your own food, which makes precautions that much easier. The dry trekking staples listed under Provisions in Chapter 4 are all safe, and just about any other food is also safe if you cook it long enough. Raw fruits and vegetables in Peru are particularly varied and tasty, however, and it would be a shame to miss them. Clean them thoroughly using ordinary water, then peel them or give them a final rinse with purified water. Avoid raw

foods that grow in close contact with the ground and cannot be peeled (such as lettuce and strawberries), or rinse them with a disinfectant solution sold in Peruvian supermarkets. Most restaurant food is safe, but you should be mindful of general cleanliness, which usually reflects kitchen hygiene. Be extra cautious about prepared food sold in markets (if there are many flies, go elsewhere), and avoid all food sold by street vendors.

Personal Hygiene

Personal hygiene is important when trekking. Don't forget to wash your hands regularly just because you are on the trail, and politely encourage guides and muleteers to do likewise. Washing up with a washcloth is also quick and easy while trekking. Keep the use of soap to a bare minimum to avoid getting it into water sources.

Skin Problems

Sunburn, windburn, and dry skin are common at high altitude. Take moisturizing cream (*crema hidratante*) and petroleum jelly (*vaselina*, sold in small containers in Peruvian shops and pharmacies) for chafed lips and skin. Bug bites are best left to heal on their own; the more you scratch, the longer they itch. Occasional rashes and fungal infections may occur; fortunately, more serious skin problems are rare. Seek medical help whenever your symptoms persist or if you develop a sore or ulcer on your skin which does not heal.

Gastrointestinal Infections

"I fart, therefore I am."

—Anonymous

Even if you take all necessary precautions, you may experience a minor

EMERGENCY CONTACTS

Emergency phone numbers change frequently in Peru and do not always work. Communications can fail on or off the trail, so self-reliance should be your first, not your last, resort. Before starting a trek, obtain current emergency numbers locally and try them before leaving town. Where there is no search and rescue service, you can get the numbers of the local police and fire stations. Take more than one number with you.

SEARCH-AND-RESCUE ORGANIZATIONS

Asociación de Guías de Montaña del Perú (AGMP)
   Peruvian Mountain Guides Association, www.agmp.pe.
Departamento de Salvamento de Alta Montaña (DEPSAM)
   specialized unit of the Policía Nacional del Perú (PNP)
   Caraz headquarters, phone 966 831 514.

PHONE NUMBERS

The following are numbers where you can call to inquire about emergency contacts, not necessarily emergency numbers themselves. Phone numbers are listed as dialed from a Peruvian cell phone. If using a satellite phone, inquire in advance about access codes.

NATIONWIDE
Tourist Police	toll free 0800 22221, Lima headquarters (01) 460 1060
Police (PNP)	105 (does not work everywhere)
Fire Department	116 (does not work everywhere)

AREQUIPA
AGMP	959 912 267, contact Carlos or Olivia Zárate
DEPSAM	(054) 627 380 / 964 610 110 / Chivay (054) 531 165
Tourist Police	office at Calle Jerusalén 315, does not have a phone

AYACUCHO (CENTRAL HIGHLANDS)
Tourist Police	(066) 315 892

CHACHAPOYAS
Tourist Police	996 940 295
Fire Department	(041) 477 049

CUZCO
AGMP	984 381 052, contact Marco Pérez
DEPSAM	966 830 413 / 984 706 454
Tourist Police	(084) 235 123

HUARAZ (CORDILLERA BLANCA)
AGMP Casa de Guías	941 946 818 / (043) 421 811
DEPSAM	966 831 514
Tourist Police	(043) 422 487

PUNO
Tourist Police	(051) 352 303

gastrointestinal upset during your visit to Peru. A bellyache, gas, or a little diarrhea are best treated with rest, dietary restraint, fluids, and especially patience. Oral rehydration solutions and salts (*sales de rehidratación oral*) are readily available in Peru but are not required for healthy adults with mild to moderate diarrhea.

Seek medical help if diarrhea persists for a week or more or if you develop a high fever or rash, have severe cramps, or pass blood or pus in your stool. If you have severe symptoms while trekking and cannot reach a medical facility, you can take metronidazole (500 mg 3 times a day) and either ciprofloxacin (500 mg every 12 hours) or azithromycin (500 mg once a day) until you reach a doctor. Recurrent episodes of bloating, with vast amounts of foul-smelling gas from above and below, suggest giardia or a related protozoal infection. Either can be treated with metronidazole.

Constipation can also be a problem on the trail. Most trekking foods have little fiber, and water can be scarce in some areas. Keeping well hydrated helps prevent constipation. Bran (*salvado de trigo*) and flax seeds (*linaza*) make a good addition to many starchy staples, and whole-wheat bread (*pan integral*) and crackers (*galletas integrales*) are available in larger towns and cities.

Upper Respiratory Infections

Cold, dry air at high altitudes irritates the upper respiratory tract. Candy can help relieve throat irritation for people who breathe through their mouth. Hoarse coughs and snotty noses are frequent among rural children and trekkers alike, as are common colds. Rest, take fluids, and be patient. For a sore throat, gargle with warm salty water. Severe cough or chest pain with high fever is reason to seek medical care. You can take ciprofloxacin or azithromycin (doses as above) until you reach a doctor.

Other Infectious Diseases

Avoiding unpasteurized milk and dairy products will decrease the risk of tuberculosis and brucellosis, both present in Peru. Milk powder (recommended for trekking), canned evaporated milk (*Leche Gloria*, available everywhere), and long-life UHT-treated milk are all safe. For insect-borne diseases, see Hazardous Animals and Plants, earlier in this chapter.

Injuries

The most important response to injury is to stay calm. Clean all minor wounds with soap and plenty of water, disinfect the skin around them with alcohol swabs, and dress them with gauze and adhesive tape. Support sprained joints with an elastic bandage, and splint injured limbs. For eye injuries, apply a drop of antibiotic (see First-Aid Kit Checklist, in this chapter) and patch the eye for one or two days, keeping the eyelid firmly closed with gauze pads and adhesive tape. After removing the patch, apply antibiotic drops three to four times a day until the eye feels normal or you reach a doctor.

Injured trekkers may benefit from a day's rest, after which they can either continue or, if necessary, make their way out. In all cases, the trekking party should stay together and move at the pace of the slowest trekker. In the event of a serious injury, make camp in the nearest secure location, and keep the injured person warm, dry, and orally hydrated. Call for assistance; if there is no cell phone coverage right there, try a higher location with line of sight to a town. If you cannot call and there are enough trekkers, two should go together to seek help as soon as possible, while one stays behind with the injured person.

After You Return Home

If you have been unwell during your travels, feel you have been at particular risk, or have been away for six months or more, arrange for a general medical examination.

IN CASE OF EMERGENCY

Before each trek, prepare a list of emergency and personal contact numbers for that area. Also see Emergency Contacts in this chapter.

Search and Rescue

Most trekkers find their own way out of most predicaments, but it is important to have backup in case something goes seriously wrong. If trekking independently, advise a reliable friend or relative of your planned trekking route and estimated date of return. Set a date by which search should begin, but remember that delays and unexpected changes of route are common. In the absence of a friend or relative, advise the manager of the hotel where you are staying or a local tour operator of your plans. You can also try your embassy. Should a serious accident occur, Peruvian authorities may contact your embassy to coordinate

and finance rescue efforts. If you are seriously delayed, try to advise your contacts of your revised plans.

The Cordillera Blanca has the most elaborate rescue infrastructure for mountaineers and trekkers; you can register with the Casa de Guías (see Emergency Contacts), and advise them of your itinerary. There are also emergency contacts in Cuzco and Arequipa. Get in touch with them before heading out independently to remote areas. Search and rescue could prove to be very expensive. If you want insurance to cover these costs, obtain it before traveling; it is not available in Peru. Keep the insurance information with you, and also leave it with your emergency contacts.

Medical Facilities

There are public and private hospitals, as well as private clinics (*clínicas*) of varying standards in all cities and larger towns (usually provincial and departmental capitals) of Peru. Smaller towns and villages may have only a modest health center (*posta médica*), if that. The best facilities, and physicians who speak languages other than Spanish, are in the largest cities including Lima, Arequipa, and Cuzco. Most Peruvians who can afford to do so travel to Lima for major medical care. You can ask your embassy or consulate for a list of doctors and dentists who speak your language. Quality medical care is expensive in Peru, so make sure you have adequate insurance.

Andean deer (taruca, Hippocamelus antisensis)

A NOTE ABOUT SAFETY

Safety is an important concern in all outdoor activities. No guidebook can alert you to every hazard or anticipate the limitations of every reader. Therefore, the descriptions of roads, trails, routes, and natural features in this book are not representations that a particular place or excursion will be safe for your party. When you follow any of the routes described in this book, you assume responsibility for your own safety. Under normal conditions, safe trekking requires the usual attention to traffic, road and trail conditions, weather, terrain, the capabilities of your party, and other factors. Keeping informed on current conditions and exercising common sense are the keys to safe and enjoyable trekking.

Political conditions may add to the risks of travel in Peru in ways that this book cannot predict. When you travel, you assume this risk and should keep informed of developments that may make safe travel difficult or impossible.

—Mountaineers Books

Opposite: *Colca Canyon (Trek 26)*

SECTION II

THE TREKS

6

SELECTING A TREK

Peru is bigger than you think. If you have limited time, consider doing treks in one area (chapter) or in a couple of neighboring ones. We are confident you will return later for others.

Treks in this section present varying levels of difficulty and run from half a day to two weeks in length. (See the Trek Summaries table at the beginning of this book.) A number of the treks are long. Most of these, however, have several possible entry and exit points. You can trek only part of a route to make it shorter. If, on the other hand, you are looking for a longer trekking experience, there are various contiguous routes that can easily be combined. Chapter maps will assist you in planning.

The routes were selected to offer innovative treks and do not include the most popular ones that may be overused and have already been described elsewhere. There are endless trekking opportunities in Peru, and you are heartily encouraged, once you feel comfortable, to strike out and discover your own.

The described treks are grouped into six chapters, corresponding to six geographical regions. Most of the regions are popular tourist destinations in their own right; not surprisingly they also offer excellent trekking opportunities. These regions are presented from north to south. The most popular trekking routes ("the beaten path") and suggested day walks ("limbering up") are listed at the beginning of each chapter. The latter include some very nice hikes that are great for acclimatization or as a complement to longer treks. Although not described in detail, they are well worth checking out.

UNDERSTANDING THE TREK DESCRIPTIONS

Each trek begins with a rating (difficulty), length, and timeframe. Treks are rated as easy, moderately difficult, difficult, or very difficult. This subjective classification is based on a combination of the trek's length, altitude, gradient, navigational challenge, trail conditions, and other factors. A range is given for the timeframe (e.g., three to four days) to allow for variations in trekking pace and style. Elevations listed are the lowest and highest points of a trek, not the beginning and end. Next is a list of required maps; these are important complements

Río Apurimac (left) and Río Blanco as seen from Choquequirao (Trek 22)

to those included in this book. (We do not recommend undertaking a trek without them, unless you have downloaded larger versions of our maps; see Using the Maps, below.)

We then list summaries of water availability, hazards and annoyances, permits and fees, and services and provisions available along the route. Next we describe the trek's special features and attractions, followed by access to the trailhead, and then a detailed account of the route and, finally, how to return after the trek. Important landmarks are boldfaced in the text where first encountered along the trekking route, and they are labeled on that trek's map (unless otherwise noted).

Because every trekker has his or her own pace, and conditions on the same trail vary from one time to another, route descriptions indicate distance, not time. Distance is measured as walking distance along the route, not line-of-sight distance between points. Trek descriptions use metric units, as used in Peru. For conversion factors between metric and English

units, see the Unit Conversion Table in Appendix C. After the first walk or two, you will be able to better gauge how long it takes you to cover a given distance over different terrains. Use the elevation profiles to help plan your treks.

Trek descriptions are easier to follow in the direction indicated. The words *trek*, *hike*, and *walk* are all used interchangeably, as are *trail* and *path*. Simple descriptive terminology is used whenever possible, but inevitably everybody has their own nuances for terms such as *steep*, *gentle*, or *undulating*. Spanish and Quechua words that refer to a type of area or geographic feature and don't have a precise English translation are used in the text and described in Appendix B. Plant and animal names are given in English (when English names exist), Spanish, Quechua, or Aymara, as well as the scientific (Latin) names.

Bearings are given in very few of the trek descriptions. They are all true north and do not account for compass declination.

USING THE MAPS

The map legend is found at the beginning of this book. Elevations on maps are shown in meters above sea level. Contour intervals range from 50 to 400 m. The scales shown on our maps are approximate and rounded to the nearest thousand meters. Common abbreviations used in the maps are: Q (*quebrada*—ravine, gully, or valley), R (*río*—river), L (*lago* or *laguna*—lake), and C (*cerro*—hill). Vehicle roads are designated as main (paved), secondary (unpaved or paved but narrow), or vehicle track (rough dirt).

Trekking routes are shown with curved arrows; straight arrows point to locations off the map. Trails fall into three categories: pre-Hispanic roads, well-defined trails, and faint trails or cross-country (off-trail) routes. Short isolated segments of an ancient road may not be shown on the maps. The distinction between the various types of trails is subjective. Sometimes, pre-Hispanic roads are indistinguishable from contemporary trails, and a wide horse trail may be used as a vehicle track. Glaciers are receding in Peru; the current altitude at which a glacier starts is likely to be higher than that shown by the glacier contours on the map.

Maps are as detailed as possible, but they cannot show all features whether or not they are described in the text, such as all forks along a route or every stone wall, gate, or stream. Larger maps of our treks and map files for upload to GPS smartphones are available from the authors at www.trekkingperu.org. You should always have a printed map in addition to the electronic one. Whatever map you use, you will need to navigate along the route, not merely follow it. To avoid carrying this entire book on the trail, you may wish to make photocopies of a particular trek description, map, and emergency contacts in Chapter 5.

7

CHACHAPOYAS

The northern highlands of Peru are full of natural beauty and archaeological riches, ideal for trekking. Nestled here amid sheer cliffs sprouting cloud forests and waterfalls is the quaint city of Chachapoyas or "Chacha," as the locals call it. Chachapoyas is capital of the department of Amazonas and namesake of a large surrounding area. The city makes a pleasant base from which to explore these surroundings. It has most services and good road links to Chiclayo, Lima, Tarapoto, the jungle, and neighboring Ecuador. Light aircraft fly between Chachapoyas and Tarapoto. The closest options for flying from Lima, then taking a bus, are via Jaén, Tarapoto, or Chiclayo. The impressive valley of the Río Utcubamba, a tributary of the Río Marañón, which in turn flows to the Amazon, is at the heart of the Chachapoyas region.

Chachapoyas has some of Peru's most fascinating and least exploited archaeological areas. It was once home to the pre-Inca Chachapoya people (AD 0–1500), and a number of their ancient cities and fortresses can be visited. Unique cliffside niches containing many sarcophagi, lost stone cities, and over two hundred

Cliff-side mausoleums at Diablo Wasi

Inca mummies found at Laguna de los Cóndores are just a few of the treasures hidden by the lush vegetation. Not to

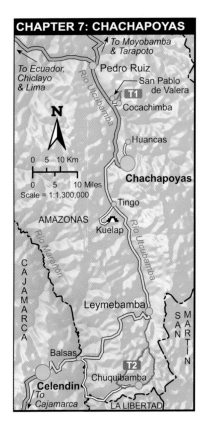

CHAPTER 7: CHACHAPOYAS

To Moyobamba & Tarapoto

To Ecuador, Chiclayo & Lima

Pedro Ruiz

San Pablo de Valera

T1

Cocachimba

N

Huancas

0 5 10 Km

0 5 10 Miles
Scale = 1:1,300,000

Chachapoyas

Tingo

AMAZONAS

Kuelap

Río Ucuyamba

Río Marañon

C A J A M A R C A

Leymebamba

S A N

M A R T Í N

Balsas

T2

Celendin
To Cajamarca

Chuquibamba

LA LIBERTAD

be missed is the superb Leymebamba Archaeology Museum, 75 km south of Chachapoyas, where many of the Inca mummies from Laguna de los Cóndores are displayed alongside a fine collection of textiles and other artifacts. The museum is along the route of Trek 2.

The beaten path. Chachapoyas is much less visited than Cuzco, Arequipa, or the Cordillera Blanca but nevertheless receives its share of tourists. All tour agencies here offer excursions to the Kuelap archaeological site, a massive citadel with over four hundred buildings in an impressive location high atop a ridge. It can be reached by vehicle (a long ride) or by cable car from Nuevo Tingo.

Alternatively, walking to Kuelap along a trail that climbs 1200 m, in 5 km, from the village of Tingo is also a good option and a demanding acclimatization hike.

Tour agencies in Chacha also offer day trips to the Gocta Waterfall (Trek 1) and trekking in the Gran Vilaya region, especially the valley of Huaylla Belén, as well as to Laguna de los Cóndores.

Limbering up. Many pre-Inca roads throughout the area, well maintained by local inhabitants, make wonderful day-hiking routes. An easy stroll from Chachapoyas to Higos Urco, returning along the road from Mendoza, makes a gentle introduction (9 km round-trip). Another easy walk is from Chacha 8 km to the village of Huancas and 5 km beyond to Huanca Urco, with fine views over the Río Sonche. Various archaeological sites can be accessed on foot. In addition to the difficult climb from Tingo to Kuelap (see above), hiking from Leymebamba to the ruins of La Congona is recommended. This moderately difficult full-day hike leads to some thirty typical Chachapoyan stone roundhouses decorated with friezes.

Featured treks. Trek 1, Gocta, is an easy, popular, and delightful walk to the world's third-highest waterfall, accessed either from Chachapoyas or the town of Pedro Ruiz. Trek 2, the Río Atuen Circuit, is a longer and moderately difficult loop through this scenic valley starting in Leymebamba. The route combines mountain passes, lakes, archaeological sites, remote villages, fantastic views, and—if you are lucky—the opportunity to see condors. Easier to spot on either trek are a variety of beautiful hummingbirds and flocks of boisterous scarlet-fronted parakeets.

1 GOCTA
THE SECRET WATERFALL

Rating: Easy 14.5-km, 1- to 2-day trek
Elevation: 1700 to 2325 m
Maps: IGN 1:100,000 Chachapoyas (13h); ESCALE Amazonas (Bongara)
Water: Available from several streams along the route
Hazards and annoyances: Cliffs (use caution near the edge when taking those unforgettable photos); wet slippery rocks by the falls. Flash flooding; keep an eye on the weather, and don't get too close to the falls. Bathing at the base of the lower tier not recommended; logs and rocks can fall, so keep a safe distance. Some biting insects.
Permits and fees: US$4 visitor's fee charged when entering at San Pablo de Valera or Cocachimba. Compulsory local guide (US$15 for group of up to fifteen visitors; consider the payment as a contribution to the community).
Services and provisions: The villages of San Pablo de Valera and Cocachimba both have community tourism projects that offer basic accommodations, guides, and pack animals. There is a very comfortable lodge in Cocachimba (see Appendix A); you can camp in San Pablo at Hotel Gocta (under construction in 2017), and simple accommodations can be found in Pedro Ruiz. Tours are available from agencies in Chachapoyas. Chachapoyas has the best-stocked shops, Pedro Ruiz has less selection, and only basic supplies are available in San Pablo and Cocachimba. Rubber boots and a rain poncho are recommended by the falls; these may be rented in San Pablo or Cocachimba.

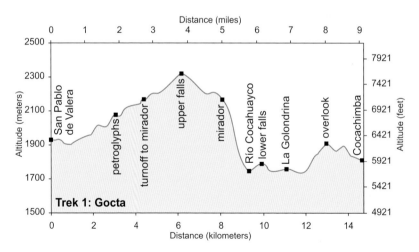

SECRETS OF THIS SIZE are hard to keep, yet the residents of the district of Valera, northwest of Chachapoyas, did not reveal the existence of Gocta, a 771-meter waterfall, until the German Stefan Zimmendorff came across it in 2002. This spectacular waterfall, surrounded by cloud forest, ranks third in the world on the National Geographic

Secrets the size of Gocta Waterfall are hard to keep.

Society's list, after Angel Falls in Venezuela and Tugela Falls in South Africa. Gocta has two tiers: the upper waterfall is 231 m high, and the lower waterfall is 540 m high. Gocta is the source of the Río Cocahuayco, a tributary of the Utcubamba, and good trails on both sides of the Cocahuayco lead to the falls. Views along the way are magnificent, and the area is rich in flora and fauna, including 110 bird species and 41 species of orchids.

Most visitors to Gocta walk along only one of the two trails that run on either side of the Río Cocahuayco. Our route includes both, starting in the village of San Pablo de Valera, above the north bank of the river; tell your guide you wish to walk on both sides. From San Pablo a trail runs along the base of impressive cliffs and leads to an excellent lookout over the falls. Beyond this viewpoint, it continues to the base of the upper falls, where you can get so close that you feel the incredible force of the water. From the lookout, a steep secondary trail descends through forest to a bridge over the Río Cocahuayco and joins the main trail on the south bank, where you can continue to the base of the lower waterfall. On the way back, the main trail along the south bank leads to the village of Cocachimba. Doing the trek from Cocachimba to San Pablo is also feasible but involves more climbing.

In order to do the trek in one day and have enough time to reach both tiers and enjoy the falls, you must start early and move fast. Spending the night before in San Pablo and/or staying in Cocachimba at the end of the walk is recommended. It is also possible to camp along the trail at La Golondrina.

Access. San Pablo de Valera is reached from either Chachapoyas or Pedro Ruiz. Near the village of Cocahuayco, 16 km south of Pedro Ruiz and 35 km north of Chachapoyas, two secondary roads go east, uphill along either side of the Río Cocahuayco. The road along the north side climbs steeply in 6 km to San Pablo de Valera, the start of the trek. The road along the south side of the Río Cocahuayco climbs more gently in 5.3 km to Cocachimba, the end of our route. Shared taxis and vans run between Chachapoyas and Pedro Ruiz, passing the turnoffs for San Pablo and Cocachimba; you can walk up from there. A taxi from Chachapoyas to San Pablo or Cocachimba costs about US$25; from Pedro Ruiz a taxi costs US$10, mototaxi US$6.

Route. At the plaza of **San Pablo de Valera**, look for the sign and follow the street past the turnoff for Hotel Gocta. It quickly becomes a well-graded trail that drops at first and then climbs gradually east through an agricultural zone; look for the *trapiche* (sugar cane mill) in this area. In 1.9 km you reach a **shelter** with excellent views of the Cocahuayco valley, the villages of Cocachimba and La Coca on the opposite side of the valley, and several waterfalls tumbling down the cliffs beyond. In another 800 m reach a **second shelter** with welcome shade or rain protection and more spectacular views of the valley. Along the way, note the impressive cliffs to your left. At 350 m past the second shelter you will find faint **petroglyphs** depicting birds and animals. Fortunately there is a sign, otherwise they would be easy to miss. About 400 m ahead is a **third shelter** with more views. Beyond this point the trail veers north and the surroundings gradually change from fields to cloud forest. In 1.4 km you reach a **signed intersection**: continuing straight to the north leads to the base of the upper waterfall; heading right, to the east, to a *mirador* or viewpoint; and beyond to the Cocachimba side. (If the weather is reasonably clear, yet it looks like it might close in, go first to the *mirador*, which is only 100 m down the trail to the east. Don't miss the window of opportunity to enjoy what is perhaps the finest view of Gocta.)

From the intersection, the trail to the upper waterfall goes through beautiful cloud forest. Take the time to spot some orchids and other flowers, moss- and bromeliad-covered trees, and giant tree ferns. Perhaps you will be lucky and a mixed-species flock of birds will go by. The climb is somewhat steeper here, and in 1 km you reach a bridge over a side stream. Another 600 m beyond is a side trail to the right; continue along the main trail for 150 m to a spectacular spot alongside the **upper falls**. To have the thundering cascade just in front of you and to feel its power make you

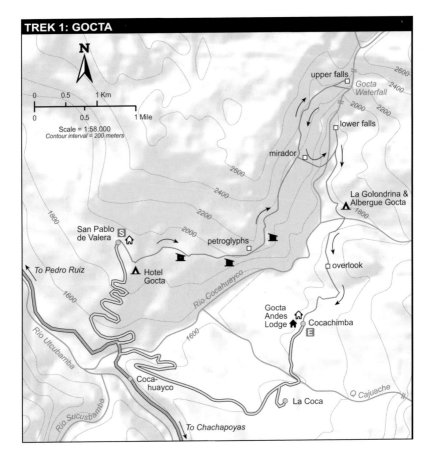

TREK 1: GOCTA

ignore the fact that you are being blown around and getting soaked. The side trail you passed leads to the river between the two tiers from where there are more views to the upper falls. If the water level is not too high, you can bathe here.

To continue to the Cocachimba side and the lower falls, return to the intersection and take the trail east, down to the *mirador*. This is the closest place from which to see the two tiers together; the view is beautiful, and it is hard to stop taking photos. From here, the trail gets narrower and drops steeply through the forest. In 550 m you reach another view of the falls and 200 m farther a pedestrian suspension bridge over the **Río Cocahuayco**, about 400 vertical meters below the fork on the upper trail. There are no signs along the trails on the Cocachimba side. Go uphill from the bridge to find the trail to the base of the lower falls; it is about 100 m ahead. Follow the main trail uphill to the north (left); in 250 m you reach a bridge over a side stream, and in another 300 m you are there, staring at the giant waterfall. It is time to put on your rain poncho. The trail leads to a pool directly at the base of the **lower falls**, an awe-inspiring sight. You cannot help but feel dwarfed as you look up, up, up and see the water turning to mist before it ever reaches the ground.

To get to Cocachimba, follow the main trail south. Although the distance between the lower falls and Cocachimba is shorter than between the upper falls and San Pablo, walking times are similar because the Cocachimba trail goes up and down more. Enjoy the forest along the way before reaching the agricultural zone. At 1.1 km south of the falls, you walk by a *trapiche* and 500 m farther is **La Golondrina**, where you can buy a drink, get a meal if you have the time to wait for it to be prepared, and stay in a very basic room or camp. Just ahead is **Albergue Gocta**, a shelter for large groups, where there is also space to **camp**. In 250 m you reach another suspension bridge over a side stream, from where you climb more steeply for 1.5 km to reach an **overlook** with nice views back to Gocta, ahead to Cocachimba, and across the river to the cliffs above the San Pablo trail. From here you descend steeply at first and then more gradually to **Cocachimba**, reached in another 1.7 km.

Return. If you have not arranged for someone to pick you up, inquire in Cocachimba if there is a vehicle going to Pedro Ruiz or Chachapoyas or ask for assistance at the tourist office. Walking down to the main road in the evening is not a good idea because public transport is usually full along the Chachapoyas–Pedro Ruiz road and you may be stuck in Cocahuayco, where there are no accommodations or places to camp.

2 RÍO ATUEN CIRCUIT
TRANQUIL TREKKING

Rating: Moderately difficult 88-km, 7- to 9-day trek
Elevation: 2218 to 3973 m
Maps: IGN 1:100,000 Leymebamba (14h); ESCALE Amazonas (Chachapoyas)
Water: Available from streams along most of the route
Hazards and annoyances: Muddy trails in the valleys
Permits and fees: None
Services and provisions: Several hotels are in Leymebamba (one opposite the museum), one basic *hospedaje* in Cochabamba, and a couple of simple *hospedajes* in Chuquibamba. Families may offer basic accommodations in their homes in villages along the route. Chachapoyas has the best-stocked shops; Leymebamba and Chuquibamba have less selection, and only basic items, if any, are available in smaller villages.

THIS IS THE MOST delightfully laid-back and flexible of our longer treks. You can end halfway at Cochabamba or Chuquibamba if you wish, or add several worthwhile side trips to the main route. (The total distance given above and the elevation profile are for the complete trek without side trips.) There is some steady climbing along the way, as well as cross-country sections where navigation skills are required, but the overall trek is not particularly difficult. Elevations and nighttime temperatures are moderate by Peruvian highland standards. The valleys are well watered and green all year, filled with hummingbirds, orchids, and other wildflowers in season (May is delightful). With a little luck you might see condors.

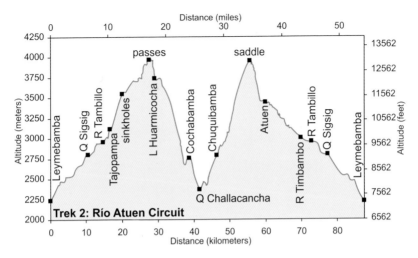

Trek 2: Río Atuen Circuit

Along the route are several interesting undeveloped archaeological sites, fragments of Inca road, lovely scenery, friendly people, and even an unusually friendly dog (see sidebar, Pastora the Shepherdess). The scenic valley of the Río Atuen, upstream from Leymebamba, is the start and end of the circuit. The route goes well beyond Chachapoyas's tourist trail and takes you through several small authentic villages. Their residents are helpful and might invite you to stay in their homes, but neither accommodations nor supplies can be relied on outside Leymebamba and Chuquibamba. You need to be as self-sufficient here as anywhere else in the highlands of Peru.

Access. There are a couple of buses a day, as well as shared taxis, between Chachapoyas and Leymebamba, a pretty 3-hour ride.

Route. From Leymebamba head south along the road to Balsas and Celendín. In 1.3 km you reach the village of Dos de Mayo; take a shortcut trail south here, uphill to the right. The trail crosses the road twice and meets it a third time at 1.4 km past Dos de Mayo, near the archaeology museum, well worth taking time to visit. About 250 m south of the museum, the road forks: the right branch heads west before dropping over endless zigzags to cross the Río Marañón at Balsas; take the left branch south, upstream along the valley of the Río Atuen. Ahead 1.3 km a signed trail branches left to Laguna de los Cóndores.

Continue south along the vehicle track on the west side of the Río Atuen. The canyon walls are higher up ahead, clothed in pretty cloud forest and often in clouds. At 6.7 km past the turnoff to Laguna de los Cóndores you reach a bridge over Quebrada Sigsig. Continue south, climbing more steeply along the road for 3.5 km, to the confluence of the Ríos Atuen and Tambillo (Tingo Grande) and a concrete bridge over the former. Do not cross the bridge; instead follow the trail on the north shore of Río Tambillo to a gate 400 m ahead on your right. There are potential camping spots in this area, or you can ask for permission to stay at a farm 450 m uphill through the gate.

A steady 2-km climb from the farm leads to a ridge and the undeveloped Monte Viudo archaeological site at 3523 m, with two-story Chachapoyan round stone houses

TREK 2: RÍO ATUEN CIRCUIT

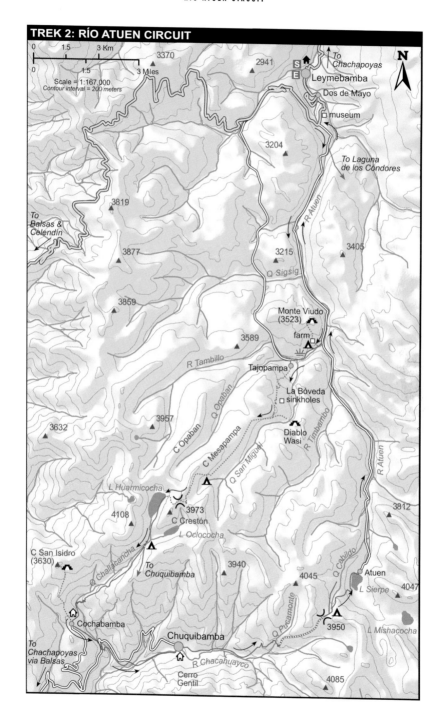

Two-story Chachapoyan stone houses at Monte Viudo

decorated with friezes, set in lovely cloud forest. Just beyond the ruins the forest opens to reveal superb views of the surrounding ridges and valleys. Monte Viudo makes a worthwhile half-day side trip.

From the gate where you entered the farm, head west upstream along the north shore of the very pretty Río Tambillo. The ground is boggy and the trail is not always easy to follow; stay close to the river's edge when you can. In 1.3 km you reach a concrete bridge over the Río Tambillo just past its confluence with **Quebrada San Miguel**. On the south side of the river the trail is drier and stonier, climbing to **Tajopampa**, with a single house, 500 m beyond the bridge. There is not much water ahead, so fill up here.

Head cross-country south and then west from Tajopampa, moving upstream and well above Quebrada San Miguel. There are many cattle trails here, but our route, at times muddy, zigzags southwest along the east slope of **Cerro Mesapampa**, between it and Quebrada San Miguel. At 3.2 km past Tajopampa you reach a gate and stone house in an area known as **La Bóveda**, the vault. Some 50 m (to the east is a large sinkhole (about 100 m deep) which might account for the toponym, with several others ahead along our route. There is also evidence of old circular terracing around the **sinkholes**, and the area is dotted with ancient stone structures.

At 1 km past La Bóveda, amid a small patch of tilled fields, a faint track heads east 900 m to flat ground overlooking Quebrada San Miguel. On the cliffs opposite are two large natural caves, and below them to the left various ancient mausoleums built into the sheer cliff face. The remains have been given the rather evocative name of **Diablo Wasi**, house of the devil. After returning to the tilled fields, head southwest, contouring along the slopes of Cerro Mesapampa. In 6.5 km you reach several excellent **camping** spots above the source of the westernmost branch of Quebrada San Miguel.

Head west up the slopes of **Cerro Mesapampa**, then south, 2.3 km to a **pass** at 3973 m separating the headwaters of Quebrada San Miguel, along which you have been climbing, and the inflow of Laguna Oclococha visible far below. The views are well worth the steady climb. Contour west 800 m to a second pass (not shown on our map) between the summits of Cerro Mesapampa on your right and **Cerro Crestón** on your left, a very nice traverse. At this second pass are great views to **Lago Huarmicocha** below. It is 700 m northwest and 225 m down past a few small patches of forest and a small pond to reach a clear trail at the northeast corner of the lake.

Follow the trail (an Inca road remnant) south, at first along the east shore of the lake, then above it. Past a stone house and corral (once an Inca *tambo*), the trail begins to descend to reach the combined outflows of Oclococha and Huarmicocha, 2.5 km from where you met the trail. Ford the outflow; there are good spots for **camping** here and a fork. The left branch climbs high above the valley, headed south and then east to Chuquibamba, a potential shortcut. Our route descends southwest along the south side of **Quebrada Challacancha**, bound for Cochabamba. It's a long steady descent through changing vegetation, from austere tussock around the lake to lush cloud forest and agricultural land below. Toward the end are views of Cochabamba and the surrounding fields. After 5.7 km of steady downhill walking from the ford mentioned above, you cross Quebrada Challacancha on a rough log bridge by a small water-powered grain mill and climb 1.4 km to Cochabamba.

Cochabamba is a delightful place, in limbo between ancient and modern times, well worth spending a day or more to explore. There is a great deal of finely cut Inca stone in the area: a few structures are still intact, some Inca stones are incorporated in the foundations of modern buildings including the church on the plaza, and many more are covered by dense vegetation. The little village has few services, but basic accommodations and meals are available from local families. There is a road to the outside world, way down and around via Balsas on the Río Marañón (it may not be passable during the rainy season), with van service and two weekly buses to Chachapoyas and, in the opposite direction, to Chuquibamba (see below). An excellent day walk from Cochabamba climbs 7.2 km to the summit of **Cerro San Isidro** (3630 m), where there are more ruins and amazing views to the gaping canyon of the Marañón below.

Head southeast from Cochabamba along a clear trail above the south side of Quebrada Challacancha. The trail crosses the road a couple of times, but the latter makes a huge detour south, so you should stick to the trail. After 2.9 km you reach a concrete bridge over Quebrada Challacancha. Ahead 1.7 km up and over a low ridge brings you to two more bridges, crossing a side stream and the **Río Chacahuayco**, respectively. It is another 3 km east along the south side of Río Chacahuayco to yet another bridge and the small town of **Chuquibamba**, nicely situated in a bowl at the base of imposing Cerro Gentil. This is the halfway point of the circuit, and you can either end the trek

PASTORA THE SHEPHERDESS

Every Peruvian *campesino* has several dogs to guard property and help herd livestock. These dogs always sound the alarm when strangers approach and can occasionally be aggressive, but they usually make friends quickly once their owner has done so. If necessary, dogs can be dissuaded by crouching to pick up a couple of stones (even when there are no stones to pick up) and, later, sharing a little of your food is often the fast track to their friendship. The latter strategy is not without its own perils, however, as we learned along the Río Atuen circuit.

Her name was Pastora (the shepherdess) and she lived on a farm near the confluence of the Ríos Atuen and Tambillo. Grateful no doubt for Daisy's offer of scraps from our breakfast, she decided to reciprocate by guiding us along our 10-day trek. She would not let herself be deterred or taken home by people we met along the way. Keeping her fed was a challenge, but Daisy is pretty resourceful in such matters and local dairy farmers were able to lend a hand. Whey and bran, it seems, are staples of the local canine diet.

Fortunately, the trek is a loop and took us past Pastora's home a second time. She had never barked during the entire ten days we hiked together, but on the last night, after returning to our campsite for dessert following a proper meal from her own bowl, she let out a single vocal farewell and headed back up the hill. The shepherdess had done her job!

here (see Return, below) or resupply and continue on to close the loop back to the Río Atuen and Leymebamba.

To continue, head east from Chuquibamba along a good trail that climbs steadily along the north shore of Río Chacahuayco, crossing several side streams along the way. At 3.2 km past Chuquibamba, the trail climbs more steeply away from the Río Chacahuayco before dropping into **Quebrada Pucamonte**, 2.5 km farther ahead.

Here the trail takes on more and more of the appearance of an Inca road, with cobbled sections, drainage ditches, and stairs, as it climbs higher along the tussock-clad slope and over a broad **saddle** at 3950 m, 3.1 km past Quebrada Pucamonte. There is some water and a flat spot to **camp** 400 m beyond the saddle. The trail divides ahead: the left branch runs north into Quebrada Cabildo; our route takes the right branch northeast down a steep slope where alpacas are grazed, then along the west shore of **Lago Sierpe** and into the quiet little village of **Atuen**, 4 km past the camp spot mentioned above.

In 2016, road construction was nearing completion between Chuquibamba and Atuen. Fortunately, some sections of Inca road along the way have been spared. The trail and Inca road fragments following the **Río Atuen** downstream from Atuen village have likewise been replaced by a vehicle road to Leymebamba. The green Río Atuen valley is nevertheless pretty and worth visiting. There are several bridges over side streams along the way. At 10 km past the village of **Atuen** you cross a larger tributary, the **Río Timbambo**, and, 2.5 km beyond, reach the **Río Tambillo**. Cross the Río Atuen on the concrete bridge just downstream from its confluence with the Tambillo. This closes the loop, leaving 14 km to return to **Leymebamba** along the same route you came.

Return. There are vans and two buses a week from Chuquibamba to Chachapoyas, a long way down, up and around, 9 to 10 hours via Balsas; once the Leymebamba–Atuen road is completed, the trip will be considerably shorter and service is likely to be more frequent. For transport between Leymebamba and Chachapoyas, see Access, above.

8

CORDILLERA BLANCA

This is Peru's premier mountain destination, offering endless trekking opportunities amid magnificent scenery and the highest summits in the country. More than two hundred snow-covered peaks over 5000 m stretch in a swath 180 km long and 20 km wide; thirty-two of them reach over 6000 m. Here are over seven hundred glaciers, the highest concentration in the tropics, their levels sadly receding year after year due to climate change. At the base of the glaciers are more than four hundred lakes, turquoise jewels enhancing the superb mountain scenery. Seven life zones above 3000 m are home to 850 plant species, as well as 210 species of birds, from condors to hummingbirds. Many of these natural wonders are protected by Parque Nacional Huascarán, and trekking permits are issued by the national park (see sidebar below).

Although the region as a whole has adopted this name, the Cordillera Blanca is but one of several mountain ranges and valleys accessed from Huaraz, capital of the Department of Ancash and hub of the area. The western range is the bare Cordillera Negra; the eastern one is the snow-covered Cordillera Blanca proper. Between the Cordilleras Negra

PARQUE NACIONAL HUASCARÁN

Some of the finest natural areas and trekking routes in the Cordillera Blanca are inside the 34,000 hectare Parque Nacional Huascarán. Trekking permits for the national park are sold at their Huaraz office (see Appendix A). In 2016 a permit cost US$22 and was valid for 21 days from purchase (ask for it to be stamped with the date you plan to enter). A 3-day ticket costs US$7 (camping not allowed) and a 1-day permit US$3. Prices and regulations are subject to change. Permits may be checked at ranger stations, trail access points, shelters, and campsites but are not necessarily sold at these locations.

Two hundred snow-covered peaks above 5000 m stretch in a swath 180 km long.

and Blanca is the Río Santa valley, called Callejón de Huaylas while it flows north before turning west to the Pacific. The valleys east of the Cordillera Blanca, their rivers draining to the Río Marañón, a tributary of the Amazon, are called the Zona de Conchucos (or just Conchucos). More mountains, in the Cordillera Oriental, lie farther east beyond the Marañón. To the southeast of the Cordillera Blanca are the snow-capped Cordilleras Huallanca and Huayhuash. The lower valleys of the Callejón de Huaylas and Conchucos are extensively populated and cultivated; and many small towns here provide access to the mountains.

Huaraz has all services for the hiker: provisions, gear purchase and rental, countless trekking agencies, a mountain center called Casa de Guías, and a trekking library and resource center at Café Andino. See Appendix A for contact information of all establishments mentioned here. There is air and bus service between Lima and Huaraz, as well as ample bus links to various cities in northern Peru. Huaraz is very well supplied

with hotels and hostels but gets busy during the months of June to September and crowded during the week prior to the July 28 national holiday. The Lazy Dog Inn is a comfortable upmarket lodge away from the bustle of the city. Caraz, 60 km down the Río Santa valley from Huaraz, is a smaller, more relaxed town with a warmer climate, also surrounded by great trekking venues. Pony's Expeditions is a useful contact here. Scattered throughout the Cordillera Blanca are six comfortable mountain lodges called Refugios Andinos.

The beaten path. By far the most popular trek in the region is the 3- to 5-day Llanganuco to Santa Cruz route, accessed from either Yungay or Caraz. This is the mainstay of most agencies and where you will find the highest concentration of groups and their impact. Another very popular trek frequented by groups is the 8- to 12-day Cordillera Huayhuash circuit, accessed from Chiquián. Also popular but seldom crowded is our Trek 9, Alpamayo, where you might meet one group a day in high season.

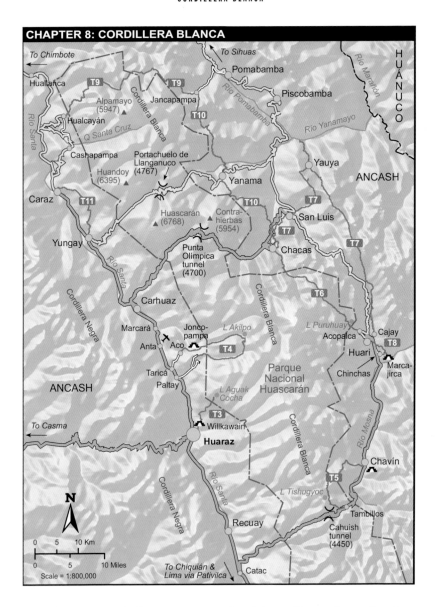

CHAPTER 8: CORDILLERA BLANCA

Limbering up. Acclimatization is important in the Cordillera Blanca, especially if arriving from the coast, and opportunities to acclimatize abound. In addition to the 3-day hikes included among our featured treks (Treks 4, 6, and 7), several other suitable excursions are found close to Huaraz. Among these is an easy 12-km-round-trip hike up to a pond called Wilcacocha and the Runtu Punta hilltop beyond. From Caraz, a moderately difficult 15-km day hike goes by the lakes of Miramar and Pampacocha, to Huaripampa or to Tzactza (Zatza); both have transport back to Caraz. Other popular day walks include Laguna Churup, accessed by vehicle from Huaraz; Laguna Auquiscocha, from Carhuaz; Lagunas Llanganuco and Laguna 69, from Yungay; Laguna Parón and Winchus (a stand of *Puya raimondii* in the Cordillera Negra), both from Caraz. **Featured treks.** Trek 3, Willkawain to Aguak Cocha, is a good 1-day route close to Huaraz, to build your stamina and get acquainted with the area. Trek 8, Marcajirca, combines a fine day walk from Huari, in Conchucos, with access to an impressive undeveloped archaeological site. Trek 11, Caraz to Yungay, is a great ridgeline day walk, high above the Río Santa valley on one side and below the glaciers of Huandoy and Huascarán on the other. Trek 4, Ishinca to Akilpo, is one of the best

short multiday hikes within easy reach of Huaraz. Trek 5, Laguna Tishugyoc, strays off the beaten path at the south end of the Cordillera Blanca, to visit one of its most beautiful lakes and take you to the Chavín archaeological site. Trek 6, Huari to Chacas, and Trek 7, Chacas to Huari via Yauya, are each worthwhile in their own right but even more spectacular when combined into a Conchucos loop including an impressive stretch of Inca road. Also well suited to be combined are Trek 9, Alpamayo, and Trek 10, Pomabamba to Chacas, which together take you from the Callejón de Huaylas across the Cordillera Blanca and down into Conchucos. From Chacas you can continue along Trek 7 to Huari, for over 200 km of uninterrupted trekking, the ultimate long-haul route in this area.

3 WILLKAWAIN TO AGUAK COCHA
TRAINING FOR THE CORDILLERA BLANCA

Rating: Moderately difficult 11.5-km, full-day hike
Elevation: 3430 to 4590 m
Maps: IGN 1:100,000 Carhuaz (19h), Huari (19i); ESCALE Ancash (Huaraz). This route can be hiked without maps.
Water: Available from an irrigation canal along the route and the lake at the top
Hazards and annoyances: Muggings have taken place between Willkawain and the Monterrey thermal baths (see map). This trek is too high if you have just arrived from sea level.
Permits and fees: Small fee charged to visit the Willkawain archaeological site, open Tuesday to Friday, 8:30 AM to 4:00 PM, Saturday and Sunday, 9:00 AM to 1:30 PM.
Services and provisions: None along the route; bring a picnic lunch from Huaraz.

"THE BEST WAY TO train for trekking is by trekking," goes the motto of one of our long-standing hiking companions. This may be overstating the case but, insofar as it makes a good point, an ideal place to train for trekking in the Cordillera Blanca is along this route. Within easy reach of Huaraz and with minimal navigational challenge, this is a fine workout to build stamina for longer more challenging trails ahead. The

route begins at a small archaeological site and climbs to a pretty little lake nestled under glacier-sculpted walls. Along the way are various introductions to the many charms of the Cordillera Blanca: fine views, interesting flora including traditional crops, polylepis trees, and miniature cacti thriving above

Andean gulls nest on an island in Lago Aguak Cocha.

4000 m. If you are lucky, you may see nesting Andean gulls on their little rookery islands in the lake.

Access. Vans run throughout the day from the corner of 13 de Diciembre and Jirón Cajamarca in Huaraz, to Willkawain, a 15-minute ride. Or take a taxi from anywhere in town for under US$5.

Route. We suggest an early start in order to include a brief visit to the **Willkawain** archaeological site as soon as it opens, leave sufficient time to enjoy the trek, and return before dark. The site, of Wari origin dating to AD 600–1100, consists of a three-story mausoleum (interestingly, there is a contemporary cemetery next door) and several smaller structures.

Follow the wide trail that begins across the road from the site. You climb gradually east past tilled fields growing lupines (*tauri*, *chochos*) and shepherds tending their flocks. At 800 m from the start the trail turns north to climb more steeply, and in another

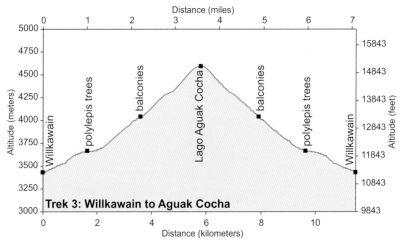

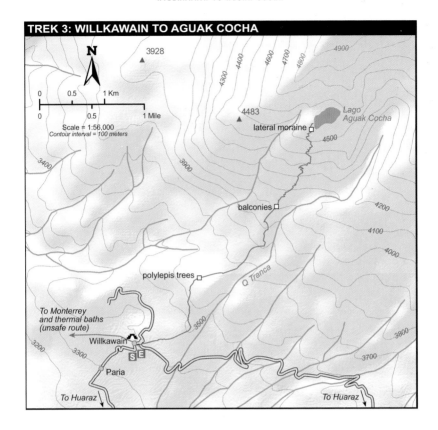

850 m you pass a small stand of **polylepis trees**, with their characteristic peeling red bark (see A Tree of Many Skins, Trek 5). Another 1.5 km of steady climbing northeast brings you to nice views back to Willkawain and Huaraz beyond, as well as the more sobering sight of a large gold mine that has denuded an extensive patch of hills in the Cordillera Negra.

Another 500 m ahead are a couple of small **balconies** above Quebrada Tranca, the large rocky drainage on your right. Look for miniature cacti no bigger than a coin at the balconies. Here you are a little more than halfway, in terms of time, to the top. The trail continues to climb steeply northeast for 2.1 km to a **lateral moraine** at 4590 m just above **Lago Aguak Cocha**. It is a short descent to the shore where, in all likelihood, you will be greeted by the raucous cries of gulls circling above. Pull out your binoculars to look for their nesting sites on the small stone islands in the lake.

Return to Willkawain the same way you came along the trail.

Return. The last van from Willkawain to Huaraz leaves at 8:00 PM. Do not walk from Willkawain to the Monterrey thermal baths (see Hazards, above).

4

ISHINCA TO AKILPO
SOMETHING FOR EVERYONE

Rating: Moderately difficult 40-km, 3- to 4-day trek
Elevation: 3010 to 5075 m
Maps: IGN 1:100,000 Carhuaz (19h), Huari (19i); ESCALE Ancash (Carhuaz); ALPENVEREIN Cordillera Blanca Süd (03/b)
Water: Abundant except along the climb to the pass
Hazards and annoyances: A 20-m section of the climb to the pass, on steep bare rock; requires caution at all times and should not be attempted in poor weather
Permits and fees: Route is inside Parque Nacional Huscarán (see sidebar for regulations). A separate minimal entry fee charged at the Joncopampa (Honcopampa) archaeological site.
Services and provisions: Refugio Ishinca (a well-maintained lodge for up to eighty climbers and trekkers; see Refugios Andinos in Appendix A) offers accommodations and good hot meals at upmarket prices. They may also sell a few snacks, but all trekking supplies should be brought from Huaraz.

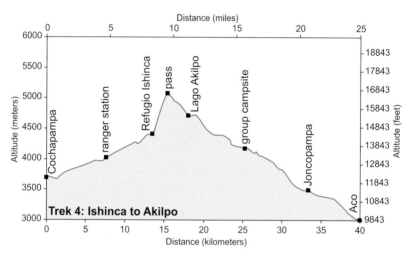

THIS ROUTE OFFERS A bit of everything, from the camaraderie of a large climbing/trekking lodge to the solitude of a seldom-visited valley, from barren recently deglaciated moraines to lush *queñua* forests teeming with life. Superb vistas of summits, glaciers, lakes, and waterfalls abound, and the great natural beauty is complemented by a small archaeological site at the end of the route. Most of the trails are well maintained and signed, but there is enough cross-country travel and a 5000-m-plus pass to provide challenge and adventure. You can also choose not to cross the pass and still enjoy a worthwhile portion of the route. It is hard to find a better "bite-size" multiday trek within easy reach of Huaraz.

Tocllaraju (6032 m)

Access. Pashpa (Pallpa) and Cochapampa can be reached by taxi from Huaraz, a 1-hour, US$25 ride. Alternatively take a Bedoya-Jangas or 10 *combi* from Jr. Tarapacá by the Huaraz market to Paltay (also called Cruce Ishinca, 45 min), from where an unpaved road leads 9 km up to Pashpa. Occasional *combis* and private vehicles run from Paltay to Pashpa; your best chance is in the morning.

Route. The unpaved road ends 2 km beyond **Pashpa** at a large open patch of ground called **Cochapampa**. This is a pretty spot with a pond and great views of various *nevados* including Huascarán, the highest summit in Peru.

Follow the wide horse trail east for 2 km from Cochapampa, descending slightly at first, then climbing gently to a saddle signed **Pelor Cotokunka**. Here a side trail, also signed, descends northwest for 1.5 km to Joncopampa. If you do not feel comfortable crossing the pass between Quebradas Ishinca and Akilpo, then you can return here on the way back and cross to Joncopampa, allowing you to visit the archaeological site at the end of the trek.

Moving forward, head east from the saddle over rocky terrain, with great views of a broad valley to the south (right) and of the *nevados* ahead. The trail crosses a low ridge and then drops to the floor of a large valley with a crystal-clear **spring** at the edge of a *queñua* forest, 2.5 km past the fork to Joncopampa. This is a very pretty spot with good **camping** near a dry streambed, 300 m farther along, convenient if you got a late start.

From the dry streambed, head 400 m south as the trail climbs steeply on the slope of a lateral moraine and then turns east again to enter **Quebrada Ishinca**. At first the canyon is narrow and the trail runs high above the rushing glacial river below. It passes through lovely *queñua* forest with many flowers and birds; keep an eye out for

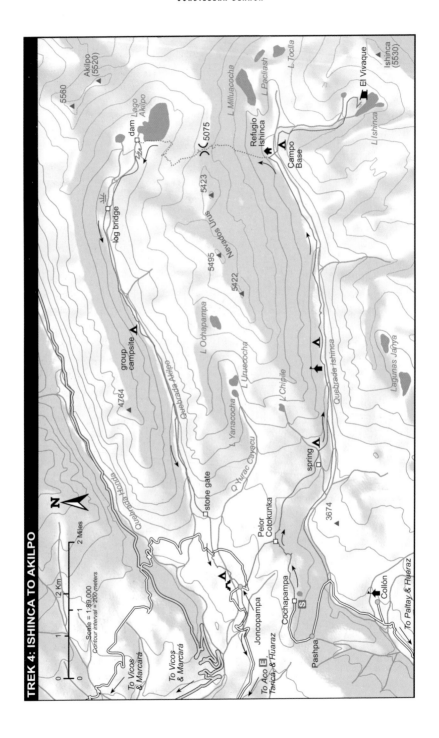

TREK 4: ISHINCA TO AKILPO

rusty-colored giant hummingbirds. At 1.2 km after the trail turns east to enter the *quebrada*, you reach a signed fork with a side trail running west to the vehicle road between Pashpa and Collón, an alternate starting point for the trek. Another 900 m ahead is a **ranger station** where tickets may be checked, but it is not always staffed.

Beyond the gate at the ranger station the canyon gets wider and flatter, with the river running alongside the trail, and there are several clear springs and side streams, as well as good **camping** possibilities. There are great views of the 800-m-high canyon walls, and soon the glaciers of Palcaraju come into view to the east, at the head of the valley.

From the ranger station it is 6 km of mostly gentle climbing to **Refugio Ishinca**, located in a wide bowl at 4400 m. The large comfortable lodge is surrounded by the glaciers of Tocllaraju (6032 m), Palcaraju (6274 m), Ishinca (5530 m), and Urus (5495 m). Treat yourself to stay or dine here, or camp in the surrounding valley known as **Campo Base**. The climbers' approach routes that fan out from Campo Base are all good options for day walks and side trips if you wish to linger. A second simpler stone shelter (no meals available) called El Vivaque is 3.5 km south at 5000 m.

Our route climbs steeply north from Refugio Ishinca to the pass between Quebradas Ishinca and Akilpo. This demanding ascent merits an early start, no later than 7:00 AM. Along the way, your efforts are amply rewarded by magnificent views of glaciated summits towering above the Ishinca valley. A small cross-country trail, sporadically marked by cairns, leaves from behind the *refugio* and is easily confused with animal tracks; 700 m ahead, at 4650 m, you reach a large rocky outcrop; follow the base of the rock to the right. Along the way, the trail becomes less distinct as it takes to the loose rock, so keep an eye out for the cairns. At 5025 m is a 20-m section of steep bare rock, a challenging scramble at the best of times and dangerous in icy conditions, snow, or high winds. After the scramble, the route to the 5075 m **pass** is a bit less steep. Once on top, the stunning 360-degree views make you forget all about the difficult climb. Note that, under normal dry season conditions, there is no ice on this route, despite the glacier contours shown on the map.

The descent on the north side of the pass is blissfully more gradual, and soon you begin to see turquoise-green **Lago Akilpo** to the northeast (right) at the base of more towering summits and glaciers. The route down crosses several flat terraces with adequate wind shelter behind large boulders and a few small seeps for water, allowing you to make a high camp here if necessary. There are fewer cairns north of the pass, but you can make your own route, descending gently north and then east from one terrace to the next, headed 2 km toward the lake. The cairns become more evident again around 4750 m, where they mark the final descent to the shore. If you are lucky, you might hear the cries of Andean gulls nesting here.

The route follows the west shore of the lake for 600 m to a large man-made rock wall, a welcome windbreak. Just beyond the wall, the natural outflow of the lake has been blocked by a small concrete **dam** and spillway. A good but narrow trail begins immediately north of the original (now dry) outflow; it is marked by cairns. Zigzags make the steep slope easy to descend as you head toward the great floodplain at the head of **Quebrada Akilpo.** Stop along the way to admire the wildflowers, which increase in variety and number as you lose elevation and the air warms.

Enjoy the solitude; Quebrada Akilpo sees much less traffic than Quebrada Ishinca. The trail, used mostly by cattle, stays south (left) of the outflow of Lago Akilpo and then turns west to cross the boggy floodplain, headed for a notch where the valley suddenly narrows. Here the trail crosses to the north shore of the main stream on a small **log bridge,** 3.5 km past the outflow of the lake. It then continues dropping gently, surrounded by high cliffs above *queñua* forest, with various spots suitable for camping along the way.

The trail continues its descent through Quebrada Akilpo, crossing the stream on rough log bridges seven times. Remember to look back for splendid views of waterfalls set against a backdrop of the glaciers of Akilpo (5520 m). At 2.5 km past the first bridge, you reach a large **group campsite** on the north side of the stream. Beyond, the trail is wider and very easy to follow, making its way through bird-filled forest growing amid large boulders—a truly magical part of the trek.

As you continue to descend, the forest thins and the canyon widens. In places, the trail is blocked by wooden barricades to prevent the passage of cattle, but they are easy to scramble around. At 6 km past the campsite you reach a stone gate at the mouth of the *quebrada,* where the trail moves away from the river and you begin to see the Joncopampa archaeological site and **Joncopampa** village beyond. It is 1 km from the gate to a vehicle road leading to the village.

The Joncopampa archaeological site is probably of Wari origin (AD 600–1100). If you arrive late and would like to explore it at leisure, there are many **camping** spots nearby. Cross the road and head 1 km southwest to reach the main ruins, surrounded by a wire fence. The village is just south on the other side of the river. You can either take a vehicle from Joncopampa to (San Miguel de) Aco or walk the 6 km through the villages of Quinranca and Shirapucru. It is mostly road-walking with a few shortcuts along the way and many nostalgic views back to the great *quebradas* and *nevados.*

Return. Vehicles run sporadically from Joncopampa to Aco, 30 minutes; and there are more frequent *combis* from Aco to Huaraz, 1 hour.

5 LAGUNA TISHUGYOC
BLUE OF BLUES

Rating: A 27-km, 4- to 5-day trek; moderately difficult around Laguna Tishugyoc, very difficult beyond the second pass
Elevation: 3200 to 4795 m
Maps: IGN 1:100,000 Recuay (20i); ESCALE Ancash (Huari); ALPENVEREIN Cordillera Blanca Süd (03/b)
Water: Abundant as far as Laguna Tishugyoc, scarce thereafter
Hazards and annoyances: Use caution on the cliffs below the second pass.

Permits and fees: The route is inside Parque Nacional Huascarán, but there are no ranger stations in this area (see sidebar for regulations).

Services and provisions: Bring all provisions from Huaraz; there is nowhere to resupply en route. Chavín, at the end of the trek, receives its share of tourism and has various places to stay, eat, and shop. Marcos Sánchez in Tambillos might be able to assist with a local guide or pack animals. There is no way to contact him in advance; ask around when you arrive and hope for the best.

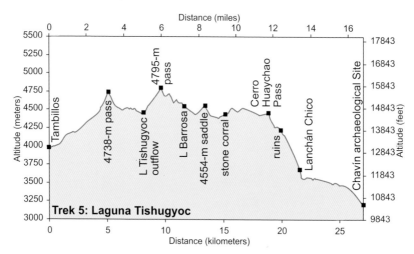

Trek 5: Laguna Tishugyoc

LAGUNA TISHUGYOC HAS A rare beauty. Its waters are a deep pure blue that is neither the turquoise of other glacial lakes nor a reflection of the sky, yet they are a faithful mirror of the white glaciers and black-, gray-, and red-rock mountains that surround it. Tishugyoc means "island lake" in the local Quechua dialect, and, indeed, it has a single island covered in exquisitely wind-sculpted *queñua* trees. The unusual color of the water is even more curious because it does not appear to contain much glacial silt; the outflow and shallows by the shore are crystal clear. The effect is spectacular and difficult to convey with words or photos; you have to see it for yourself.

Making a loop around Tishugyoc and returning the way you came is a delightful 2- to 3-day trek in itself. For those seeking more of a challenge, the route described below includes a seemingly dead-end pass (it isn't), difficult off-trail navigation, and a long stretch without water. The rewards are ample, including outstanding views of many glaciated peaks and bottomless green valleys, as well as a visit to an apparently untouched archaeological site.

Access. Many buses and shared taxis run from Huaraz to Chavín and other destinations in Conchucos and can drop you off in Tambillos, 5 km beyond the 4450-m-high Cahuish road tunnel, a 2-hour ride. Leave Huaraz before 7:00 AM in order to reach one of the campsites above the east shore of Laguna Tishugyoc on the first day.

Route. From **Tambillos** walk 1 km west along the paved road, back uphill toward the tunnel, until you reach a good trail on the north (right) side. The trail climbs above the road and runs west parallel to it for another kilometer before turning northwest to begin climbing through **Quebrada Chicchis**. It is a steady climb through this pretty valley, crossing several small streams along the way. Ahead 2.6 km the trail turns north, climbs more steeply, and enters a small patch of *queñua* forest before crossing a somewhat loose **scree** field to an unnamed first **pass** at 4738 m, 600 m beyond the scree. There are excellent views from the pass, including your first glimpse of Laguna Tishugyoc. Two faint trails go around the lake on either side of it and meet at the north end.

Descend gradually north. Several terraces between the pass and lake make adequate camping spots with small muddy seeps for water, but it is worth continuing on to better sites ahead. At 1.1 km from the pass, start contouring over the *ichu*-clad terrain before climbing to a ridgeline above the east shore of the lake. This ridge separates **Laguna Tishugyoc** from the deep valley of its outflow, Quebrada Hualpish. The ridge is covered in pretty *queñua* forest with several small ponds and great views west over the amazingly blue water to the glaciers of Nevados Yanamarey. There are very good **camping** spots here, 2 km beyond the pass. By a dry pond near the camping area, a poor trail branches east to descend through Quebrada Hualpish to the village of Machac on the paved road from Huaraz to Chavín. Parts of the descent are very steep, and there are many cliffs along the way, so this route is not recommended.

Beyond the fork, the trail (at times vague) follows the ridgeline north, dropping gradually to the source of **Quebrada Hualpish** at the outflow of the lake, 600 m ahead. This is a section to be savored, with lovely forest and more wonderful views. You can scramble down to the lakeshore, but cliffs prevent you from following the shore to the outflow, which should be reached along the ridgeline. The outflow is ankle deep and easily forded. Just beyond is a small but splendid spot for **camping**, graciously sheltered by *queñua* trees.

Past the outflow the trail climbs slightly along the north shore of the lake. If you wish to make a loop and return to Tambillos, follow the north shore west through a patch of *queñua* forest and then head south above the west shore, passing between Tishugyoc and the smaller Laguna Yanacocha, below the twin waterfalls formed by the outflow of the latter lake.

To continue to Chavín, from the outflow of Laguna Tishugyoc follow the trail above the north shore of the lake toward the *queñua* forest mentioned in the previous paragraph. Before you reach a small stream coming from the 4795-m pass to the north, leave the trail and climb cross-country, steadily north, to the crest of a broad *ichu*-covered ridge running parallel to the stream. Continue north along the crest of the ridge to an altitude of 4600 m, where the *ichu* gives way to sandy and rocky terrain. Turn northwest here and head toward the drainage coming down from the pass. You cannot reach the drainage directly because it is flanked by rock walls at this level, but before you reach these, you come to a small corridor amid the rocks, 1.1 km past the outflow of Tishugyoc, which climbs north to meet the drainage 150 m ahead.

The beauty of Laguna Tishugyoc is difficult to convey—you have to see it for yourself.

In the drainage the terrain turns to scree and talus, with a few larger boulders along the way. Stay on the east (right) side of the drainage. Despite all the fractured rock, the footing is reasonably stable, and steady cautious climbing brings you to an unnamed **pass** at 4795 m, 450 m beyond where you entered the drainage. Along the way are countless superb views back south to Tishugyoc, and another spectacle awaits at the pass. Spread out before you are a vast array of glaciated peaks including Huantsán (6395 m), towering above a deep green valley, a tributary of Quebrada Shongo.

Just beyond the pass is a rocky terrace that seems like the end of the line, with no obvious way down over the sheer cliffs below. Explore the west side of the terrace, and you will find a small corridor leading down over crags to a sandy chute that winds its way steeply down to a large **weeping wall** on a vertical red rock face, an important landmark about 50 vertical meters below the pass. Just past the red weeping wall you reach a broad platform. There are many potential ways down here and no trail. Our route contours northeast at 4700 m near the base of the cliffs, undulating slightly to cross the many low stone ridges carved by past glaciation. From the platform aim for an *ichu*-covered slope that climbs to the east. At the top of this slope is a **spring** amid the rocks with wind-sheltered flat ground nearby, a great **campsite** with outstanding views, 800 m beyond the pass.

Turn northwest at the spring and descend along a cattle trail to the next level of the glacier-carved slope. After 550 m, the cattle trail turns east (right) and disappears. Continue to contour east and northeast crossing many low ridges until, after 700 m, you reach a slightly higher ridge above **Laguna Barrosa**. This smaller lake has the same beautiful blue color as Tishugyoc and is surrounded by large *queñua* trees. Follow the ridge north for 300 m down to the outflow of the lake, where there is flat but exposed ground for **camping**. Be sure to take water here.

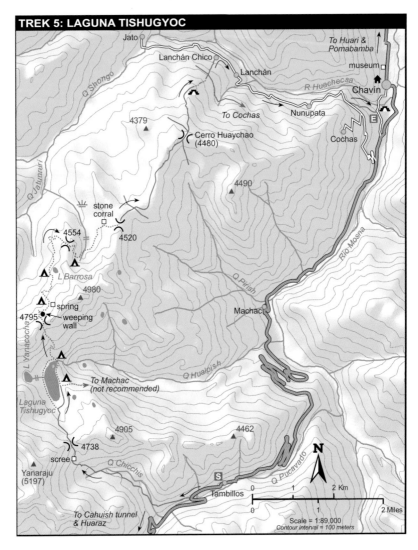

TREK 5: LAGUNA TISHUGYOC

After crossing the shallow outflow, climb northeast to a small notch between the surrounding hills. From the top you can see a patch of *queñua* forest growing on a scree field below, for which you are headed. It looks like an impossibly steep descent, but hidden in a cleft between a large boulder and the rock face on your right is a convenient natural stairway. The scree is a bit loose but crossed by a faint trail; sadly, it was made by loggers, and the once-rich forest is succumbing to their axes.

Beyond the forest, the terrain turns to gently undulating *ichu* as you contour high above Quebrada Jatunruri to the north (left). Continue east over several low *ichu*-covered ridges and dry drainages until you reach a higher stonier ridge that rises southeast toward a clearly visible saddle. Climb to this **saddle** at 4554 m, 1.8 km beyond the outflow of Laguna Barrosa. Splendid views of an unnamed valley flanked by a cirque of rocky peaks await you at the top. It is a straightforward descent southeast along the steep *ichu* slope to the valley floor, passing an impressive rock spire along the way. There are pretty camping spots at the boggy head of the valley, 550 m from the saddle. Here is the first water since Laguna Barrosa and the last until you reach Lanchán Chico, 10 km ahead, so take as much as you can.

Contour northeast from the head of the valley across a couple of small scree fields. In 1.2 km you reach a large **stone corral** on the far side with great views back to the cirque and a waterfall. Climb east from the corral to a broad **saddle** at 4520 m with views of the valley of the Río Mosna to the east. Turn north (left) and follow a trail for 500 m to a four-way intersection; here one trail descends southeast toward Machac, another runs northwest toward Quebrada Shongo, and our route continues northeast along the ridgeline toward Cerro Huaychao.

This area is heavily grazed, and you might meet a few herdsmen. The trail runs along the west side of the ridge toward Cerro Huaychao, or you can follow the ridgeline for the best views. Just before a series of rocky outcrops, 1.6 km past the four-way intersection, the trail crosses from the west to the east side of the ridge. It continues to contour for another 1.1 km to the base of the **pass** on **Cerro Huaychao**. Here it meets another trail descending toward Machac; we climb north to the 4480-m pass with more glorious views.

Beyond the pass, look for a trail headed north along a ridge on the east (right) side of the valley below; do not follow the large trail going northwest. A good landmark if it is still there, 850 m beyond the pass, is a stunted plantation of pine and *queñua* trees. Follow the ridgeline 350 m north from these unhappy saplings to reach a fragment of trail crossing from the west to the east (left to right) side of the ridge and leading to an impressive set of unexcavated **ruins** at 4225 m. There are many buildings and corrals of rough stone here, covering a large area and suggesting a site of some importance, possibly dating to Wari times (AD 600–1100).

From the ruins descend steeply northeast on vague trails until you reach the first tilled fields, a few scattered huts, and an intersection 1.2 km from the ruins. The right branch contours and climbs to the village of Cochas, a considerable detour. We continue straight ahead and northeast down to the hamlet of **Lanchán Chico**, 500 m ahead. Lanchán Chico is just above the road between Chavín and Jato, a narrow precarious vehicle track running high above the valley of the **Río Huachecsa**. Walking the 5 km east to Chavín via **Nunupata** is safer than riding one of the few vehicles that pass through. There is a good shortcut near the end, past Nunupata, where a clear trail descends from the road to the Chavín **archaeological site**, clearly visible below. It is well worth taking time to visit this site, as well as the excellent archaeology **museum** on the north side of the town of **Chavín**.

Return. From Chavín you can get a bus or shared taxi to Huaraz, 3 hours away. There are also shared taxis that run north to Huari, 1 hour away; from Huari, you can connect to Treks 6, 7, and 8. Farther north is Pomabamba, access to Treks 9 and 10.

A TREE OF MANY SKINS

As you walk along a high barren valley and suddenly see a green patch in the distance, get close and observe; it is likely to be a polylepis forest. Walk in and you will be transported into a fairy-tale land of gnarled trunks and branches. Polylepis, from the Greek *poly* (many) and *lepis* (flakes or scales), is a genus of trees and shrubs in the rose family, native to the Andes from Venezuela to Argentina. About twenty-eight species have been described; fourteen of them, including three endemics, can be found in Peru. They get their name from their mutlilayered reddish bark, which protects them from low temperatures and fires.

Polylepis are slow-growing, often stunted trees, although some species can reach 20 m in height. They are evergreens, well adapted to high altitudes, with dense clusters of small thick leaves and small flowers pollinated by the wind. Most species grow in a transition zone between lower forests and higher Andean vegetation, at altitudes between 3500 and 5000 m. *Polylepis tarapacana* grows up to 5200 m, the highest naturally occurring tree in the world. Four species can be found in Parque Nacional Huascarán: *P. sericia* and *P. incana* along rivers in sheltered lower valleys, *P. weberbaueri* and *P. racemosa* at higher altitudes. In all forests you will notice bright red and yellow flowers of the *pupa* (*Tristerix* spp), a parasite that attaches to polylepis branches and eventually kills them.

The polylepis has many native names including *queñua, quenua, quenual, quewiña, lampaya, pantza,* and *coloradito*. In many of the high areas where they grow, they are the only available source of wood, making them vulnerable to loggers. Unfortunately, they also make excellent charcoal. Their habitat has been reduced to the less-accessible slopes where they are out of reach of people and their herds. The destruction of polylepis forests has also affected the birds that live in them, including the giant hummingbird (*Patagona gigas*), the world's largest hummingbird. The polylepis is protected by Peruvian law, and trekkers can do their share to help preserve surviving forests. Do not use them for firewood, and please resist the temptation to collect some of that amazing red bark; the trees need it more than you do.

6 HUARI TO CHACAS
INTRODUCTION TO CONCHUCOS

Rating: Moderately difficult 37-km, 3- to 4-day trek
Elevation: 3070 to 4530 m
Maps: IGN 1:100,000 Huari (19i); ESCALE Ancash (Huari, Asunción)
Water: Keep bottles full for climb from Lago Puruhuay; water abundant thereon
Hazards and annoyances: Parts of the trail and some camp spots muddy. Cattle frequent, with the curious habit of following trekkers, looking for food scraps and even urine, licking the ground where you pee (perhaps desperate for salt?). They are persistent but not aggressive.
Permits and fees: This route is inside Parque Nacional Huascarán; see sidebar for regulations.
Services and provisions: There are simple hotels, restaurants, and well-stocked shops in Huari and Chacas, but nowhere to resupply en route. Specialty items should be brought from Huaraz. Some Huaraz agencies might offer this trek.

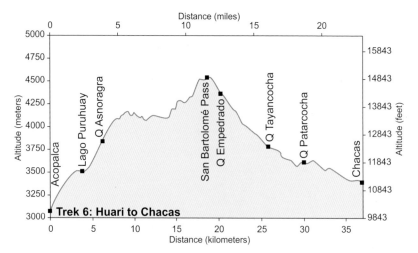

LESS FREQUENTED BY TREKKERS and climbers than the Callejón de Huaylas or the Cordillera Blanca, Conchucos has a character of its own. People here are a bit more reserved at first but nonetheless soon warm up to visitors. The landscape is gorgeous: lakes and emerald green valleys beneath tussock-covered hillsides, rocky slopes, and glaciers. Huari, the starting point of this trek, is a regional center that makes a convenient base for several hikes in the area, starting with this fine introduction to the Conchucos backcountry.

This trek follows a good trail and is occasionally used by groups but is not crowded. Keep in mind that national park signs along the route may indicate line-of-sight directions and distances to landmarks, rather than travel distances along trails leading to

PADRE UGO'S PARISH

Chacas is dominated both physically and socially by the works of Padre Ugo de Censi, a Salecian priest who arrived from Italy in 1976 and founded various craft workshops to provide employment for local people. Chacas woodworking is especially well known and can be seen in the large church and many ornate balconies such as that of the *municipio* on the plaza. Wood carvings from Chacas are exported worldwide, and other craft products range from furniture and religious art to fine cheese. Padre Ugo's Operazione Mato Grosso also runs six comfortable climbing and trekking shelters in the Cordillera Blanca, including those at Ishinca (Trek 4) and Contrahierbas (Trek 10).

The church-sponsored model of development in Chacas has been criticized as paternalistic by some, but its success is the visible envy of the surrounding region. Foreign visitors to Chacas are automatically assumed to be connected with the parish, and the first question asked of trekkers is usually *"Son italianos?"* ("Are you Italian?").

them. In addition to the route described here, there is ample scope for off-trail exploration nearby, for example around Lagunas Sacracocha and Ventanilla, as well as up Quebradas Tayancocha, and Patarcocha. However, some of the terrain is soft and boggy, hence especially fragile. If you wish to trek off the trail, then stay on higher rocky ground in order to minimize your impact.

Access. Several buses run daily between Huaraz and Huari, a nice 4- to 5-hour ride. From Huari an early-morning van goes to Acopalca in 15 minutes, or take a taxi: US$3.50 to Acopalca, US$14 to the Lago Puruhuay visitor center.

Route. From the village of **Acopalca**, a vehicle track and a wide trail both climb steadily northwest along the south side of Río Puruhuay. The trailhead is hidden behind some houses; ask around for it. The trail meets the road after 2.2 km. Then follow the road left and go left at the first fork, right at the second to reach the national park visitor center, 1.7 km past where you met the road. Nicely situated on the south shore of **Lago Puruhuay**, the visitor center has a paid camping area, and meals may be available. To continue along our route, take the left branch at the second fork mentioned above or return there from the visitor center; do not follow the lakeshore trail north from the dock.

Follow the trail, climbing steadily north above the west shore of the large scenic lake. In 2.4 km you cross **Quebrada Asnoragra**, a deep ravine and reliable water source. A bare stone **shelter** and trash-strewn camping area are 650 m ahead. Beyond the shelter, climb more gently north along the undulating trail to cross a broad ridge after 1.4 km, with views down into a deep green valley to the north. This unnamed drainage is a tributary of Quebrada Cachichinan, main inflow of Lago Puruhuay. The trail contours northwest above the south side of the unnamed valley to reach a good **campsite** with a reliable spring, 1.5 km past the ridge.

Continue contouring northwest past more camping possibilities and a pretty little **farmstead** 3 km ahead, with forested Cerro Rosario coming into view on the north side of the valley. The trail continues northwest, climbing steadily for 5 km to **San Bartolomé Pass** at 4530 m. The surrounding landscape has been scoured into low rocky ridges by past glaciation, and there are fine views along the way.

Beyond the pass the trail descends gradually northwest into the *ichu*-covered valley of **Quebrada Empedrado**, fording the drainage 2.5 km ahead. Another 1.5 km brings you to the outflow of Lago Yanacocha near its confluence with Quebrada Empedrado. Here are several pretty waterfalls on the bare rock above the trail and ahead are two more confluences of Quebrada Empedrado: with Quebradas Yanallullimpa and Pucallullimpa, respec-

Lago Puruhuay

tively. Together they form **Quebrada Asnocohuana**. Here is a good **camping** spot 900 m beyond the outflow of Lago Yanacocha.

The trail continues west along the south side of Quebrada Asnocohuana, through pretty *queñua* forest, at times high above the river. In 3.1 km you reach a concrete bridge known as Puente Taulle, over **Quebrada Tayancocha**. The forest thins out ahead, and Quebrada Asnocohuana becomes the **Río Arma**, with two lovely waterfalls to be seen as you trek high above its gorge. The next major tributary is **Quebrada Patarcocha**, 4.2 km ahead, with a locked shelter and a pasture suitable for camping downhill behind the shelter. The *quebrada* is crossed on a locked bridge, and there are several gates that may be locked along this section of trail. Agency groups must pay local communities for right-of-way, but individual trekkers are welcome to work their way around these obstacles.

After Patarcocha the trail climbs briefly north, then contours along the east flank of **Cerro Gella**, moving away from the Río Arma. Here the first crops and pastures come into view. At 4.5 km past the locked shelter you cross a large mudslide, unstable in the wet season, and 500 m farther meet a vehicle track. This track runs northwest for 1.8 km through the little village of **Cushuruya** to the center of **Chacas**. Chacas is a charming hillside town, looking up at the *nevados* of the Cordillera Blanca. It is a wonderfully relaxed place to rest up after the trek, before returning to the buzz of Huaraz or resupplying and continuing on along Trek 7 or 10, the latter in reverse.

TREKS 6 & 7: HUARI TO CHACAS & CHACAS TO HUARI VIA YAUYA

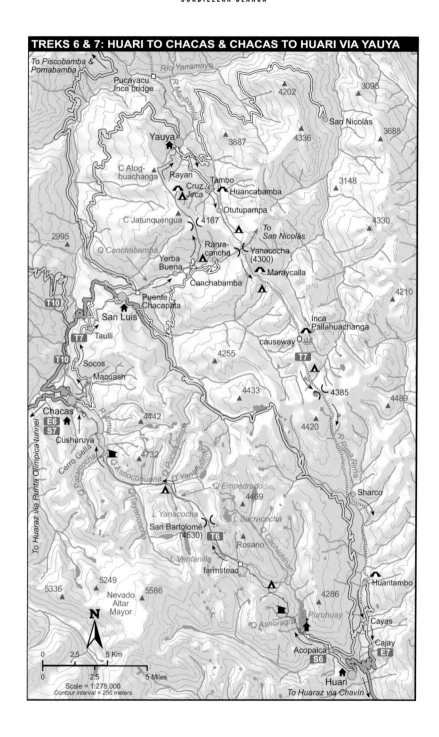

Return. Two daily buses and shared taxis run from Chacas to Huaraz, an unforgettable 4-hour ride via the 4700-m-high Punta Olímpica tunnel. If continuing along Trek 7, vans run throughout the day to San Luis in 45 minutes, or it is a pleasant hike.

7 CHACAS TO HUARI VIA YAUYA
THE GREAT INCA CAUSEWAY

Rating: Moderately difficult 86-km trek; 3–9 days
Elevation: 2940 to 4385 m
Map: IGN 1:100,000 Pomabamba (18i), Huari (19i); ESCALE Ancash (Asunción, Carlos Fermín Fitzcarrald, Huari)
Water: Generally abundant, except as noted below
Hazards and annoyances: Inquire in advance in Yauya if it is safe to cross the Inca bridge at Pucayacu.
Permits and fees: None
Services and provisions: Chacas, San Luis, and Huari each have several hotels, restaurants, and well-stocked shops. Services are more basic in Yauya. Specialty items should be brought from Huaraz.

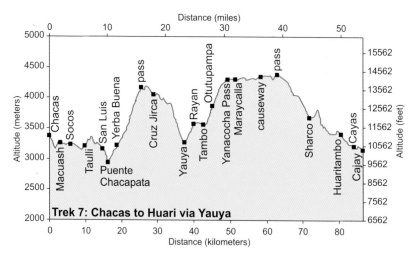

Trek 7: Chacas to Huari via Yauya

OF THE MANY OUTSTANDING features of the Capac Ñan or Great Inca Road (see Chapter 1), one of the most impressive are the causeways that carried it over marshy terrain. These highlight the monumental nature of the road because, in many cases, they were not strictly necessary. Inca engineers could have detoured around such bogs, but instead they built the road perfectly straight through them, over stone culverts that permitted the free flow of water beneath the roadway and have kept it intact for hundreds of years. The Inca did not deign to make detours for man or nature!

A spectacular causeway is but one small part of the extensive stretch of Capac Ñan this route follows, south from the rebuilt Inca bridge over the Río Yanamayo toward the next major span over the Río Mosna. This was the main line between Cuzco and Quito, and the grandeur of the ancient road is evident along much, if not all, of the trek. It is complemented by several Inca and pre-Inca archaeological sites and splendid views of the Cordillera Blanca along the way.

The length of this trek is very flexible. After completing Trek 6 or 10 you can resupply in Chacas or San Luis and continue on along the complete route described below. Alternatively you can travel by bus from Huaraz to Chacas and start fresh there, or in either San Luis or Yauya. You also have the option of bypassing Yauya, thus saving 2 days, and there are several places to finish the trek before the end. You could hike from Yauya to Sharco, for example, in 3 or 4 days.

Access. For bus service between Huaraz and Chacas, and Chacas to San Luis, see Trek 6, Return, above. There is one bus around midday between San Luis and Yauya, an impressive 2.5-hour ride.

Route. In Chacas ask for the trail to Macuash; it starts near the furniture workshop on the east side of town. The trail descends steadily east, first crossing the little Río Shuyayacu and then the larger Río Arma at the bottom of the valley, 1.6 km from town. Both river crossings are on good bridges. From the Río Arma a trail climbs steeply north for 1.6 km to Macuash, where it meets an unpaved road also coming from Chacas. Follow the road northwest and north as it contours high above the Río Arma on your left, with terrific views of glaciated summits in the Cordillera Blanca behind the deep valley. After 2.8 km the road passes the village of Socos, then Taulli 4 km farther ahead.

Leave the road at the north end of Taulli and follow a trail northeast (right), climbing steeply to a ridgeline reached in 2 km. Here are more great views and the trail turns east, becoming an unpaved road 1.1 km ahead, just past the little village of Gonzajirca. It is 1.9 km farther to the plaza of San Luis. San Luis is a convenient supply center (visit the dairy for good cheese and other provisions) but not the safest or friendliest town in Conchucos, so there is not much reason to linger.

Leave San Luis along the steep street, heading east down from the market, and ask for the way to Puente Chacapata. This concrete footbridge crosses the drainage at the bottom of the valley, 1.5 km from town. Take the trail on the far side, going left at the fork to follow Quebrada Canchabamba upstream, crossing it several times in its lower sections. The valley is populated and the trail well used, so there are plenty of opportunities to ask for directions along the way. Everybody knows the way to Yauya.

In 2.5 km from Puente Chacapata you reach the hamlet of Yerba Buena and 1.2 km farther an important fork. The right (southeast) branch runs to the larger village of Canchabamba from where you can climb to Yanacocha Pass via Ranracancha, a substantial shortcut that avoids Yauya. Our route takes the left (east) branch past a large mudslide to a concrete footbridge, 1.2 km past the fork. Take the right branch of the

The east side of the Cordillera Blanca at sunrise

next fork, immediately after the bridge, and climb steadily northeast. There are various side trails here but usually someone to ask. In 400 m you cross a vehicle track (right goes to Canchabamba) and 550 m farther pass a school with a large adobe wall. Here the trail begins to climb more steeply north past several potential **camping** spots. There is no water, but you can ask for some at one of the houses or ask permission to camp in someone's pasture.

The population at last begins to thin out, and the trail climbs 3.4 km north from the school to a broad 4167-m **pass** at the base of **Cerro Jatunquengua**. Do not descend into the valley; contour northwest from the pass along a faint path, crossing the *ichu*-covered slopes toward the impressive pre-Inca ruins of **Cruz Jirca**, 2.7 km ahead. The site is 750 m off the trail on the right and consists of high concentric stone walls topped with a large cross. The vantage point offers superb views in all directions, from the heights of the Cordillera Blanca to the depths of the Río Yanamayo. It makes an inspirational **camp** spot even though the nearest water is a small seep 1.3 km back along the trail toward the pass.

From Cruz Jirca return to the trail and follow it northwest along and below the ridge-line for 2.4 km to a small stone shrine with wooden crosses. A further 450 m ahead are the remains of a stone structure on **Cerro Atoghuachanga**, where you turn northeast to begin descending through fields and pastures toward Yauya, clearly visible in the valley below. You cross an unpaved road in 3.2 km and reach **Yauya** 1.2 km farther ahead.

Yauya is a pleasant little town with basic services, well worth spending some time to visit, especially for a side trip to see the **Inca bridge** over Río Yanamayo at **Pucayacu**. The 40-m-long bridge was rebuilt near its original location in 2006 using steel cables with a wooden floor and natural fiber cords along the sides, a reasonable facsimile of the original structure. (See Trek 19 for an Inca bridge built with ancestral techniques and materials.) The floor and sides are replaced every year before a festival held in November (confirm dates in advance). It's a long, thirsty 1000 m down and back up, 16 km round-trip, along a good trail running north to the bridge. Start early; it gets very hot at the bottom.

Leave Yauya from the high school, headed southeast along a vehicle track 2.9 km to **Rayan** and taking advantage of several shortcuts along the way. As you climb there are views left to the deep valley of the Río Maribamba and back to the even deeper canyon of the Río Yanamayo. The Maribamba valley is cultivated and populated. The next village along the way is **Tambo**, 2.6 km ahead, with the small archaeological site of **Huancabamba** behind the soccer field.

The vehicle track ends at Tambo. Climb steeply south along a trail through a planted pine forest to the next village of **Otutupampa**, 2.5 km ahead. You can ask to camp at the soccer field here, or next to someone's home; be sure to take water. Leaving the settled part of the valley, the trail climbs steadily south and east along the south side of the drainage to reach an artificial pond surrounded by flat ground suitable for **camping**, 2.2 km from Otutupampa.

Another 1.2 km brings you to the first easily identifiable segment of Capac Ñan, and from here on you travel the Royal Inca Road! Follow it first to a pass marked by an *apacheta*, 200 m ahead, then another 500 m to **Yanacocha Pass** at 4300 m. Here is an important intersection with a contemporary trail: to the west (left) it descends to Ranracancha and Canchabamba; to the northeast (right) it heads toward San Nicolás.

Continue southeast along the Capac Ñan for 2.2 km to the larger archaeological site of **Maraycalla**, with twenty-four adjacent structures and several outlying ones. Another 1.4 km ahead are two small ponds with good **camping** nearby and outstanding views of glaciated summits in the Cordillera Blanca. The Inca Road continues southeast 4.8 km to modest ruins at **Inca Pallahuachanga** and, more significantly, the two most amazing segments of Inca roadway along the route. Past the ruins is a spectacular 12-m-wide ramp with intact stone paving for almost 500 m and, beyond, a 700-m-long stretch of Inca **causeway** running straight as an arrow through a beautiful wetland. In addition to the majestic causeway (note the functioning stone culverts), the wetland, home to large flocks of puna ibis and Andean lapwings, is well worth a leisurely stroll.

Beyond the marsh the Capac Ñan is less well preserved but remains easy to follow south over undulating terrain. There is plenty of flat ground here for **camping** with various seeps and bogs for water. The Inca Road climbs southeast to one final **pass** at 4385 m, 4.2 km after the marsh, and begins a long gradual descent. The Inca Road starts to fade on the way down, but there are many fine views, and 4.4 km beyond the pass you cross a footbridge over the **Río Rima Rima** (Cuchimachay). The valley becomes increasingly cultivated and populated ahead.

Continue descending on the west side of the valley for another 4.4 km to a vehicle bridge by the village of **Sharco**. You can end the trek here and take a van to Huari (three daily, a 30-minute ride) or continue hiking along any combination of several roads and trails. Our choice is to stay on the Capac Ñan, following it south along the east side of the Rima Rima valley. From Sharco you climb away from the river, then drop back down to it. In 7.5 km you reach the extensive **Huaritambo** ruins, 1.1 km before the spread-out village of the same name. Huaritambo has road links to Huari, so you can also end the trek here.

From Huaritambo village the Capac Ñan descends gently south along the east side of the valley. It once passed below the villages of Cayas and Cajay, both of which can be reached on contemporary trails and also have road transport. To persevere at all costs along the increasingly faint Inca Road involves hiking through tilled fields and precariously steep slopes above the river, an anticlimax and not recommended. It is 3.7 km from Huaritambo village to **Cayas**, and a further 2.5 km to **Cajay**, where the paved road begins and there is more frequent transport to Huari.

Return. To reach Huari from one of the several possible endpoints, see above. For bus service between Huari and Huaraz, see Trek 6, Access.

8 MARCAJIRCA
THE WARI PENTHOUSE

Rating: Moderately difficult 11.5-km, full-day hike
Elevation: 2830 to 3800 m
Maps: IGN 1:100,000 Huari (19i); ESCALE Ancash (Huari)
Water: Take a full bottle from Huari; the only places to refill are well along the way down.
Hazards and annoyances: If returning to the highway at dusk, it's best to take a taxi from Puente Huayochaca rather than walking up through the peripheral neighborhoods of Huari.
Permits and fees: None
Services and provisions: None along the route. Bring a picnic lunch from Huari.

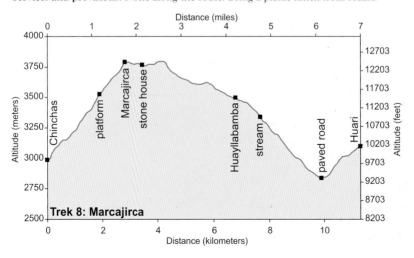

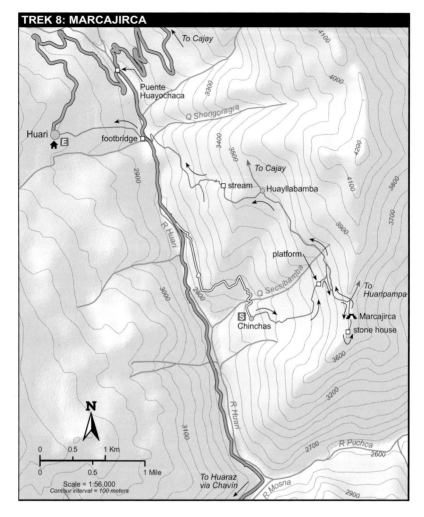

THE WORLDWIDE FAME OF celebrity archaeological sites like Machu Picchu (Chapter 10) and Kuelap (Chapter 7) has tended to eclipse the myriad undeveloped ones throughout Peru. Trekkers soon learn, however, that it's hard to take a step anywhere in Peru without stumbling on something of archaeological significance. Marcajirca is a good case in point: an impressive, minimally developed, and little-known site spectacularly located on a narrow ridge 1000 m above rushing rivers on three sides. Objects from Marcajirca have been dated from approximately AD 700, placing its origins in the Wari era. (In the usual confusion of toponyms, Wari refers to the ancient civilization and Huari to the contemporary town.) The site contains residential, public, and funerary sectors, including many small stone mausoleums called *chullpas*. Views from Marcajirca are as impressive as its structures. It must have been quite a privilege to live (and die) up in this "Wari penthouse."

Chullpas *at Marcajirca*

There are several routes to Marcajirca. This trek follows a steep direct trail up and a longer, more gentle one down, which allow you to take a taxi from Huari to the trailhead at Chinchas and then hike all the way back to Huari without arranging a pickup. It offers an ideal acclimatization hike before undertaking longer routes in the area, as well as a great bird's-eye view of Conchucos geography. The varied flora en route is an additional treat.

Access. To reach Huari from Huaraz, see Trek 6, Access. Taxis charge US$7 for the 25-minute ride from Huari to Chinchas.

Route. Leave Huari by taxi, van, or bus around 7:00 AM to make the climb before it gets too hot, and to have enough time to explore the ruins. From the plaza of the sleepy little village of **Chinchas**, climb steeply east along a trail past homes and tilled fields. A house 250 m from the plaza proudly displays a portrait of a *chullpa* to encourage you along your way. Just beyond it is a T-intersection where you go right. Follow the trail south for 150 m to the next fork, where you go left. The trail now runs due east past a few more intersections for 900 m, where it veers north. As you gain altitude the views back to the Cordillera Blanca become ever more spectacular. After 550 m headed north you reach a small **platform** with stone retaining walls. From the platform the trail runs northeast 200 m to a fork, where you go south (right) for 400 m to meet a larger and better-graded trail.

Still climbing steeply, head south and east along the larger trail past a rock face covered with interesting vegetation ranging from lichens to orchids. Look for *achupallas* (*Puya angusta*), with spiny leaves resembling pineapple tops (they are in the pineapple family) and *cucharillos* (*Oreocallis grandiflora*) with large cream and pink flowers. Soon the first stone structures of Marcajirca come into view, and at the ridgetop you meet another big trail running north–south. Northbound (left) it goes to the village of Huaripampa on the east side of the ridge; south (right) it runs through the **Marcajirca** archaeological site. In all, it is an 800-m climb over 2.8 km from Chinchas up to Marcajirca at 3800 m, a good grunt and well worth the effort.

Spread out along the ridgeline for 500 m are a large assortment of stone structures, mostly on the east side, including the base of an impressive tower and an amphitheatre, as well as many reddish stone *chullpas*. The *chullpas* often have intact stone roofs, some crowned with living plants like locks of unruly hair. Follow the ridgeline south for 650 m to a contemporary **stone house**. Here are some of the best views of the plunging valleys of the Ríos Huari, Mosna, and Puchca, below. You could wander through the site all day, but be sure to leave enough time (3 to 4 hours) for the hike back.

Return north along the ridge. At the fork between the wider trail and the steeper narrower one along which you came, follow the wider trail as it contours north and west. Views of Huari dwarfed by the glaciers of the Cordillera Blanca are all the more spectacular in the afternoon light. In 2.5 km of gentle descent from Marcajirca you reach the little village of **Huayllabamba**, where the trail forks: north to Cajay (see end of Trek 7), reported difficult due to landslides, and west along our route to Huari. The trail down is not too steep but it is rocky, with many "ball bearings," little stones that roll out from under your boots. At 900 m past Huayllabamba is a small **stream** for water. Another 600 m brings you to a larger trail. Follow it northwest (right) for 1.5 km to **Quebrada Shongoragra**, where you meet the paved road between Huari and Huaraz via Chavín. A few meters north up the paved road, a trail branches west to cross the Río Huari on a wooden **footbridge**. Follow the trail climbing steadily west for 1.5 km up to **Huari**.

Return. If you arrive late at the paved road, or prefer not to make the final climb along the trail, then you can instead follow the pavement north for 1.2 km to Puente Huayochaca, where taxis wait for the short ride up to Huari.

9 ALPAMAYO
CROSSING THE CORDILLERA BLANCA

Rating: Difficult 57-km, 6- to 10-day trek
Elevation: 3130 to 4868 m
Maps: IGN 1:100,000 Corongo (18h), Pomabamba (18i, optional); ESCALE Ancash (Huaylas, Pomabamba); ALPENVEREIN Cordillera Blanca Nord (03/a)
Water: Abundant along most of the route, but fill bottles before climbing to passes.
Hazards and annoyances: Remoteness and isolation; see trek introduction below.
Permits and fees: This route is inside Parque Nacional Huscarán; see sidebar for regulations.
Services and provisions: Caraz is the nearest tourist center with a variety of hotels, restaurants, and well-stocked shops. Pomabamba has a more modest but adequate selection. Specialty items should be brought from Huaraz. There is nowhere to resupply past Hualcayán, at the start of the trek. Tour operators in Caraz and Huaraz offer this trek.

THIS TREK IS A splendid combination of the wild and the organized. It traverses the heart of the Cordillera Blanca alongside some of its most impressive mountains and glacial lakes, crossing five 4500-m-plus passes. Yet the trail is excellent along most of the route, there are large designated campsites, and signs are generally helpful. An optional side trip takes you higher and farther off the beaten track, but all parts of the route offer plenty of physical challenge, incomparable mountain vistas, and many "wow moments." Of course the perfect pyramidal summit of Alpamayo is the star of the show.

The large group campsites and good trails also belie the fact that you are crossing mountain wilderness with little or no population, hence nowhere to resupply or seek assistance in an emergency. Although you may meet a few trekking groups along the

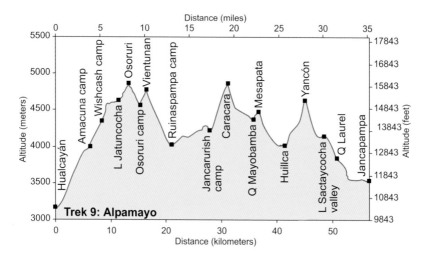

Trek 9: Alpamayo

way, you must be entirely self-sufficient. Navigation is generally straightforward, but there is even more confusion than usual about toponyms here, with totally different names for major landmarks used by different maps. Alternative names are given in parentheses in the route description below.

Access. There is frequent van service along the paved road between Huaraz and Caraz, a 90-minute ride. From Caraz to Hualcayán, one or two crowded vehicles may leave around midday from Paradero Santa Cruz behind the market; service is irregular so, ask around. Taxis charge about US$30 (negotiable) for the 2-hour ride. Alternatively, take a vehicle from Paradero Santa Cruz to Cashapampa (more reliable service than Hualcayán, 1 hour) and walk 10.5 km, mostly along the road with a couple of shortcuts, from Cashapampa to Hualcayán, adding a day to the trek with heavy packs.

Route. Hualcayán is an agricultural village quite used to seeing trekkers. It has an undeveloped **archaeological site** nearby, basic shops, and a **camping** area on the outskirts of town. There are no hotels but you might be able to find accommodations in a private home. It is a good idea to ask around here or make previous arrangements through a tour operator in Caraz, for pack animals and a muleteer to haul your gear for the first day's climb, and to get an early-morning start.

Pick up the trail by the water reservoir of **Hualcayán**, east of the village. The initial climb north is tough, gaining almost 1500 m in 11.5 km to Lago Jatuncocha (Atuncocha, Cullicocha). The trail roughly follows an irrigation channel and crosses it several times, either on footbridges or at shallow fords. There are many zigzags with shortcuts, but the way up is sufficiently steep that, unless you are feeling exceptionally acclimatized and energetic, it is best to stick to the trail. As you climb there are nice views back over Hualcayán and its extensive archaeological site, surrounded by a patchwork quilt of tilled fields. Farther west the Cordillera Negra rises dramatically above the Río Santa plunging into the depths of the Cañón del Pato.

At 5.6 km past Hualcayán you reach a *queñua* forest romantically named Bosque del Amor and the large **Amacuna camp**. Continue climbing north 2 km to **Wishcash camp**

Nevados Santa Cruz behind Lago Jatuncocha

and, just beyond, wonderful views of emerald-green Lago Yanacocha far below. Here the trail turns east and reaches a fork 500 m past Wishcash: right goes to Lago Yuracocha; take the left fork to follow our route over increasingly rocky terrain. After 1.3 km you cross an irrigation canal and continue east on the trail, contouring alongside a rock wall on your right. The scene ahead is an impressive one, with your first views of the glaciers of Nevados Santa Cruz ahead and a smooth granite cliff dropping 150 m to Lago Coyllorcocha (Azulcocha) far below on your left. Continue east 800 m along the trail, climbing to the shore of **Lago Jatuncocha**. There is an exposed **camping** area near the lakeshore, and a dam and control station at the outflow 500 m north. If your group is not too large, the guard might invite you to spend the night at the station.

From Jatuncocha the trail continues north, at first over smooth bare rock, then turns sharply east to climb steadily through more vegetated terrain with great views: over Jatuncocha to the smaller Lago Rajucocha and Nevados Santa Cruz to the east, as well as the Cordillera Negra to the west. The trail then heads north again, to climb to **Osoruri Pass** (4865 m), 1.9 km from the outflow of Jatuncocha. There are two parallel branches of the trail running through a pretty little valley before the pass.

Beyond Osoruri the trail descends gently north over rocky terrain, past a dry lake, to a spring 650 m ahead, a potential campsite. The trail continues north 400 m to cross a ridgeline, bringing Quebrada Los Cedros into glorious view beneath the snows of Nevados Milluacocha. The trail turns northeast at the ridgeline and drops steeply over switchbacks 1.1 km to the **Osoruri camp**. Fill your water bottles here and climb steadily northeast for 1.1 km to **Vientunan Pass** (4780 m). The trail zigzags gradually down from Vientunan; avoid shortcuts here to minimize impact on the steep fragile slope. In 3.3 km

you reach a fork: north (left) to the tiny hamlet of Calicanto (Alpamayo) on the north side of **Quebrada Los Cedros** and east (right) along our route. Just past the fork you cross a small stream with a few flat spots to **camp**, thanks to ancient terracing. The terracing extends throughout the *quebrada*, suggesting a much larger population in times gone by.

The trail contours east along the south side of **Quebrada Alpamayo**, as Los Cedros is called upstream, gradually bringing more and more magnificent glaciated summits into view: first Tayapampa (5675 m), then Jancarurish (5601 m), Alpamayo (5947 m), and Quitaraju (6036 m). These and the glacial river snaking its way through the valley make for many unforgettable scenes in the changing light. After 1.2 km from the fork to Calicanto you reach the large **Ruinaspampa camp**, with many ancient stone structures nearby. From Ruinaspampa, the trail begins to climb along a lateral moraine, rising above the valley floor and bringing the route ahead to Caracara (Gara Gara) Pass into view. The entire valley has good camping possibilities.

Continue east 7 km from Ruinaspampa to a signed fork: the east (left, Caracara) branch descends to the **Jancarurish camp** and continues along our route; the south (right, Tayapampa) branch turns the corner around the ridge ahead, bringing the upper Quebrada Alpamayo into full view. It is definitely worth going at least this far in order to see the perfect pyramid of Alpamayo at the head of the valley. Waterfalls sprout from the glaciers of Alpamayo, and the splendid scene is worthy of camera, binoculars, and a long, deep breath.

For a 2- to 3-day **side trip**, continue south on the right branch along a lateral moraine high above Lago Jancarurish, to an **old base camp** no longer used by mountaineers. If you stash your gear near the camp, you can enjoy an additional full-day hike along a

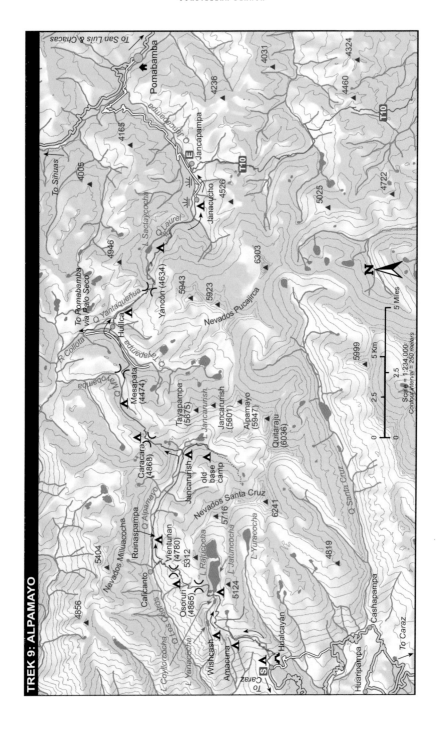

TREK 9: ALPAMAYO

smaller trail heading south and west to the base of the glaciers on the east side of the Nevados Santa Cruz. The final section is very difficult and marked only by cairns. Return to Jancarurish camp the same way you came. The 13-km-round-trip side trip (not included in our elevation profile) is a good option if you have sufficient time and provisions.

From Jancarurish camp, head east to cross Quebrada Alpamayo on a small concrete bridge, a bit hard to find so look for it in advance from above. Follow cairns through the flats on the north side of the *quebrada*; the trail becomes clear when it starts to climb north. It's steady going on good trail, the higher sections marked by cairns. **Caracara Pass** (4868 m, the highest of the trek) is reached 3.2 km from Jancarurish camp. Not surprisingly, the most amazing views and the iciest winds are at the top. The trail descends north from the pass 300 m to a shallow lake with flat ground and reasonable wind shelter for **camping**.

At the lake the trail turns east to zigzag down the steep slope into the large valley of **Quebrada Mayobamba** where there are more **camping** possibilities. After 4.6 km you ford the *quebrada* and begin to climb gently east to **Mesapata Pass** (4474 m), 1.1 km ahead. This, the lowest pass of the trek, offers some of the most amazing views of the red-rock Nevados Pucajirca to the southeast. Descend gently southeast and then east along the north side of **Quebrada Tayapampa**. After 1.8 km you meet a vehicle track. Follow it east for 1.8 km and then leave the road to cross a concrete footbridge over the *quebrada*, upstream from its confluence with Quebrada Yantaqueñua to form the Río Collota, draining a broad glacial valley filled with livestock. Just past the footbridge is one of the three houses of **Huillca**, the first signs of settlement in many days. There is unlimited space for **camping**, but no supplies of any kind are available.

From Huillca climb gently southeast along the south side of **Quebrada Yantaqueñua**. The trail is easily lost in the flats of the valley, but 2.3 km past Huillca it crosses to the north side, becomes clearer, and climbs ever more steeply to **Yancón Pass** (4634 m), 1.3 km ahead. At the top is a stone wall that makes a very welcome windbreak. Descend carefully southeast from the pass; the first 30 m are on very steep, hard-packed glacial sand. Ahead is a very pretty valley above **Laguna Sactaycocha**, with several small ponds and plenty of flat ground to **camp**, 3.5 km from Yancón Pass. You can't help but notice the abundance of life at the lower altitude; flowering plants are everywhere and bird-song fills the air.

The trail again becomes clearer ahead as you descend southeast over a series of level platforms, the result of successive stages of glacial retreat, interspersed with steep zig-zags over what were once terminal moraines. After 2.2 km from the campable areas mentioned above, you descend steeply alongside a boulder field on your right, then reach a lovely valley with ancient stone structures and a waterfall in **Quebrada Laurel** (Yanajanca), the outflow of Sactaycocha. The trail, not always clear, follows the nar-row Quebrada Laurel downstream south for 2.2 km to the broad, flat, and boggy **Jancapampa valley**. Explore upstream from where you emerge onto the flats to find a footbridge over a branch of Río Jancapampa or make a calf-deep ford. Even here, at the end of the trek, more wonders await: dozens of splendid waterfalls tumble down the east face of Nevados Pucajirca, carrying the meltwater from their glaciers.

Tupatupa Pass (4385 m)

The trail is difficult to follow in the boggy valley. Look for the hamlet of **Janacucho**, just a small cluster of houses to the southeast, 1.5 km from the footbridge mentioned above. Groups sometimes **camp** nearby and, unfortunately, children here have learned to beg. Follow the vehicle track 2.3 km east from Janacucho to the village of **Jancapampa**.

Return. Two vans a day ply the rough 17-km track between Jancapampa and Pomabamba, at 7:00 AM and 1:00 PM, a pretty 1-hour ride. In Pomabamba you can either resupply and return to Jancapampa at 6:00 AM or noon to start Trek 10 or catch a bus to Huaraz, an impressive 8-hour journey back across the Cordillera Blanca via Punta Olímpica tunnel. From Pomabamba to Caraz, change buses in Carhuaz. A rest, warm shower, and comfortable bed for the night are all available in Pomabamba before moving on.

10 POMABAMBA TO CHACAS
LAID-BACK CONCHUCOS

Rating: Moderately difficult 60-km, 5- to 7-day trek
Elevation: 2875 to 4385 m
Maps: IGN 1:100,000 Corongo (18h), Pomabamba (18i), Huari (19i); ESCALE Ancash (Mariscal Luzuriaga, Yungay, Asunción); ALPENVEREIN Cordillera Blanca Nord (03/a)
Water: Abundant along most of the route
Hazards and annoyances: None
Permits and fees: None

Services and provisions: Pomabamba has simple hotels, restaurants, and well-stocked shops. The comfortable Andes Lodge Peru (see Appendix A) in Yanama is a place to pamper yourself, and the town also offers more basic accommodations, meals, and opportunities to resupply. Small towns along the second half of the route offer only basic provisions.

IT IS UNUSUAL TO find a multiday trek that is off the beaten track and offers breathtaking views of the Cordillera Blanca, yet is not too physically demanding. The three very scenic passes along this route are all under 4400 m, which is modest by Peruvian standards. Many of the climbs, although long, are on good trails and relatively gentle slopes. You can end the trek in Yanama or take a comfortable break there, about halfway along the route.

The second half of the trek is especially laid-back, with plenty of easy road-walking and several towns and villages where you can finish early. If you prefer a slightly longer trek with more physical challenge, then we suggest including a side trip to the gorgeous Refugio Contrahierbas at 4120 m (see Refugios Andinos in Appendix A) with outstanding views toward Huascarán and surrounding *nevados*. Note that the *refugio* is not always open and it can be difficult to inquire in advance, so you should be prepared to camp outside in the cold.

Both Pomabamba, at the start, and Chacas at the end of this trek are excellent places to resupply and make connections to other treks in the Cordillera Blanca. As in Trek 9, there is a great deal of discrepancy over toponyms among the various maps and local usage; see Trek 9 introduction, above.

Access. The trailhead is at Jancapampa; see Trek 9, Return, above.

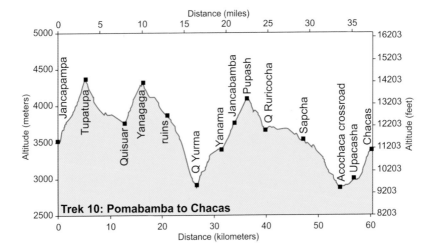

Route. Climb steeply south along the trail from **Jancapampa**, following the east side of **Quebrada Nañayoc** past tilled fields and a few houses. There are lovely views west to the snows of Nevados Pucajirca to help you keep cool. In 2.3 km you reach a flat spot between the main drainage and a side stream. It makes a good **campsite** if you arrived on the afternoon bus from Pomabamba. Continue climbing south for 1.7 km and cross the drainage, which may be dry, from the east to the west side. A further 1.1 km of steady ascent through *ichu*-covered terrain brings you to the very broad **Tupatupa Pass** (4385 m), with great views in all directions.

From Tupatupa the trail descends steadily south 1.1 km to a small heart-shaped pond. The trail ahead is more difficult to follow; stay on the larger branch that continues descending south; do not contour toward a boulder field to the east. As you descend, enjoy the great views west to the glaciers of Taulliraju (6303 m) feeding waterfalls at the head of Quebrada Tuctubamba (Tingobamba). There are nice **camping** possibilities near a pretty patch of mixed forest, 3.2 km after the pond. The trail continues descending south on the east side of **Quebrada Tuctubamba**. In 1.9 km you reach and ford **Quebrada Ingenio**, just downstream from its source at the confluence of Quebrada Tuctubamba and the outflow of Laguna Huecrococha. If Quebrada Ingenio is running high, you can instead cross the outflow of Huecrococha on a pedestrian bridge upstream from the confluence.

A wide trail runs along the south side of Quebrada Ingenio, part of the popular Llanganuco–Santa Cruz trekking route. Follow it east 1.4 km to the tiny hamlet of **Quisuar** (Quishuar). There is not much here except access to the Yaino archaeological site, some 6 km northeast and well off our route. By Quisuar take a turnoff south (ask for the trail to Yanagaga). The trail climbs steeply south 1 km to cross an irrigation canal and reaches the double saddle of **Yanagaga Pass** (Yamagaga, Yanagrajirca, 4312 m), 2.4 km farther ahead. The best 360-degree views are at the second saddle, including the colossus of Huascarán and the five summits of Contrahierbas. From Yanagaga descend

TREK 10: POMABAMBA TO CHACAS

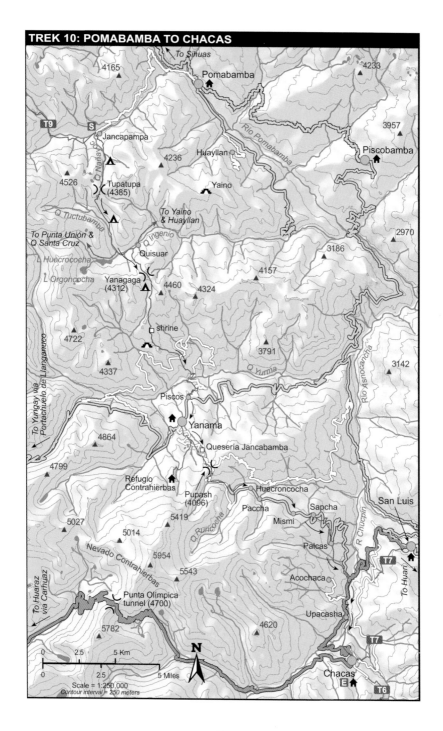

To Sihuas

4165

Pomabamba

4233

T9

S

Jancapampa

Rio Pomabamba

3957

Piscobamba

4236

Huayllan

4526

Tupatupa
(4385)

Yaino

Q Tuctubamba

To Yaino
& Huayllan

2970

To Punta Unión &
Q Santa Cruz

Q Ingenio

3186

L Huecrococha

Quisuar

4157

L Orgoncocha

Yanagaga
(4312)

4460

4324

4722

shrine

3791

4337

Q Yurma

3142

Rio Asnocancha

Piscos

Yanama

Queseria Jancabamba

4864

4799

Refugio
Contrahierbas

Huecroncocha

San Luis

Pupash
(4096)

Paccha

Sapcha

5027

5419

Mismi

R Chucpin

5014

Q Ruricocha

Nevado Contrahierbas

5954

Palcas

To Huari

T7

5543

Acochaca

To Huaraz
via Carhuaz

Punta Olímpica
tunnel (4700)

Upacasha

5782

4620

T7

N

0   2.5   5 Km

0   2.5

5 Miles

Chacas

E

T6

Scale = 1:250,000
Contour interval = 250 meters

To Yungay via
Portachuelo de Llanganuco

gently south along the east side of the valley past several springs and **camping** possibilities nearby.

At 4.4 km from Yanagaga is a small Catholic **shrine** built on pre-Hispanic foundations. There are extensive undeveloped **ruins** nearby and, all around them, tiny contemporary stone dwellings. Past and present merge before your eyes! Beyond the ruins are many forks and a veritable maze of trails all headed down into the deep valley ahead. In 2.8 km past the ruins you cross a vehicle track and meet it again 2.1 km farther along. Follow the road right for 750 m to cross the vehicle bridge over **Quebrada Yurma**; it then zigzags its way south to Yanama with several good shortcuts along the way. The spread-out hamlet of **Piscos** is 1.2 km past the bridge, and **Yanama** is 3.6 km farther ahead. The latter is a pleasant, friendly little town with good services where you could enjoy a hot shower and comfortable bed overnight, or get transport if you wish to finish the trek early.

From Yanama climb south, then southeast along the wide trail toward Jancabamba, which shortcuts the zigzags of an unpaved road headed the same way. In 1.8 km you reach a prominent fork: southwest (right) to the lovely **Refugio Contrahierbas**, a worthwhile 6-km-round-trip **side trip**, especially when the lodge is open; and southeast (left) along our route, 800 m to the *quesería* (cheese factory) at **Jancabamba**. This is a great place to stock up unless, as sometimes happens, they have just sent all the cheese to the city. The trail climbs southeast from Jancabamba along the west side of the valley, crossing the road several times. **Pupash Pass** (4096 m) is 2.4 km beyond the *quesería* and offers magnificent views of a glacial valley flowing down from Nevado Contrahierbas.

The trail continues to shortcut the zigzags of the road on the way down from the pass. At 3.7 km after Pupash you cross the glacial stream of **Quebrada Ruricocha** on a footbridge next to a rustic soccer field. After you return to the road on the far side of the *quebrada*, it's 7.2 km of road-walking past the hamlets of **Huecroncocha, Paccha**, and **Mismi**, to the larger village of **Sapcha**. If you wish to camp along the way in this populated area, then ask permission to do so near someone's home. Leave the road at Sapcha and ask for the best trail toward Chacas; there are many options. One route, wide and easy to follow, descends gently southeast, then south, 3.1 km to **Palcas** and 3.9 km farther to the paved road below Acochaca on the west side of the Río Chucpin. Acochaca village proper is uphill and farther west.

You could end the trek at the Acochaca crossroad and take motorized transport to Chacas. To finish on your own steam, walk up along the paved road 2.6 km south to **Upacasha**. Follow a trail to cross the Río Chucpin on a pedestrian bridge 1 km south of Upacasha, then climb 2.6 km south and southeast to the center of **Chacas**. You can connect here to Trek 6 (in reverse) or Trek 7.

Return. If you finish the trek in Yanama, take one of the two vans a day that leave for Yungay (on the Huaraz-Caraz highway) after midday for a beautiful 3-hour ride over the 4767-m Portachuelo de Llanganuco Pass. From Yanama to Pomabamba, take a taxi to Puente Llacma on the San Luis-Pomabamba road and wait for a bus there. From the Acochaca crossroad, shared taxis run to Chacas in 15 minutes. For onward transport from Chacas, see Trek 6, Return.

11 CARAZ TO YUNGAY
ALONGSIDE THE GIANTS

Rating: Moderately difficult 22-km, full-day hike
Elevation: 2250 to 3625 m
Maps: IGN 1:100,000 Carhuaz (19h); ESCALE Ancash (Yungay); ALPENVEREIN Cordillera Blanca Nord (03/a)
Water: Water in irrigation canals along the route is not clean; bring full bottles from Caraz. You can buy drinks at a few small shops in villages or ask for water from homes.
Hazards and annoyances: None
Permits and fees: None
Services and provisions: Caraz and Yungay are both large towns with most services; Caraz is larger with more selection. No services along the route; bring a picnic lunch.

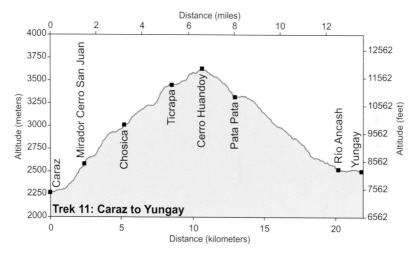

FEW ACCLIMATIZATION HIKES HAVE views as spectacular as this one. It is quite a feeling to walk alongside the towering summits of Huandoy (6395 m) and Huascarán (6768 m, Peru's highest mountain), among other beautiful glaciated peaks. This full-day hike on trails and back roads follows a broad ridge east and then south, high above the Río Santa valley between Caraz and Yungay. The ridge separates the Río Santa from the Ríos Llullán and Ancash, behind which are the giant mountains. In addition to spectacular views, the route offers a glimpse of rural life in the Callejón de Huaylas.

At first glance this may seem like an easy stroll through the countryside, but the long and physically demanding route climbs almost 1400 m to then descend 1100 m. It also offers unexpected navigational challenge because of the many roads and paths in the area. You could in fact follow vehicle roads all the way, but that would make the trek even longer, and the challenge is precisely in finding the right shortcuts. Our

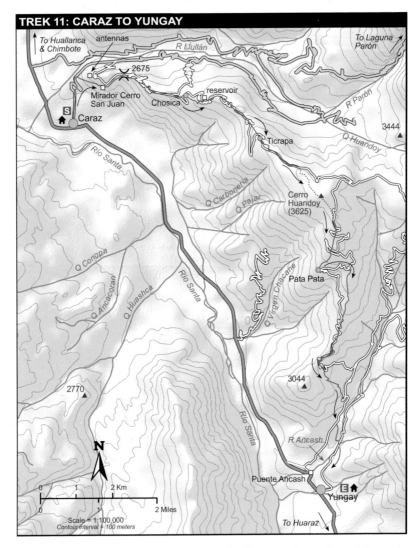

TREK 11: CARAZ TO YUNGAY

GPS-uploadable map (see Chapter 3) is helpful; older maps do not show all the roads. In addition, there are usually people to ask along the way. You will hopefully feel stronger and wiser at the end of the day.

Access. See Trek 9 for transport between Huaraz and Caraz; the same vans pass through Yungay to pick up passengers en route. This trek is best done while staying in Caraz or Yungay; it is too long to ride in from Huaraz and return there the same day.

Route. From the main plaza in **Caraz**, take Jirón Sucre uphill. Where the street ends, continue up along the pedestrian walkway and stairs in front of a school. At the top, 750 m from the plaza, cross the road and take the horse trail that veers left. Follow the signs to **Mirador Cerro San Juan**, a large shrine with a lookout over the city, 2 km from

Twin summits of Huascarán (6768 m), Peru's highest mountain

the plaza. Do not head for the sign reading "Caraz Dulzura" and the antennas behind it. Taking the right branch at forks will lead you to the main San Juan shrine.

Continue east, then northeast on the trail just below the shrine. In 700 m it climbs gradually to a **saddle** at 2675 m with views of the Río Llullán valley to the north and the Río Santa valley to the south. Here you meet the road coming from the antennas; follow it right a short distance. Just beyond the saddle take the trail going uphill along the ridge to the southeast. You meet the winding vehicle road several times along the way. Here are the first great views of Huandoy and other glaciated peaks. In 1 km from the saddle the terrain levels off and you once again reach the road by cultivated fields and houses, entering the very spread-out hamlet of **Chosica**.

Continue 300 m east along the road, then follow an irrigation canal lined with alders, on the right of the road. The canal at first runs parallel to the road, then shortcuts and crosses it 500 m farther along, at the Chosica church and school. Continue climbing southeast on the trail for 600 m over stone steps of an ancient road, to a small **reservoir** that is the source of the irrigation canal. From here the terrain is steeper, more bare, and the views more open. Climb toward the top of the hill to the northeast and later to the southeast along a track that often crosses the winding road; at times you walk right on the road. Be sure to look back at the Cordillera Negra and Río Santa valley laid out in all their splendor. In 2 km the terrain levels off and you reach the first houses of **Ticrapa**. Continue along the ridge, then down to the school 600 m ahead.

From the school, follow the road for 1 km, then leave it and climb cross-country southeast for 1.1 km to the top of **Cerro Huandoy** at 3625 m, not to be confused with the eponymous giant Nevado Huandoy. The views from this spot are magnificent. Follow the ridgeline through cultivated fields to the southeast, then south. In 900 m you reach a road. Follow it south, taking advantage of several shortcuts to avoid the wide zigzags. In 1.5 km you reach the little village of **Pata Pata**. Follow the road 1 km east to a hairpin bend, then leave it for a trail heading south. The trail crosses the road several times until it ends at the road, 2 km ahead.

Continue south along the road for 1.1 km, then leave it to make a large shortcut along a stony trail following a ridgeline down to the valley of the Río Ancash. In 1.4 km you again meet a branch of the road, just before it reaches the valley floor. Follow the road 1.6 km southwest to a populated area. From here, the road continues 1.8 km to Puente Ancash, a bridge on the paved highway between Yungay and Caraz. To continue to Yungay, look for a trail to the left of the road; it runs 500 m between white stone walls to an improvised log and cement bridge over the **Río Ancash**. Another 150 m east past the bridge is a road; follow it south (right) to **Yungay** 1.7 km ahead.

Return. Vans run frequently between Yungay and Caraz, a 20-minute ride, and also from Yungay to Huaraz, 40 minutes. If you stay on the road instead of crossing the Río Ancash at the end of the hike, you can also catch the same vans on the paved road at Puente Ancash.

9
CENTRAL HIGHLANDS

Located between the Cordillera Blanca and Cuzco, the often-overlooked Central Highlands await trekkers who appreciate the unbeaten path. In addition to gorgeous scenery, this region features important pre-Inca and Inca archaeological sites and roads, colonial cities, renowned folklore, and splendid crafts. At the heart of this extensive area spanning various departments is the congenial city of Ayacucho, originally called Huamanga. It has fine colonial architecture, its own gastronomy, craft workshops, and outstanding Holy Week processions.

The Sendero Luminoso movement was conceived at the University of Ayacucho, and the Central Highlands were among the areas most severely affected during the insurgent campaign (see Two Decades of Terror, Chapter 2). For a better understanding of this violent period, visit the Museo de la Memoria ANFASEP (see Appendix A) in Ayacucho. Since 2000, peace has returned and, despite the scars left by this terrible period, people in the Central Highlands are very friendly and welcoming.

The treks included in this chapter are in two regions located some distance apart. In the north is an area of historical importance around Jauja, a pre-Inca and Inca city. Peru's first colonial capital, Jauja is accessed from Lima, either by paved highway or daily flights. In the south is the splendid Sondondo valley, with endless terraced slopes, friendly villages, and excellent condor-sighting opportunities. Andamarca, the largest town in Sondondo, is accessed from Puquio,

Andamarca is the gateway to the splendid Sondondo valley.

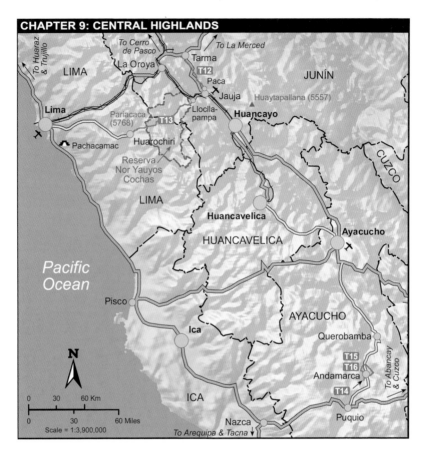

CHAPTER 9: CENTRAL HIGHLANDS

along the Lima–Nazca–Cuzco Highway. Both Jauja and Andamarca can also be reached from Ayacucho along spectacular, hair-raising paved roads. Public transport is available along all these routes.

The beaten path does not exist here. The closest thing to a popular trekking destination in the Central Highlands is Huánuco Viejo, ruins of a large Inca city along the Capac Ñan. A few trekkers visit these ruins on tours organized by agencies in Huaraz, in the neighboring Cordillera Blanca (Chapter 8).

Limbering up. The hill southwest of Jauja, reached along a refurbished stone stairway, has pre-Inca ruins and offers fine views of town and the Mantaro Valley. There are great day-hiking opportunities around Huarochiri (albeit at the end of a long trek), including one to Chuicoto to the southwest, with fragments of Inca road and pre-Inca *chullpas*.

In the Sondondo valley, the best place to observe condors is at the Mirador de Cóndores, 13 km from Andamarca along the road to Mayobamba. Viewing is best around 7:00–9:00 AM, so arrange for transport (US$20 for a taxi from Restaurante Cielo Azul). From the Mirador, it is a nice walk back to Andamarca, taking shortcuts along remaining sections of ancient trail, or continuing to Mayobamba to join Trek 16.

HUASQUI TO LAGUNA PACA

Aqaymarka is an imposing rocky ridge and natural lookout across the Río Negro Mayo from Andamarca. There are three trails leading to the top with magnificent views. Follow the beginning of Trek 16 across the river and go right at the second intersection.

Featured treks. Ancient roads figure prominently in this chapter. Trek 12, Huasqui to Laguna Paca, follows varied segments of the Capac Ñan, the main line of the Great Inca Road, through beautiful scenery and an impressive archaeological site. Trek 13, Llocllapampa to Huarochiri, follows one of the most inspirational pre-Hispanic roads in all of Peru through the Nor Yauyos Cochas Reserve. Trek 14, Puzapaqcha Waterfall, is a scenic day walk from the town of Andamarca to a sacred cascade. Trek 15, Luichumarka Maquette, a half-day walk from Cabana, leads to an intriguing ancient scale map, etched into the rock. Trek 16, Sondondo Circuit, connects several villages in the valley, taking in the region's many attractions.

12 HUASQUI TO LAGUNA PACA
FOLLOWING THE CAPAC ÑAN

Rating: Moderately difficult 50-km, 3- to 4-day trek
Elevation: 3400 to 4222 m
Maps: IGN 1:100,000 Tarma (23l), Oroya (24l); ESCALE Junín (Jauja)
Water: Scarce except in towns and at a few springs near *estancias*; fill your bottles whenever possible.
Hazards and annoyances: Public safety concerns in the peripheral neighborhoods of Tarma and the area around Incapatacuna Pass; camping by the pass not recommended.
Permits and fees: None
Services and provisions: Tarma and Jauja have ample supplies and services. Basic provisions are available in towns along the route. Huaricolca has a municipal *hospedaje*, and Paca offers simple lodgings.

THIS IS SOMETHING OF a bittersweet trek, highlighting both the past glories of the Capac Ñan (The World's Greatest Road, Chapter 1) and—in places—its current state of neglect and decay. Along the way are beautiful scenery, villages, *estancias*, and archaeological sites. The hiking is not too strenuous, but navigation can be challenging, especially as more and more modern roads encroach on the ancient one.

Two possible trailheads for the trek are accessed from the city of Tarma. Once a mountain resort and sanatorium for *limeños*, Tarma has a lovely plaza but is otherwise bustling, noisy, and dirty. At the end of the trek, Jauja is a smaller more congenial place to spend time.

You can start hiking in either Huasqui, 8.5 km west of Tarma, or Tarmatambo, 8 km south of Tarma, along the road to Jauja. The former route has more views and an impressive retaining wall along the Inca road at the beginning; the latter is a day shorter. Past Tarmatambo, the route runs mostly parallel to the paved Tarma–Jauja road, with frequent transport, so you can make the trek as long or short as you like.

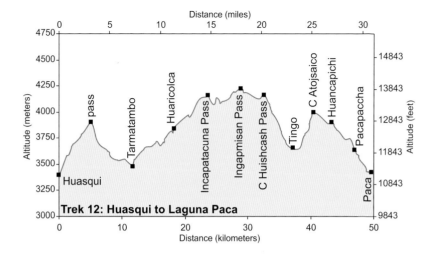

Trek 12: Huasqui to Laguna Paca

Access. Tarma is easily reached by bus from Lima, Jauja, or Huancayo. To start hiking in Huasqui, take a shared taxi or bus from the corner of Vienrich and Castilla in Tarma and get off past Huasqui village, at a *capilla* where the road makes a sharp left turn. To start in Tarmatambo, take a shared taxi or van there from the gas station at Jr Francisco Bermúdez and Av Francisco de Paula Otreo in Tarma. Although there is a trail from Tarma to Tarmatambo, walking through the peripheral neighborhoods is not advisable.

Route. From the chapel outside **Huasqui**, cross the road and walk downhill to the nearest houses. Look for a narrow lane between the houses and follow it climbing steadily northeast, passing below the cemetery. In about 500 m you reach a remnant of the Capac Ñan, identifiable as a wide swath along the hillside with a stone retaining wall. The surface is badly deteriorated and in parts overgrown, especially with agaves, so at times you walk next to it. Follow it east and then southeast. On this stretch is one of the highest retaining walls along the entire Capac Ñan. In 2.8 km you reach a series of stone mounds and, 1.9 km beyond, a **pass** at 3896 m. Along the way are excellent views of the flower-growing valley below and Tarma in the distance.

From the pass, descend south 1.2 km along ancient road fragments, to cross **Quebrada Auquibamba** (reported dry year-round), where there are remains of a stone bridge. Just beyond is a vehicle track; follow it east and south, contouring above the spread-out village of Carhuacátac, staying right at the forks to reach **Tarmatambo** in 5.5 km. This section has more fine views of the valley below and back to Tarma.

Tarmatambo was an important Inca administrative center. Spread over several hills in an attractive location, it is built on ancient stone terraces, sadly marred by incredible amounts of trash. For a place to stay, ask at Bodega Ely by the main plaza. A signed path along an old canal leads 1 km to Cerro Marca Marca, the hill south of town with **ruins** of twenty-two *colcas*, two of which have been restored. There are more ruins higher up the hill, which require several hours to visit.

Vicuñas come to drink at Incapuquio, the Inca spring.

The Great Inca Road climbs 700 m southeast from the center of Tarmatambo to **San Juan Pata**. This neighborhood can also be reached from the *colcas* by heading 350 m east; look for the church. Continue southeast above the paved road; stay right at the first intersection and left at the second. After 2.3 km the Capac Ñan disappears, replaced by the paved highway. Follow it southeast for 2.5 km to **Parque de los Novios**, a small plaza on your right with a statue of a bride and groom. Leave the paved road here to follow a secondary road south. Shortly it divides; both branches go south and rejoin 1.1 km ahead, by the main plaza of **Huaricolca**. This nice, friendly village has a municipal guesthouse and provides access to rock formations and a cave with rock art at Pintish Machay, southwest up Quebrada Cruzhuahuán.

To continue along our route, cross to the east side of the *quebrada* at Huaricolca and climb to a **reservoir** surrounded by a concrete wall 400 m ahead. From here a vehicle track climbs gently southeast along the valley of **Quebrada Licuhuichay**. Follow the track until it drops to meet the paved road at a hairpin bend, 2.4 km past the reservoir. Here the highway goes left and we go right, following a nice Inca road fragment southeast; unfortunately it soon deteriorates. Continue climbing southeast through the straw-covered valley, at times along remains of Inca steps. It is 3 km to **Incapatacuna Pass**, at 4173 m, also known as La Cumbre. Shortly before the pass, you cross the highway; between here and where you meet it again at the pass itself is a magnificent stone stairway, 14 m wide—the Capac Ñan in all its glory! A vehicle track branches east immediately before the pass, toward Palca on the road from Tarma to La Merced.

From the pass, an excellent segment of Inca Road, which maintains its monumental width, heads southeast on the south side of the drainage, undulating through the open straw-covered *puna*. After 1 km it crosses a gully, and 1 km farther a second one, both branches of **Quebrada Tranquilla** (dry in August). Narrower ahead, the Inca road rises to an area called Suacancha and follows the west side of a third branch of Quebrada Tranquilla to two springs at its source, another 1 km ahead. There are several *estancias* nearby, where you could ask permission to camp. The area is called **Incapuquio**, the Inca

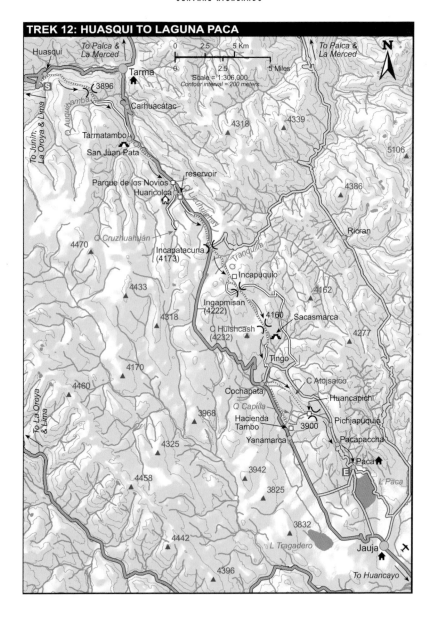

TREK 12: HUASQUI TO LAGUNA PACA

spring, and you might see vicuñas drinking here. Follow their lead and take water; there is none ahead until Tingo. Unfortunately the ancient road is used as a vehicle track here.

Beyond the second spring are a house and stone corrals, and the Capac Ñan is less distinct. Go southwest from the spring to a vehicle track, and soon after leave it to head southeast up a narrow stony valley that shortly opens up. Climb southeast to large tilled fields where *maca* is grown and the ancient road has been shamelessly plowed under.

FIESTA DE SANTIAGO

In the finest traditions of Andean syncretism, the ancient practice of marking domestic animals with colored tassels to identify their owner blends with the annual Fiesta de Santiago honoring Saint James the Apostle. It is celebrated in several parts of Peru but nowhere as intensely as the Central Highlands, especially the department of Junín. This is a happy holiday with much music, dance, food, and drink, when Santiago (also called Tayta Shanti) and the  apus are thanked for their protection and the fertility of the land and herds.

Traditions, dates, and duration of the festivities vary greatly. Preparations may begin in June with the blessing of corn to be used during the festival, bonfire parties, and youngsters going from house to house playing traditional instruments. On the night of July 24 an altar is prepared with the image of Santiago, laden with offerings including coca leaves inscribed with the names of each cow and bull, and ear ribbons from the previous year. At midnight a *pago* (sacrifice) is made to *Pachamama* and the *apus,* with the offerings buried as tribute. Before dawn, torches are passed by each animal to expel evil spirits, followed by Catholic mass. On the main day, July 25, cattle are fed a mixture of coca, *chicha,* and *quinua,* and colorful ribbons are placed in their ears during a ceremony called *señalacuy* or *cintachicuy.*

The rituals are accompanied by joyful dancing with much flirting. This is a time when young couples meet, and fertility is not only for the animals. In many communities festivities continue for two weeks into August.

At 2.1 km from the spring, near a couple of *estancias,* you reach the **Ingapmisan Pass** at 4222 m and a vehicle track.

Cross the track and continue southeast, descending at first, then across the level *puna* with more *maca* fields. A vehicle track runs on top of the Capac Ñan, but edges of the Inca road are still noticeable under the vegetation. Cross another vehicle track, 2.4 km from the pass. Eventually the Capac Ñan becomes more distinct. Climb 1.4 km along it to a broad pass at 4160 m, below **Cerro Huishcash**. Here are lovely views including the glaciers of Huaytapallana (5557 m), northeast of Huancayo.

The Capac Ñan descends south before once again becoming a vehicle track. In 1.4 km it loses all semblance of an ancient road. On a hill to the east are the ruins of **Sacasmarca.** Descend 3 km along the vehicle track, with lovely views of the valley, to the linear village of **Tingo**. There are no services here, but vans go to Jauja, and there is a choice of routes ahead. Ours crosses one drainage east and heads south to scenic Laguna Paca. Another route follows one more segment of the Capac Ñan southeast alongside contemporary roads.

From Tingo follow the unpaved road south and look for a pedestrian bridge on your left, 1.5 km from the plaza. Cross the bridge and follow the river south. Cross a dry *quebrada* and head for a street between the houses. Follow it southeast across two more *quebradas*. At the third one, 600 m past the bridge and just north of the hamlet of **Cochapata**, the two routes divide. The Capac Ñan is said to reappear past Cochapata, running south 2.2 km to **Quebrada Capilla**, where it is lost. At 500 m past Quebrada Capilla is **Hacienda Tambo** near the town of Yanamarca, 13 km from Jauja by paved road with plenty of transport. From Quebrada Capilla a trail climbs northeast about 3 km to join our route to Paca described below.

To head for Paca, at the third *quebrada*, just north of Cochapata, climb east on a large trail to a *quebrada* with eucalyptus trees. Continue climbing southeast above the south rim of the gully to a small saddle at 3980 m, 1 km from the start of the climb. Ascend briefly east, then contour cross-country southeast along the straw-covered flanks of broad **Cerro Atojsaico**; the views are lovely. In 2 km you reach an area with many old stone corrals. Turn east to descend to a flat area called **Huancapichi**, and a broad **pass** at 3900 m, 1.1 km ahead. Here you meet the trail coming up from Quebrada Capilla.

From the pass, descend gradually southeast along the trail amid pastures and cultivated fields to the spread-out village of **Pichjapuquio** (Five Springs), 1.9 km ahead. In 350 m you reach an unpaved road coming from Tingo. Follow it south (right) for 650 m, then continue along a trail going south, just east of the road; it avoids many hairpin bends. In 600 m you reach the picturesque village of **Pacapaccha**, with a waterfall nearby. From Pacapaccha, descend southeast along the wide trail with lovely lake views, crossing the road a few times, to **Paca**, 2.8 km ahead. This resort town on the shore of **Laguna Paca** has weekend homes and several *hospedajes*, but many are closed midweek.

Return. There is regular van service from Paca to Jauja, 10 km south.

13 LLOCLLAPAMPA TO HUAROCHIRI
STAIRWAY TO HEAVEN

Rating: Difficult 102-km, 9- to 11-day trek
Elevation: 2710 to 4829 m
Maps: IGN 1:100,000 Oroya (24l), Yauyos (25l), Huarochiri (25k); ESCALE Junín (Jauja), Lima (Huarochiri)
Water: Available throughout
Hazards and annoyances: None
Permits and fees: None
Services and provisions: Most supplies available in Jauja; bring specialty items from Lima or Huancayo. Llocllapampa has a simple Hospedaje Municipal and shops. Hacienda Cochas produces cheese, has a basic shop (closed weekends), and might

provide accommodation. There are basic shelters at Laguna Escalera and Tambo Real; at the latter llamas for hauling gear can be hired. Tanta, 7 km south of the route, is the largest town in the area, with simple lodgings, eateries, and shops. Basic services are also available in San Juan de Tantaranche and San Pedro de Huancayre. Huarochiri has simple lodgings, restaurants, and well-stocked shops, but many are open only on market days: Wednesday and Saturday.

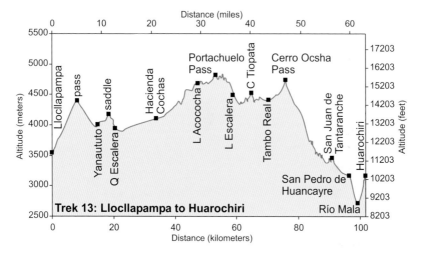

AMONG THE ANCIENT ROADS connecting the highlands and the coast, the one from Jauja to Pachacamac stands out for its historical significance, monumental 1800-step stairway, and excellent state of preservation. Starting well before Inca times, pilgrims traveled it between the great sanctuaries of Pariacaca, southwest of Jauja, and Pachacamac, south of today's Lima. Worship of Pariacaca, one of the most venerated *apus* in Peru, is described in the 16th-century *Manuscrito de Huarochirí* (see *Dioses y hombres de Huarochirí* and *Ritos y tradiciones de Huarochirí* in Appendix A). So great was the *apu*'s prestige that all wars are said to have been suspended during its annual festival. The sanctuary of Pariacaca was destroyed by the Spaniards, and even its location has been lost, but reverence of the *apu* endures. Herdsmen who travel this route offer tributes to it at *apachetas* along the way, and tributes are also paid during the Fiesta de Santiago (see sidebar in this chapter). At the end of the trek in Huarochiri, a massive colonial church sits on a stone platform of Inca or pre-Inca origin.

The grandeur of the ancient road is complemented by wonderful scenery. The route crosses the continental divide between the watersheds of the Río Mantaro, a tributary of the Amazon, and the Río Cañete, draining to the Pacific. The beautiful snow-covered peaks of Pariacaca (5768 m and 5730 m) and Tunshu (5660 m) dominate a landscape dotted with lakes and rivers.

Several vehicle tracks run through the area, and those looking for a shorter walk can start at Canchayllo, Yanaututo, Hacienda Cochas, or Portachuelo Pass (where the most spectacular section begins). You can also end early at Tanta, San Juan de Tantaranche, or San Lorenzo de Quinti.

Access. Vans run all day from the old train station in Jauja to Llocllapampa, a 30-minute ride. On Sunday and Wednesday at 1:00 PM, a bus goes from Jauja to alternate starting points at Canchayllo, Hacienda Cochas, Portachuelo Pass, and Tanta. To start at Yanaututo, hire a taxi in Canchayllo or Jauja.

Route. From the plaza in **Llocllapampa**, follow the street left of the Municipio uphill to the south. It becomes a winding vehicle track with shortcuts. In 2 km, by the hamlet of **Antapata**, the road turns east toward a mine visible on the left. Leave the road above Antapata and climb south through the pretty valley. In 2.3 km you pass under two powerlines. Turn southwest; in 1 km you reach some *estancias*. To the northwest is the hamlet of **Esperanza**. Continue 500 m south up the valley to a notch at 4231 m. Ahead the straw-covered terrain is flat and the trail is lost. The route described below goes south of Cerro Yanacorral. We were later advised that the ancient road, although not always evident, runs north of this mountain and the two routes meet at Tambojasa.

Head southwest from the notch, crossing two branches of a small stream; take water here. Then climb cross-country 1.9 km to the 4393-m **pass** visible ahead. Here is your first view of the majestic peaks of Pariacaca, surrounded by a myriad of smaller mountains to the west and separated from you by a vast plateau. Descend gradually west and then southwest, undulating over several low ridges and dry *quebradas*. In 2.6 km from the pass you cross a deeper *quebrada* with water and areas suitable for **camping**.

Continuing northwest and west, look for a stony chute to cross the next *quebrada* and a natural bridge across the one after. In 2.6 km, by an *estancia*, you cross another stream. This general area is known as **Tambojasa**. Some 400 m from the stream, you reach remnants of the ancient road and follow it southwest. It fades in and out, crosses several small *quebradas*, and goes by a large stone corral to reach a larger drainage (dry in August) in 2.7 km. This is **Yanaututo**; nearby are several *estancias*, with friendly shepherds and their flocks. Cross the drainage and a powerline, to reach a vehicle track 550 m ahead. The road comes from Canchayllo; there is no public transport, but a taxi can be hired in Canchayllo if you want to start trekking here.

Cross the road and climb southwest 500 m to a **saddle** at 4148 m. Continue over a hill to a large open plateau with views of Pariacaca. Proceed southwest cross-country, past a couple of old corrals and a few *Puya raimondii* plants (see Queen of the Andes, Chapter 2). In 1.7 km from the saddle you reach the rim of deep narrow **Quebrada Escalera**, just above its confluence with Río Cochas. You can see stone steps and the Inca road emerging across the canyon. Look for trail fragments descending into the gully. After crossing a small side stream, you reach a cave on the right, 500 m from the rim. In this section you also find impressive ancient stone steps, overgrown with straw. Cross Quebrada Escalera (dry in August) 100 m past the cave. Climb out of the *quebrada* along the larger, clearer ancient trail that then contours around the ridge separating Quebrada Escalera from the broad Río Cochas valley; the views are lovely. In 1.4 km, above an *estancia*, you cross an old railway line; stripped of rails and ties, it now looks like a vehicle track.

Inca stairway above Laguna Escalera

Descend to the **Río Cochas** valley and continue southwest (upstream) along a trail, clear at times and lost at others, running between the ex-rail line and the east shore of the river. In 2.6 km are a couple of uninspiring tin sheds, and there are unlimited **camping** possibilities throughout the valley. Cross under a high-tension powerline in 900 m, then follow an irrigation canal to its intake. Just past some stone corrals, 4.1 km from the powerline, is a flimsy pedestrian bridge across the main river. This is also the last good **camping** spot until Hacienda Cochas, since the river enters a gorge ahead.

In principle, you can continue on either side of the river. On the east side, where the ancient road ran, are a number of fences and *quebradas* to cross; on the west side it is all road-walking, 4.5 km to **Hacienda Cochas**. This farm dating to the 1940s was once run by a US mining company. Its large buildings, abandoned hydroelectric plant, antique bathtub, and former telephone system all speak of faded glory. With agrarian reform it became a community cooperative, home to a large herd of Junín sheep, the only breed developed in Peru.

At the hacienda, cross to the south side of Río Cochas on a vehicle bridge. As before, the Inca trail fades in and out along the plain. Here it runs west, just south of the vehicle track, with some fences across it. Follow either the trail or the road for 1.1 km from the bridge to cross a small stream, where the road turns south. Continue west through boggy terrain to ford **Quebrada Antaracra** 900 m ahead. Take water here and head for a broad straw-covered ramp that climbs gradually southwest above the boggy ground, the outflow of a pretty little pond with reeds and waterfowl, visible from the top of the ramp. Follow the trail west, below **Cerro Yuraccancha**, at times climbing gently, at others contouring along balconies where livestock graze. In 2.2 km you cross a seasonal stream. Climb northwest, with nice views of the mountains to the north, to a small notch between the rocky ridges, at 4393 m, 2.8 km ahead.

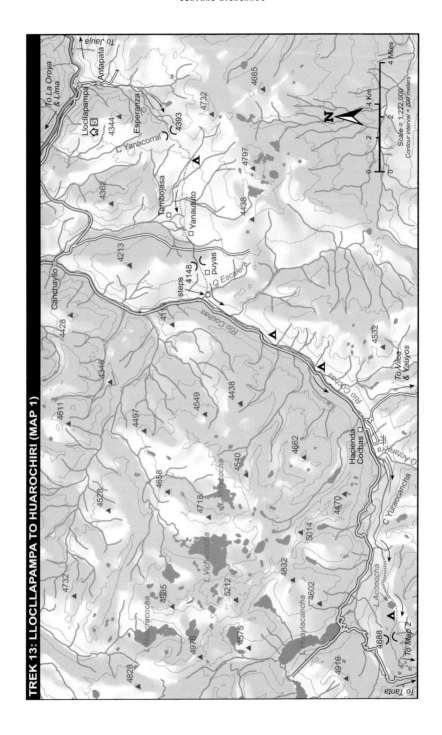

TREK 13: LLOCLLAPAMPA TO HUAROCHIRI (MAP 1)

Descend west alongside a bare rock face on the right, down a steep slope covered in high straw. Below are a stream and *estancia*. Follow the trail, which contours well above the *estancia*, then climbs along the east side of the stream and crosses it, 1.1 km past the notch. After the stream the ancient road gradually becomes clear as it contours west and at times southwest. There are lovely views of Laguna Huaylacancha and Nevado Tunshu. The Inca road climbs southwest to another notch at 4679 m, 3.1 km from the stream, with more great views.

From the notch, descend to the broad, flat basin of **Laguna Acococha** where many llamas and alpacas graze, and **camping** is possible. The Inca road disappears here. Head west cross-country along the south shore of the lake, and continue in the same direction to climb to a low **pass** at 4688 m, separating the Acococha basin from a much larger one at the headwaters of Quebrada Shacucrumi. This is the continental divide, 1.4 km past the notch before Acococha. Contour around the cirque of **Cerro Shacucrumi**, following bare rock balconies at about 4650 m. Then climb south through an area with many ponds and an *estancia* to **Portachuelo Pass**, at 4816 m, 4.6 km from the pass after Acococha.

At Portachuelo you meet the vehicle road from Canchayllo to Tanta. Follow it south (left) for 550 m to a sign marking the start of the next section of Inca road. Leave the vehicle road to follow the Inca road south; it is faint at first but then more distinct. Cross two ridges and later a scree field with views down to several ponds, then climb steeply to a **pass** at 4829 m marked with a large *apacheta* 1.6 km from the car road. This is a truly spectacular and inspirational place, with views of the glaciated summits of Pariacaca and the blue waters of several lakes. Cairns line the beginning of a ridge northwest from the pass. It is worth taking the detour, a short steep climb, for even better views of Pariacaca. Below the pass is a small lake, surrounded by good **camping** spots.

From the pass, descend steadily southwest along the ancient road, then curve around the north edge of a valley and climb briefly to another saddle at 4702 m before dropping south on stone steps to a pretty pond, 2.5 km from the pass with the *apacheta*. Just after the pond begins a steep descent along **Escalerayoc**, the monumental Inca "stairway to heaven." In 1.1 km it winds its way down to **Laguna Escalera**, 170 m below. There is a **shelter** above the south shore of the lake, a welcome refuge from the elements but sadly vandalized. There are also **camping** possibilities nearby. Southwest, 260 m from the bottom of the stairway, is **Cuchimachay**, a cave at the base of a huge boulder with fine rock art depicting camelids, dated to 4000–2000 BC. It is by the last boulder, a little hard to find but worth the effort.

Continue southwest along the ancient road from Cuchimachay through the rocky valley of the outflow of Laguna Escalera. The drainage becomes the inflow of the next and most beautiful of the many lakes along this trek, deep-blue **Laguna Mullucocha** with a solitary island. After crossing several branches of the inflow, you emerge above the north shore of the lake, 1.5 km from Laguna Escalera. Head west to cross the outflow of Laguna Atarhuay (not visible), which tumbles over lovely waterfalls into Mullucocha. Continue south along the Inca road which crosses a scree field and looks more like a horse trail. It climbs steadily along the west side of the lake to its south end,

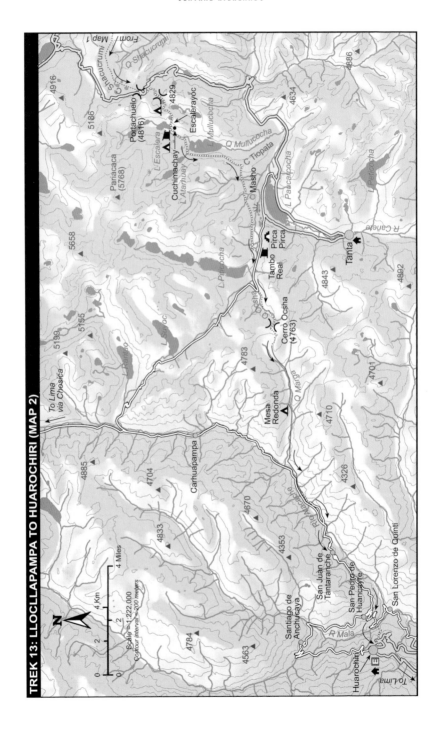

TREK 13: LLOCLLAPAMPA TO HUAROCHIRI (MAP 2)

2.8 km ahead. Continue climbing southwest above Quebrada Mullucocha, the lake's outflow, and the eponymous hamlet. In 1.5 km you cross west over the ridge, a lateral moraine called **Cerro Tiopata**. Ahead is the large basin of **Laguna Paucarcocha**.

To end the trek or resupply in Tanta, south of Paucarcocha, you can either cross the dam at the east end of Paucarcocha and follow a vehicle road south or follow the north shore of the lake to another car road and take it south to town. To resume the trek from Tanta, go to Tambo Real; there is no need to go back to Cerro Tiopata.

To continue the trek from Cerro Tiopata, descend west along the straw-covered slopes to cross a couple of seasonal streams. Stay above the swampy valley on your left. Follow a long stone wall and pass to the north of the hamlet of **Masho**. In 3.8 km from Tiopata you see the extensive **ruins** of **Pirca Pirca** on the south side of the valley. Continue west for another 1.5 km, then descend south and ford the river by the remains of an Inca bridge. You reach a vehicle track and a shelter similar to the one by Laguna Escalera, at **Tambo Real**, 400 m ahead. Just northwest of the shelter are the ruins of a small Inca *tambo*. Across the road from the shelter is an *estancia* with a herd of exceptionally large llamas that may be hired for trekking.

West of Tambo Real, the Inca road has been turned into a vehicle track. Follow it west for 1.3 km to a fantastic view of **Laguna Piticocha** with the peaks of Pariacaca and Tunshu beyond. Continue along the vehicle track for another 900 m; where it turns to cross **Quebrada Ocsha**, leave the road and go west cross-country on the south side of the *quebrada*. In 1.3 km you reach a stream and should take water. Follow the stream south, cross it, and continue climbing southwest alongside it. You are headed to the right of a white hill amid several dark ones. After 900 m, at an altitude of about 4630 m, turn west and climb more steeply along increasingly evident fragments of Inca road to **Cerro Ocsha Pass** at 4763 m, marked by a small shrine to Pariacaca, 650 m ahead. There are several passes nearby; the correct one is 400 m north of the white hill. Be sure to follow the Inca road fragments; the shrine is not visible until the pass. There are wonderful views back to Pariacaca, for the last time, and ahead to Quebrada Marga.

Head west down into **Quebrada Marga** and, once in the valley, stay south of the stream. Where the valley narrows, 4.2 km from the pass, cross to the north side and continue west above the stream to a round flat area called **Mesa Redonda**, suitable for **camping**. Beyond, at Shaulla, uphill from the trail, are other campable areas with stone corrals and water. Look for a trail going down steeply to ford Quebrada Marga 2.5 km from the previous crossing. It is ankle deep in the dry season, and just downstream is a pool for a cold dip. From the ford, scramble up the slope on a small trail that soon meets a larger one. Follow it west above the south bank of the stream. In 2.5 km you will be high above Quebrada Marga's confluence with the **Río Atacache**, and 2 km farther you reach an Inca road fragment threatened by road construction. It is a lovely 500 m stretch with stone steps cut into the rock face. Continue 2 km southwest on the vehicle track (under construction) to a pedestrian bridge and cross it to another road on the north side of the valley. Follow the road 2 km west, with a good shortcut, to the pleasant town of **San Juan de Tantaranche**.

Except for a few shortcuts along short Inca road fragments at the beginning, it is all road-walking for 6 km from San Juan de Tantaranche to **San Pedro de Huancayre**, a pleasant village in a pretty location above the confluence of the Río Atacache and Río Mala. There are several ways to continue from San Pedro: (1) 5.5 km south by road to San Lorenzo de Quinti, where there are more services and transport; (2) 6.5 km north by road to Santiago de Anchucaya, crossing the Río Mala on a vehicle bridge and returning 8.5 km south to Huarochiri, a long way around; (3) down to San Lorenzo, then across the Río Mala on a vehicle bridge and road-walking back up to Huarochiri, a total of 11.5 km and a long way down and back up; and (4) along remnants of the Inca road west, fording the Río Mala (if it is low enough) and up to Huarochiri as described below.

To finish on the Inca road, from the southwest corner of the plaza in San Pedro, go one block south and turn west; this street leads to a wide trail heading west. Soon you reach a T intersection; go left to descend southeast, later south, and finally southwest. The trail crosses the car road to San Lorenzo de Quinti several times, and you also walk briefly along the road.

When you are close to the river, head cross-country downstream to ford the **Río Mala** by a bend in the river, 2.5 km from San Pedro. On the west shore, look for a small trail going uphill to meet a larger one heading south. It leads to a beautifully preserved segment of Inca road winding its way up over stairs and splendid S-curves, to **Huarochiri**, 2.3 km from the ford. The ford and ancient road make for a nontrivial finale worthy of this wonderful trek.

Return. There are daily buses from Huarochiri to Lima, a 5- to 6-hour wild and spectacular ride. To finish early, San Lorenzo de Quinti also has a daily bus to Lima; San Juan de Tantaranche has a bus to Lima on Monday, Wednesday, and Saturday; and from Tanta a bus goes to Jauja on Monday and Friday at 1:00 PM.

14 PUZAPAQCHA WATERFALL
A SOURCE OF LIFE

Research assistance by César Abad and Froilan Ramos

Rating: Moderately difficult 15-km round-trip, full-day hike
Elevation: 3470 to 3800 m
Maps: IGN 1:100,000 Querobamba (29o); ESCALE Ayacucho (Lucanas). Route can be hiked without these reference maps; an elevation profile is not provided.
Water: Available from irrigation canals and streams
Hazards and annoyances: Steep slopes on the approach to the falls; use caution and do not attempt to cross the river if the level is high.
Permits and fees: None. Do not bathe under the waterfall, considered sacred by the local community; doing so would be a serious offense to their sensibilities.
Services and provisions: None along the route; take a picnic lunch from Andamarca.

THE MOST REMARKABLE FEATURE of the Sondondo valley is the extensive ancient terracing of its slopes. Over the centuries, one culture after another modified its surroundings to create this productive and strikingly beautiful landscape. Some 5600 hectares of agricultural terraces were built mainly by the Wari nation; some were improved by the Incas. To bring life to the terraces, reservoirs and elaborate irrigation and drainage systems were devised. At higher altitudes, springs were diverted to expand *bofedales* where camelids graze. Perhaps most astonishing is that many of these terraces, canals, and *bofedales* are still in use.

Following old trails amid terraces and stone walls, this trek leads from Andamarca to Catarata Puzapaqcha, a 140-m-high, multitier waterfall along the upper Río Negro Mayo. It brings water and life from the *puna* at the base of Apu Osqonta, one of

Puzapaqcha Waterfall (photo by César Abad)

two Sondondo mountain deities. Initiation ceremonies for Andamarca's *danzantes de tijeras* (see Scissors Dance, Trek 16) are held at Puzapaqcha. The route described leads to the base of the falls. Along the way are ancient stone irrigation canals. Views of Andamarca and the terraced valleys around it are spectacular. With a little luck, condors may be seen.

Access. One trail starts at the south end of Andamarca; another starts 4.5 km south of town at a hairpin bend on the paved road to Puquio, where a sign marks the trailhead. The route described below follows the trail from the south end of town, with excellent views in the morning light. You can either return the way you came or make a loop by walking back along the road. For a shorter hike, take a *mototaxi* from Andamarca to the trailhead on the road and make the loop in the opposite direction. Either way, be sure to start early to have enough time to enjoy the falls and the return trip. The route to or from the road requires fording Río Negro Mayo, which may not be possible in the wet season.

Route. From the southwest corner of the plaza in **Andamarca**, follow the street south. At the edge of town it becomes a trail and veers southwest. In 650 m you reach some **water tanks** on the left. Go south (left) on the trail that starts behind the tanks. If this trail is very wet, you can continue along the trail you came on until you reach

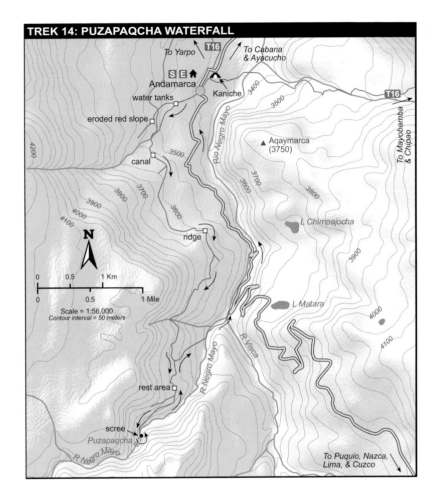

TREK 14: PUZAPAQCHA WATERFALL

To Yarpo · T16 · To Cabana & Ayacucho
S E ♠
Andamarca
Kaniche
water tanks
eroded red slope
canal
3500
Rio Negro Mayo
3400
3500
T16
To Mayobamba & Chipao
▲ Aqaymarca (3750)
3700
3600
3800
L Chimpajocha
3900
4200
4100
4000
3900
3600
3700
3600
ridge
N
0   0.5   1 Km
0   0.5   1 Mile
Scale = 1:56,000
Contour interval = 50 meters
L Matara
4000
4100
R Visca
R Negro Mayo
rest area
scree
Puzapaqcha
R Negro Mayo
To Puquio, Nazca, Lima, & Cuzco

some houses on the right. By an eroded red slope, cut left across the fields to meet the direct trail from the tanks.

In 1 km from the tanks, you cross a modern **irrigation canal**. Continue southeast to **a fork** shortly after the canal, and take the left branch south. It climbs gradually, then contours east. Along the way are ancient canals, still in use. In 1.4 km you reach a **ridge** with fantastic views over the Rio Negro Mayo valley back to Andamarca, and a plethora of terraces. Continue around the ridge, and gradually descend south, past **a fork** where you take the right branch, to another intersection by a small stream, 800 m past the ridge. Take the right branch, climbing southwest to reach another stream in 1 km. This part of the trail gets less use and is a bit overgrown; look out for cacti.

Continue south from the stream, undulating, then climbing, to reach a flat **rest area** with a sitting log, 1.2 km ahead. In 100 m you reach an intersection. Take the larger trail south (left), then southwest descending along the stony slope to ford the **Río Negro**

Mayo 850 m from the intersection. On the south side of the river, climb to the left of a large **scree** field, then cross it on the well-defined trail where it is most stable. The base of **Puzapaqcha** is 150 m ahead. Enjoy the amazing views!

Return. Andamarca is about 7.5 km from Puzapaqcha along either the route described above or an alternative trail and the paved road, as indicated below. To return along the latter, go back the way you came past the intersection and rest area. About 500 m past the rest area (on the way back), where the trail you are on goes north, look for a faint trail descending northeast. You are headed toward the north end of some terraces on the opposite shore of the river. Shortly after crossing a larger trail and 650 m after leaving the upper trail, ford the **Río Negro Mayo**. Climb northeast along a larger trail, past the top of more terraces. Cross the ridge ahead and continue northeast to descend to a pedestrian bridge over the **Río Visca**, just above its confluence with the Negro Mayo, 700 m past the ford mentioned above. The paved road is 150 m ahead. Follow it northeast (left) 4.5 km to Andamarca. There is not much traffic on the Andamarca–Puquio road to get a *mototaxi* or hitchhike, so you should count on walking all the way back.

15 LUICHUMARKA MAQUETTE
PERU'S FIRST MAP?

Rating: Easy 7-km-round-trip, half-day hike
Elevation: 3319 to 3534 m
Maps: IGN 1:100,000 Querobamba (29o); ESCALE Ayacucho (Lucanas). Route can be hiked without maps; an elevation profile not provided
Water: Bring from Cabana
Hazards and annoyances: Spiny vegetation
Permits and fees: None
Services and provisions: None along the hike. There are a couple of good hostels, restaurants, and well-stocked shops in Cabana.

MOST TREKKERS LOVE MAPS, and finding an ancient stone map along the trail is pretty amazing. Scattered about the Sondondo valley are a number of *maquettes* or scale models, believed to date to Wari times. It is likely that these engraved boulders were models, used in planning the transformation of an area. Perhaps they were replicas, not-so-instant photos of an existing landscape. Or maybe they were just decorations. Carved into the rock are miniature terraces, ponds, and irrigation canals. According to the chronicles, the Incas used clay or sculpted-stone models in planning structures and for military strategy. The Mochica, on the coast, also had maquettes. The model-building tradition has not been completely lost. Today, one *maquetero*, Sr Julián Cuaresma, remains in the Mayobamba area (see Trek 16), continuing the tradition he learned from his father and grandfather.

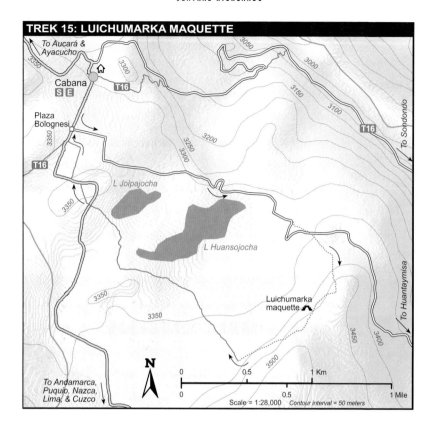

TREK 15: LUICHUMARKA MAQUETTE

This short hike takes you from the town of Cabana (along Trek 16), by a couple of nice lakes rich in waterfowl, to the Luichumarka maquette, atop one of the hills to the southeast of town. Here is the largest maquette found to date in the Sondondo valley, 15 by 20 m. The volcanic rock on the hilltop has been sculpted into a 3-D model with a clear likeness to the landscape found in the region. Was this the first map of Peru?

Access. Cabana is 30 minutes by van north of Andamarca.

Route. From the southeast corner of the main plaza in **Cabana**, follow Jirón Huamán Poma south, uphill to Plaza Bolognesi. At the top of Plaza Bolognesi, turn east and follow a dirt road headed toward Huantaymisa; there are a couple shortcuts at the hairpin bends ahead. In 1.1 km from the start, you will be above a lake called **Laguna Jolpajocha** and, 700 m beyond, the larger **Laguna Huansojocha**. Binoculars are helpful to see the many birds amid the *totora* reeds (rushes) near the shore. Among the species found here are the speckled or yellow-billed teal, giant coot, common moorhen, Andean gull, ruddy duck, silvery grebe, and, during the rainy season, Chilean flamingo.

After the next hairpin bend, 800 m from Huansojocha, leave the road and go along a faint trail to the southeast and then south to climb among the scrubby vegetation to the ridgeline. One of the spiny cacti is the *ullo* (*Corryocactus brevistylus*), with a conspicuous round fruit. Follow the ridgeline southwest. Some 800 m from the road, at an altitude

The stone maquette at Luichumarka

of 3480 m, is a flat rock platform on the north edge of the ridge, overlooking the lakes and Cabana. Look carefully and you will see that the platform and surrounding rocks have been carved into a scale model of the landscape; this is the **Luichumarka maquette**. The views of the real full-size landscape from here are also gorgeous.

Return. You can return to Cabana the way you came, or make a loop by continuing to the southwest, climbing a few meters at first, then descending along a faint trail that meets a larger trail between two stone walls, 700 m from Luichumarka. Follow this trail to the northwest (right), past the south side of Laguna Huansojocha and the west side of Laguna Jolpajocha, to meet the paved road between Cabana and Andamarca in 1.8 km. Cross the road and continue along the trail as a shortcut, then follow the road 1 km to the main plaza of Cabana.

16 SONDONDO CIRCUIT
TIMELESS VALLEYS

Rating: Moderately difficult 48-km, 3- to 4-day trek; 65 km and up to 8 days including all side trips
Elevation: 2980 to 4205 m
Maps: IGN 1:100,000 Querobamba (29o), Santa Ana (29ñ); ESCALE Ayacucho (Lucanas)
Water: Available from streams and towns along most of the route
Hazards and annoyances: Spiny vegetation including long-needled cacti; use caution along crater rims
Permits and fees: None

Services and provisions: Andamarca and Cabana have a couple of simple places to sleep and eat, and well-stocked shops. Services in other towns are more basic. Transport is available to and from most towns.

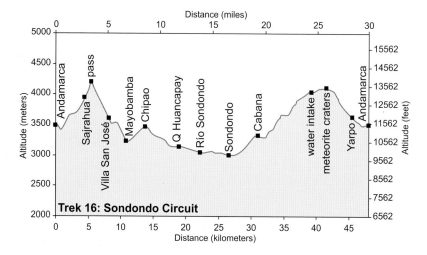

Trek 16: Sondondo Circuit

THE SELDOM-VISITED SONDONDO REGION offers an incredible variety of attractions. Start with wonderful scenery, endless ancient agricultural terracing (much of it still in use, see Trek 14), and unique scale-model landscapes carved in stone (Trek 15). Here too are several Wari and Chanca archaeological sites, ancient roads, lakes, waterfalls, and hot springs, not to mention the highest concentration of condors in the country. Stands of *Puya raimondii* (see Queen of the Andes, Chapter 2), meteorite craters, miniature volcanoes, and an exceptionally rich cultural heritage round out the wonderful cornucopia. Although Sondondo is off the tourist trail, it is easily accessible along the overland route from Lima to Cuzco via Nazca.

This trek connects several Sondondo towns and villages that have basic or better services. You can therefore travel light (but do take a tent and sleeping bag), and there is considerable flexibility regarding the route and length of the walk. The circuit described starts and ends in Andamarca, the main town of the region. In addition to trekking around the circuit, several side trips are possible. The duration of your trek will depend on how many side trips you take and where you begin and end the walk. Although the hiking is not particularly difficult, navigation in parts can be tricky, and the first and last days are most demanding. For a much easier alternative you can take motorized transport to Mayobamba or Chipao, start the trek there, and end in Cabana. There are plenty of opportunities to interact with friendly villagers along the route, and the chance of seeing condors is very good, not only at the designated *mirador* but throughout the trek.

Access. See chapter introduction.

Route. The trek begins in Andamarca (the Chanca ruins of Kaniche here are worth visiting). From the northeast corner of the main plaza, walk a block north, turn east for three blocks, then north again, and look for a trail starting on the right. It leads down to a pedestrian bridge over the **Río Negro Mayo**, 700 m from the plaza. Continue on the trail on the opposite shore, climbing steadily to the east; sections are rocky. At the first fork go right (the left branch goes to the road to Mayobamba). At the second fork go left (the right branch goes toward Aqaymarka). In 1.5 km from the bridge, you reach a spot where water is spilling from an irrigation canal, and just beyond it, a T intersection by a patch of white crumbling soil. Take the narrower trail to

Río Sondondo valley

the left, descending to the north into an unnamed *quebrada*, 400 m ahead. Follow the gully upriver for 400 m, cross the stream, and look for a trail going up the north rim. The stony trail with overhanging bushes climbs east and ends abruptly at a stone wall, 700 m from the stream. Cross over the wall, shortly after take the left trail northeast through the bushy vegetation 200 m to a second wall. Beyond it lie the broad pastures of **Sajrahua**. These commons are heavily grazed during the dry season, when many people from Andamarca walk up every day to milk their cows and make, on the spot, a unique dumbbell-shaped cheese.

Continue cross-country, staying to the north (left) side of the pastures, climbing gradually east. Look—or ask—for a walled spring, 550 m from the start of the open pastures. This is the last water until Villa San José, far on the other side of the pass. Cross a small depression to a ridge with a stone corral just to the southeast. Continue climbing to the east toward a stone wall running east–west. Near the wall, 400 m from the spring, look for a trail. You are headed for the pass between Cerro Curtaya on the left and an unnamed rocky summit on the right. The climb looks steep, but the trail goes along the slopes diagonally to the southeast and then zigzags, making the ascent more gentle. Some 500 m from the start of the trail, you reach the **pass** at 4205 m. There are fantastic views back to the Negro Mayo valley and ahead to the Mayobamba valley, with the peaks and glacial fragments of Apu Carhuarazo (Qarhuarazo) towering above.

A small clear trail descends southeast from the pass. In 400 m is a fork; go left and descend northeast to reach some vegetation and beyond it an area of white soil near

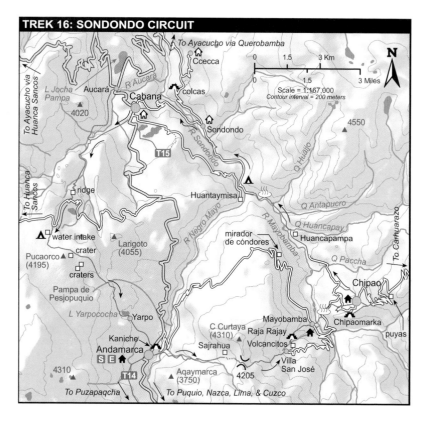

TREK 16: SONDONDO CIRCUIT

which is a *cobertizo*, 800 m from the fork. Ahead lies an area of eroded slopes, *quebradas*, and cliffs, so it is important to keep to the trail. Just 150 m east of the *cobertizo* is an easily missed fork; go right to continue east and then northeast, descending along zigzags into a dry gully to your right. Stay along the northwest slope of the gully until you cross it 900 m past the fork. Climb out of the gully to reach an agricultural area and the hamlet of **Villa San José**, 600 m ahead. There are no services here, but you can camp in the grassy plaza in front of the church or ask for permission to stay in the school.

A vehicle track runs from Villa San José to Mayobamba, but it is more interesting to follow the trail going down steps at the edge of town and continuing to descend to the northeast, to reach the fenced-off **Volcancitos** (Little Volcanoes), to the left of the trail 700 m ahead. These are cold to lukewarm springs, bubbling up in lively fashion; their mineral crusts have taken the form of miniature volcanoes 10 to 50 cm in height. The wide trail continues down to Mayobamba, but it is worth taking a longer and more challenging route via the **Raja Rajay** ruins. Head to a cluster of houses above the volcanoes and from there along a small trail that crosses the terraces and drops into an unnamed *quebrada* to the north. There is a wooden footbridge to cross the stream. Continue along the trail that climbs, at times a bit precariously, to the north rim. In 1.1 km, you emerge at a low wall with a vast area of impressive stone structures on the far side. This is an undeveloped site from the Chanca period, with some later Inca influence.

From the ruins, a good trail drops into the next unnamed *quebrada* to the north and follows it northeast to the town of **Mayobamba**, 1.6 km ahead, on the west shore of the Río Mayobamba. There are basic services, and an incongruous four-story hotel was under construction in 2016. From Mayobamba, cross the river on a pedestrian bridge. Here are a simple hotel and thermal baths, crowded on weekends. Climb east past the bathhouses and a dirty natural hot pool, to the road to Chipao, 1 km ahead. Follow the road northeast for 600 m, then take the trail uphill to the east for 1.3 km to **Chipao**. This larger town with a nice plaza and services offers good side trips. There is transport to Puquio via Mayobamba and Andamarca four times a week.

Side trips from Chipao. Southwest of Chipao are the extensive Chanca ruins of **Chipaomarka** spread over a scenic ridgeline. The trail begins behind the high school; the ruins are 1 km from and 130 m above town. Starting early, this walk can be combined with a visit to a beautiful stand of *Puya raimondii* (see Queen of the Andes, Chapter 2), without going back to town. The **puyas** are 3 km from and 560 m above Chipao, to the northeast, on a ridge on Cerro Quenajaja, above two hills with crosses. The trail crosses a vehicle road several times. To go directly to the puyas from Chipao, pick up the trail southeast of town and follow it past the cemetery to the first cross, then toward the second cross (not reached) and the road. To go to the puyas from Chipaomarka, follow the ridge east to a canal and a larger trail. Take the latter downhill, then turn right to climb to the cemetery. The combined loop is 7 km long, and the views are magnificent.

Continuing on the main trek, from the northeast corner of the main plaza in Chipao, go north three blocks to a shrine where several roads and trails meet. Follow the trail leading northwest. At a fork 500 m ahead, take the left branch and continue 600 m northwest, to reach a vehicle track. Continue along it in the same direction to ford **Quebrada Paccha** in 1.1 km. In another 1.1 km, leave the track and descend toward the Río Mayobamba. In 2016, the vehicle track ended just beyond. There were plans to extend it but also opposition on the part of those who would like to conserve the old and very pretty *camino de herradura* ahead. Follow this trail to the north, cross a stream, and continue northwest to the remains of an old hacienda at **Huancapampa** and ford **Quebrada Huancapay** just beyond, 1.6 km after leaving the vehicle track.

The trail continues descending gradually along the shore of the river, crossing a number of clear streams flowing out of the craggy cliff sides above, nesting grounds of many condors. These majestic birds are best seen in the early-morning sun, spiraling upward as they catch the thermals. At 1.7 km past Huancapampa you ford yet another stream amid *saywas* (small stone cairns). Here the trail gets narrower and drops right to the edge of the river, where it makes a couple of very scenic bends. In 750 m, next to the cold rushing river is a small bubbling hot pool with a cement retaining wall, a tempting spot for a warm soak. A further 600 m brings you to the roadhead of a vehicle track coming from Sondondo; it is due to be connected with the track from Chipao. Some 500 m beyond, the Mayobamba and Negro Mayo rivers meet to form the **Río**

SCISSORS DANCE

A unique tradition of the Central Highlands is the Danza de las Tijeras, part of the UNESCO World Heritage Trust. To the sound of harps, violins, and the rhythm of two large scissor-like blades that they click in their right hand, elaborately attired dancers perform a series of complicated steps and pirouettes. This artistic expression is said to have originated in the 16th century as a camouflaged way of worshiping the *apus* and *auquis* (benevolent spirits).

Dancers are proud and highly regarded representatives of their communities, not mere performers but intermediaries between the *apus* and people. After rigorous training and initiation, they dance at religious and agricultural festivals and are responsible for blessing water sources. Sometimes a duel is held between two groups of dancers and their musicians, which can last as long as ten hours. In Andamarca, Señor Froilan Ramos, a senior dancer, has an exhibit about the Scissors Dance at Mirador de Andamarca.

Sondondo. There are several terraces suitable for **camping** ahead; water from the side streams is cleaner than the main river. The vehicle track continues just above the river, 4.1 km to the village of **Sondondo**. Just south of the plaza you can visit the remains of the house of chronicler Felipe Guamán Poma de Ayala (see Aboriginal Cultures, Archaeology, and History, in Appendix A). *Mototaxis* go between Sondondo and the town of Cabana, providing the only motorized transport.

Side trip from Sondondo. A combination of road- and trail- walking takes you to the sleepy hamlet of **Ccecca**, 5 km to the north. It seems like the quintessential village lost in time, with a large colonial stone church, tile-roofed adobe houses, and just a handful of people in the street. Here is a *hospedaje municipal*. Scattered along the way between Sondondo and Ccecca are many Inca *colcas*, large round stone granaries.

To continue the main trek from Sondondo, descend west through lanes to a pedestrian bridge over the **Río Sondondo**, 1 km ahead. On the west bank, a vehicle track climbs to **Cabana**. Taking a couple of shortcuts along the way, it is 3.7 km ahead. There are many nice views of the valley and surrounding terraces. You can end the trek in Cabana; several daily vans run from here to Andamarca or Ayacucho.

Side trips from Cabana. Trek 15 to Luichumarka starts here. You can visit **Aucará**, 1.9 km northwest along a paved road with shortcuts. Aucará has a colonial church, basic places to stay, and provides access to **Lago Jocha Pampa**. You can either return to

Cabana from Aucará or take a trail 3.6 km along the west shore of the Río Aucará to join the route described below.

To continue from **Cabana**, from the main plaza go uphill to Plaza Bolognesi, turn right for one block, then left. By a basketball court and school, take a wide trail headed southwest along the broad valley of the **Río Aucará**. In 1.6 km from the start, you cross a cement irrigation canal and 1.2 km farther meet the trail from Aucará. From here, climb steadily toward the *puna*. In 400 m cross a smaller canal; take water here, as in the dry season there is none for quite a ways ahead. Near an adobe house, the trail crosses the drainage, and 700 m from the smaller canal you reach a fork where you go left (southeast) and then again southwest. In 1.2 km you reach a flatter area and a dry stream where the trail fades.

Continue due south; shortly the trail starts again, with a couple of branches all climbing to the south, offering great views back to Cabana and beyond. In 1.4 km you reach a **ridge** at 3920 m, where Carhuarazo comes into view to the east and Laguna Jatunputaja below to the south, and 250 m farther, a vehicle track. Turn right on the road to go southwest and then south, past a metal gate, to a hairpin bend 1.6 km ahead. Leave the road and follow a trail south 400 m to a **water intake** for a canal supplying Andamarca. There are interesting rock formations nearby and wind-sheltered spots suitable for **camping**. Take water from the stream feeding the canal; there is none ahead.

From the water intake go south, cross the stream, and follow a trail south to a four-way intersection 600 m ahead. Turn left and follow one of the small parallel trails leading southeast to cross in 250 m another stream feeding the canal. From here the trail climbs 800 m east to Pachapamancan (The Earth's Pot), an area with three large meteorite **craters**. The trail runs past the north rim of the first crater (about 130 m long, 80 m wide, and 70 m deep). Be careful along the edge of the crater, as parts are overhung. This is an inspirational spot where *danzantes de tijeras* are initiated (see Scissors Dance). It is worth making a detour to the top of a straw-covered hill called **Pucaorco**, 400 m south, for excellent views of the crater and surroundings as far afield as Carhuarazo. Continue east 600 m from the first crater to a broad saddle. The second, perfectly round, crater (90 m in diameter, 40m deep) is 180 m to the southeast, and a third smaller crater (40 m in diameter, 20 m deep), lodged in a dramatically steep location, is 100 m south of the second crater.

From the craters, return to the parallel trails; these turn southeast from the broad saddle, at first over a low ridge, and then descend increasingly steeply along a sharp ridgeline. Views are gorgeous here; with binoculars, you can see Chanca ruins on the flat triangular summit of Cerro Larigoto to the northeast. In 1.6 km from the second crater, just before you reach the drainage of **Pampa de Pesjopuquio** (may be dry), turn left (east) to cross a low stone wall. Continue along the trail, dropping east on the north side of the drainage. In 200 m it turns south and drops more steeply to cross the stream, then continues descending steadily southeast and south to reach the flats around algae-laden **Laguna Yarpococha.** Here is the hamlet of **Yarpo**, 2 km past the drainage of Pesjopuquio. From Yarpo, an excellent stone trail gradually descends southeast, past terraces, to **Andamarca**, 2.5 km ahead.

10

CUZCO

Fame is nothing new to Cuzco. Once the navel of the Inca universe, later a jewel in the Spanish colonial crown, Cuzco's current incarnation as a top international tourist destination does not seem out of place. More surprising, perhaps, is that despite the inevitable Disneyfication that comes with over a million visitors a year, the department of Cuzco continues to offer trekkers a wealth of authentic experiences beyond the grasp of mass tourism. The restored Inca citadels and Inca roads of the area are legion, but Cuzco is also home to three massive glaciated cordilleras, turquoise mountain lakes, plummeting canyons, countless remote villages, and a living ancestral way of life. We were delighted to find that we could still get lost here.

The city of Cuzco has all services, many geared specifically to the tastes of international visitors. There are over thirty flights a day to Lima, Arequipa, and Puno, as well as extensive road connections and long-distance bus routes. You can purchase anything from food supplies to topographic maps (see Chapter 3) and specialized trekking gear in Cuzco, and of course tour agencies and operators are

too numerous to count. South American Explorers and the guides' association, AGOTUR, can provide a list of guides, porters, and muleteers (see Appendix A). At the very least, Cuzco is a hub from which to stock up, organize, and set out into surrounding trekking venues. If you don't mind the crowds, Cuzco also offers unlimited opportunities to immerse yourself in the multifaceted glories of the city, past and present, at a vast array of museums, churches, and monuments.

The beaten path. The most-visited archaeological site in South America and one of the most heavily used trekking routes in the world are Machu Picchu and the Classic Inca Trail leading there, respectively—so much so that authorities have had to implement regulations to mitigate crowding. The Classic Inca Trail is limited to five hundred trekkers a day and cannot be hiked independently; tours should be booked several months to a year in advance. Trekking on alternative Inca trails in the vicinity of Machu Picchu, including several variations of the Salkantay Trek, is offered by many agencies, and these routes also get busy. Trekking groups also frequent the Lares valley and, to a much lesser extent, the Ausangate Circuit and the trail to the archaeological site of Choquequirao. Parts of the latter two routes are shared by our Treks 21 and 22, respectively.

Limbering up. Since many visitors arrive in Cuzco by plane from sea level, taking time to acclimatize to altitude is especially important. There are many more day-hiking opportunities here than we have room to mention, let alone describe. Raqchi (Racchi), an impressive and popular archaeological site located 115 km southeast of Cuzco, provides access to good day hiking: an easy 4-km walk along a Capac Ñan fragment to reach the ruins from the village of San Pedro and a more demanding 6-km climb from the site to the three craters of extinct Quimsachata Volcano. Treks 17 and 18 are both good acclimatization hikes in preparation for more strenuous high-altitude routes. From Chinchero, at the end of Trek 18, a moderately difficult 10-km full-day trek runs north to Huayllabamba in the lower Vilcanota valley and is described in *Exploring Cuzco* by

Peter Frost (see Explorers and Trekkers in Chapter 1 and also Appendix A). From Huancacalle, the start of Trek 23, an easy 7-km half-day loop runs to the archaeological site of Vitcos and back through Rosaspata and Yurac Rumi.

Featured treks. To the north and west of the city of Cuzco lies the lower Vilcanota valley, better known as the Sacred Valley of the Incas and farther downriver as the Urubamba valley. Here are Trek 17, Cachiccata, and Trek 18, Huchuy Cuzco, both gentle routes to get acquainted with this justifiably famous area. Farther afield in the same direction and framed by the Cordillera Vilcabamba and the Apurímac Canyon, are Trek 22, Choquequirao to Huancacalle, and Trek 23, Huancacalle to Machu Picchu. When combined, these make a long and beautiful traverse between the two legendary Inca sites. To the southeast of Cuzco is the valley of the upper Vilcanota and the Cordillera Vilcanota, crowned by the spectacular massif of Ausangate. Trek 21, Vilcanota to Carabaya, is the longest in this book, crossing between these great

Vitcos, one of the final strongholds of the Incas

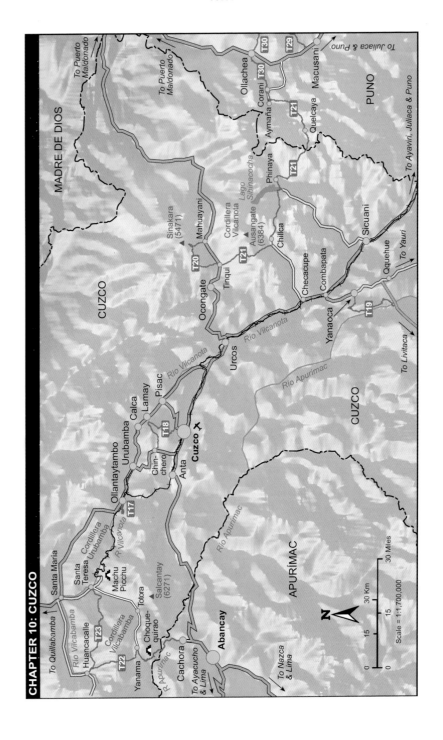

CHAPTER 10: CUZCO

cordilleras. Also situated southeast of Cuzco, Trek 19, Q'eswachaca, and Trek 20, Qoyllur Rit'i, take you back through time to witness two of the most impressive and enduring events in the region's annual calendar.

17

CACHICCATA
QUARRY OF THE TIRED STONES

Rating: Easy 14-km round-trip, full-day trek
Elevation: 2830 to 3545 m
Maps: IGN 1:100,000 Urubamba (27r); ESCALE Cusco (Urubamba)
Water: Available from a couple of small streams along the route; take water from Ollantaytambo for the initial climb
Hazards and annoyances: Frequent train traffic (use caution when walking back along the tracks), as well as chaotic vehicle traffic between the train station and the center of Ollantaytambo
Permits and fees: None
Services and provisions: Ollantaytambo is a major tourist center with most services, but none are available along the hike. Take a picnic lunch from town. For a treat at the end of the trek, upmarket Café Mayu at the train station has snacks and meals made with ingredients from their own garden.

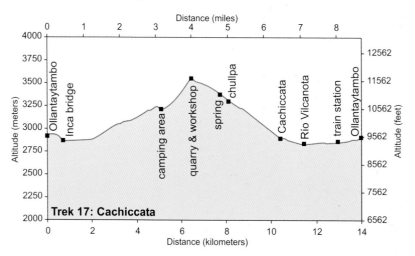

OLLANTAYTAMBO LIES AT THE heart of the Sacred Valley of the Incas. Many visitors arrive by road from Cuzco to see the imposing archaeological site here and continue on by train to Machu Picchu. The living Inca architecture in town is every bit as

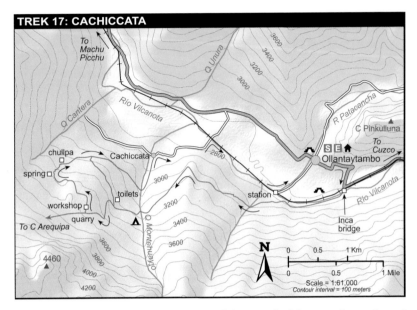

TREK 17: CACHICCATA

impressive as the monumental ruins. Homes and shops north of the main plaza are housed in original Inca structures. The massive stones used to build Ollantaytambo were quarried in an area called Cachiccata on the hillside south of town, on the opposite side of the Río Vilcanota. The quarry may seem close, but consider that the immense blocks had to be transported entirely by manual means, without the use of wheels. Little wonder that a few remained behind. They have been nicknamed *las piedras cansadas*, "the tired stones."

This is a gentle and relaxed day hike. Tour groups use the route, but it seldom gets crowded. The surroundings offer more than their share of sights: vast agriclutural terraces by the rushing river against a backdrop of snowy mountains, while the tourist trains dart back and forth below. The trek takes a full day with time to explore the quarry at leisure. If your day pack feels heavy along the way, then think of the Inca laborers who transported the tired stones.

Access. Ollantaytambo has frequent road and rail service from Cuzco and throughout the Sacred Valley.

Route. From the main plaza of **Ollantaytambo**, follow Calle Principal east. It soon becomes the main road to Cuzco and turns south to descend to the railway tracks and the **Río Vilcanota** (also called Río Urubamba). At 500 m from the plaza, where the paved road makes a hairpin bend east (left), continue straight ahead to cross the tracks and a suspension bridge built on Inca stone foundations (**Inca bridge**).

On the south side of the river, follow the large signed trail to climb gently west. Along the way note the extensive agricultural terraces on the north bank, just above the railway tracks. As you climb, more and more of the valley comes into view, as well as the glaciers of Nevado Verónica to the northwest. At 3 km past the bridge the trail turns away from the river and you climb more steadily southwest. Another 1.1 km brings you to **Quebrada Montehuayjo**, a small stream running through a stone channel, and then a **camping** area with a roof for shade. Just beyond the camping area is a boulder field where some stones might have been quarried and the first "tired stones" can be seen.

The trail forks past the boulder field: the right branch goes to a **toilet** block and a shortcut to Cachiccata village (which bypasses the quarry); go left and climb more steeply over the zigzags ahead. In 1 km from the fork you reach the **quarry** with many partly cut and worked stones throughout the area.

Tourist train beneath the terraces of Ollantaytambo

While the main trail climbs west from the quarry toward a notch in the ridge of Cerro Arequipa, our route runs north (right) passing what must have been a workshop and storage area; cut stones that were destined to be steps and cobbles are clearly seen. Beyond the workshop the stone-lined path offers wonderful views of the valley and river below, framed by various snow-capped peaks—an especially beautiful sight in the lengthening afternoon light. Navigation is a little trickier up ahead as the stones lining the path end and you descend gently northwest, passing an area of overgrown stone structures. At 1.2 km from the quarry you reach a cool, clear **spring** where the trail veers northeast and, 500 m farther, a small round stone structure (possibly a *chullpa* built atop a large boulder). Both the spring and the *chullpa* are a few meters off the trail on your left as you descend.

At 500 m past the *chullpa* you reach a larger zigzag trail. Follow it east for 1.2 km to cross Quebrada Montehuayjo. Here the trail turns north and descends to the little village of **Cachiccata** with an impressively small church, 650 m ahead. Follow the unpaved road 1 km east from Cachiccata to a bridge over the Río Vilcanota. On the north side turn southeast (right) to follow the rail line 1.5 km to the **train station**. It is 1 km farther along Avenida Ferrocarril to the plaza of Ollantaytambo.

18 HUCHUY CUZCO
THE INCA'S COUNTRY ESTATE

Rating: Moderately difficult 42-km, 2- to 3-day trek
Elevation: 3700 to 4472 m
Maps: IGN 1:100,000 Urubamba (27r), Calca (27s); ESCALE Cusco (Calca)
Water: Available from streams along most of the route but can be scarce during the dry season; fill up whenever you can.

Hazards and annoyances: Possible public safety issues in walking from Cuzco to the trailhead or starting the trek in Qenqo; better to take motorized transport to Puca Pucará (see Access, below) or inquire in advance at one of the iPerú tourist offices in the city.

Permits and fees: Entry to the Puca Pucará and Tambo Machay archaeological sites at the start of the trek requires the *Boleto Turístico de Cuzco* (BTC, see Appendix A); US$43 for multiple sites in 10 days, or US$23 for fewer sites for 1 day. You can bypass these two sites if you wish (see Route, below), but all visitors must pay a US$7 entry fee at Huchuy Cuzco.

Services and provisions: There are hotels in Chinchero, Calca, and Lamay, as well as community accommodations in Pucamarca and Huchuy Cuzco. Supplies are best purchased in the city of Cuzco; there is nowhere to resupply en route.

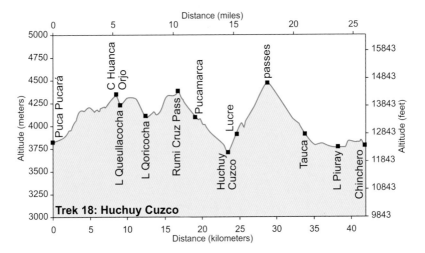

FACED WITH A BEWILDERING array of excellent trekking opportunities, many visitors to Cuzco might ask where to begin. It is hard to think of a better brief introduction to the landscape, archaeology, and people of the area than this trek. The trailhead is just outside the city of Cuzco, and you can end in Lamay, Chichero, or Calca, all of which have frequent transport links back to the city.

The trek runs from two impressive archaeological sites in the hills around the city of Cuzco, north to the Vilcanota valley, and then west to the vast plateau around Lago Piuray and the town of Chinchero. Chinchero is a popular tourist destination known for its weaving, church, and Inca ruins. The most impressive archaeology, however, is found halfway along the trek at the site of Huchuy Cuzco, perched high above the Río Vilcanota. Huchuy Cuzco means "little Cuzco," and it is easy to think of it as the Incas' country estate, a luxurious secluded villa to escape the bustle of the imperial capital. Shall we join the emperor along the way to his rural retreat?

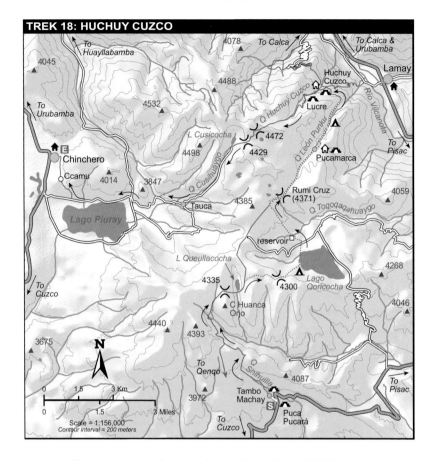

TREK 18: HUCHUY CUZCO

Access. You can take a taxi from anywhere in Cuzco (about US$10) or one of several buses or vans from Calle Pututi, to Puca Pucará, a 15-minute ride. The El Huerto bus serves this route. Buses going to Pisac, Calca, and other destinations in the Sacred Valley can also drop you off at Puca Pucará, although they might charge the fare all the way to their final destinations.

Route. If you would like to visit the archaeological sites at the start of the trek, then begin at **Puca Pucará**, the red fort, on the east (right) side of the paved highway from Cuzco to Pisac. The name comes from its appearance at sunset, not the color of the stones. From Puca Pucará follow the paved highway 500 m north (toward Pisac) to the entrance to **Tambo Machay**, which is on the left side. Past the fine masonry wall and the spring for which this site is famous, continue northwest along the south side of **Quebrada Shihuilla** (also called Puncu Puncu) to cross it as described below.

If you prefer to skip the archaeological sites, then take the unpaved side road that branches northwest (left) from the paved highway, directly across from Puca Pucará. This side road climbs to the village of Tambo Machay, located above the eponymous ruins, and becomes a trail which reaches the crossing of Quebrada Shihuilla (mentioned above) 1 km past the paved highway.

Cross the *quebrada* and follow the trail, climbing gently northwest for 2 km to a notch in the ridge that separates it from an unnamed *quebrada* to the north. The trail turns left at the notch to follow the ridgeline west, past several other notches, and then contours along the north side of the ridge. The *quebrada* below is pretty, and there are views back to the urban landscape of Cuzco. At 3.5 km after the first notch you meet a trail coming from Qenqo. Continue north and cross the headwaters of the unnamed *quebrada* you have been following, then climb steadily to an *apacheta* and turn northeast to reach a **pass** on **Cerro Huanca Orjo**, 1.6 km past the intersection with the trail to Qenqo. From the pass at 4335 m you can look ahead to **Laguna Queullacocha** with a concrete dam at its outflow and large herds of llamas grazing the surrounding hills.

The trail is less distinct after the pass. Head down 550 m to the dam and cross the small spillway, then take a large trail headed north. Following this trail all the way to Rumi Cruz Pass is the most direct route to Huchuy Cuzco, but despite the detour and more difficult navigation, we prefer to go east via the pretty scenery and campsites of Lago Qoricocha. To do so, leave the large trail after 550 m and climb northeast, then east, cross-country to a **pass** at 4300 m, 1.4 km past where you left the large trail. Here are great views north to the snowy crags of Nevado Colque Cruz, among other summits of the Cordillera Urubamba, and Lago Qoricocha below.

Mosaic of terraces below Huchuy Cuzco

Descend steadily cross-country alongside large potato fields to the west shore of **Lago Qoricocha**, where there are several good **camping** spots 1.3 km beyond the pass mentioned above. Cross an inflow of the lake near the shore and head north, across a vehicle track and under a high-tension powerline, to a small **reservoir** with an earthen dam at the head of **Quebrada Toqoqaqahuaygo**, 1.5 km from Laguna Qoricocha. Cross the dam and contour west at the base of the tussock-covered hill to pick up a trail that veers northwest to a wooden bridge over a deep irrigation canal, 450 m past the earthen dam. The trail now climbs steadily northwest to the top of a small valley where it grows faint. Continue northwest cross-country heading for a wide, unrestored Inca road that is soon visible ahead, 1.4 km past the wooden bridge.

Follow the Inca road north and east across a couple of small *quebradas* to reach **Rumi Cruz Pass** (4371 m), 900 m beyond where you met the Inca road. The pass is marked by three large *apachetas* built on stone platforms and has great views in all directions. The Inca road beyond has been restored. Follow it northeast, descending gently to the village of **Pucamarca**, 2.4 km after the pass. Pucamarca has community tourism and a small cluster of ruins. Continue another 1.8 km farther down along nicely restored Inca road, through the beautiful canyon of **Quebrada León Punku** (the lion's gate), and you reach well-preserved terraces on the right that make a good **campsite**.

Past the terraces the Inca road descends more gently north, staying high above the west side of the *quebrada*. At 1.7 km past the terraces it turns sharply west (left) and takes to the slopes of the much wider valley of the **Río Vilcanota**, now looking more like an ordinary trail. Views are superb: down to the turquoise blue water of the Rio Vilcanota making its way through the fertile green valley against a backdrop of snowy peaks in the Cordillera Urubamba to the north. The trail descends west past extensive terraces to **Huchuy Cuzco**, 1.3 km ahead. Take time to enjoy the well-restored archaeological site. Note the unusual mixed stone and adobe construction. You can stay with a family in community accommodations at Huchuy Cuzco or camp on their grounds.

True to its name of "little Cuzco," there are four main roads emanating from the main plaza of Huchuy Cuzco: one southeast along which you have arrived; a second east, descending 4 km to Lamay; a third leading northwest to Calca (10.5 km, difficult); and a fourth heading southwest for 18 km to Chinchero, along the route described ahead. You can choose to finish the trek along any of these routes.

To continue southwest, walk uphill through the ruins to pick up a large trail climbing steeply along the south side of **Quebrada Huchuy Cuzco**. After 850 m you reach the Inca terraces of **Lucre** on the south side of the valley and a fork in the trail. Take the larger left branch, which zigzags south above Lucre and in 2 km returns to Quebrada Huchuy Cuzco. Continue southwest 1.9 km to a windy **pass** at 4472 m with fantastic views of distant snowy peaks and several ponds to the south. Contour southwest on a wide trail above the nearest pond for 850 m to a second **pass** (4429 m) and descend gradually into the valley surrounding **Lago Cusicocha** nestled beneath massive rocky cliffs.

A vehicle track descends from Cusicocha through **Quebrada Cusihuaygo**, and our trail runs southwest parallel to and at times alongside the track. It is a gentle 4.4 km descent from the second pass to the village of **Tauca**, the last section reforested with pines. Shared taxis run sporadically from Tauca to Chinchero. Alternatively, it is a pleasant stroll along the north shore of **Lago Piuray**, through the little village of **Ccamu** with a final stretch of Inca road (here called *Runa Ñan* or "the people's road"), to **Chinchero**, a total of 8 km from Tauca. Chinchero already sees its share of tourism and may become even busier once the new airport for Cuzco opens nearby.

Return. There are frequent buses and vans to Cuzco from the cities of the Sacred Valley passing through Chichero, Calca, and Lamay throughout the day; all are 30- to 60-minute rides.

19

Q'ESWACHACA
THE LAST BRIDGE

Rating: Moderately difficult 45-km, 3- to 4-day trek
Elevation: 3650 to 4270 m
Maps: IGN 1:100,000 Livitaca (29s), Sicuani (29t); ESCALE Cusco (Canas)
Water: Available from streams and at villages along the route
Hazards and annoyances: The rope bridge is safe to cross for about 6 months after it has been rebuilt each year (i.e. from June through November). Don't risk it at any time during high winds, after heavy rain, or if the bridge is sagging badly.
Permits and fees: Women are not allowed near the bridge while it is being rebuilt but are welcome to watch from above and to use it after it has been inaugurated. Tourists may be charged a fee to watch the bridge construction; this varies from year to year.
Services and provisions: There are simple *hospedajes* in Yanaoca, Pongoña, and Qquehue and *tambos* in Ccotaña and Perccaro. The area is quite populated, so it is best to ask in villages for permission to camp near someone's home. Cuzco offers the most elaborate shopping, and there are well-stocked shops in Sicuani (see Access, below). There is less selection in Yanaoca, and villages along the route offer, at most, basic items.

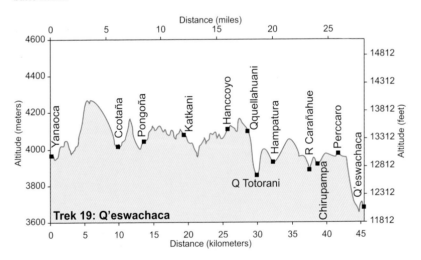

THE DEEP CHASMS AND rushing rivers so characteristic of Andean geography were a formidable challenge to the construction of Inca roads, and rope bridges were the answer. The most famous of these crossed the canyon of the Río Apurímac not far from the current road between Cuzco and Abancay. It was 45 m long, suspended 36 m above the water, and was maintained over six hundred years, long enough to be seen by and sketched by several 19th-century explorers.

In an environment of intense solar radiation and heavy rains during part of the year, straw fiber degrades rapidly and rope bridges had to be rebuilt at regular intervals. Today that tradition is carried on in only one place, at Q'eswachaca, also on the Apurímac, about 200 km upstream from the bridge mentioned above. Every year in early June, two weeks before Inti Raymi (confirm dates locally), some four hundred families from four communities join forces for four days to reconstruct their Inca bridge using ancestral techniques and materials. In 2014 the bridge at Q'eswachaka was declared a UNESCO World Heritage Site. *The Last Bridge Master* (see Appendix A) is a documentary film about the bridge and its builders.

Each family is required to contribute forty arms' length of cord made of twisted *q'oya*, a tough, flexible, highland straw. Exactly thirty strands of cord are carefully laid out alongside each other and twisted again into a thicker rope, which is in turn braided into the heavy cables that form the floor of the bridge. Only the *chacacamayoc* (bridge-master) knows all the secrets of the process, handed down through

Inca bridge over the Río Apurímac (Clements Markham, 1910).

countless generations of his family. Throughout the construction period, a small group of Andean priests make offerings of coca leaves, alcohol, and incense to *Pachamama* to propitiate a successful and accident-free effort. Once complete, the bridge is inaugurated with great ceremony, and the event is culminated with a daylong festival of food, drink, music, and dance. A few Cuzco agencies offer tours to Q'eswachaca on this final day.

In order to place the Q'eswachaca bridge in context, this trek follows the Apurímac canyon upstream through various small communities, a few days prior to the annual reconstruction. There are many roads and trails along the route; navigation is not always easy, and you should ask for directions whenever possible. As you advance, the canyon becomes an imposing presence, and talk among villagers turns to the forthcoming event. Nearer still you see the *q'oya* being harvested and twisted into cord. It is worth staying three or four days at Q'eswachaca to witness the entire process, a fascinating glimpse of ancient civil and social engineering. Even if you cannot make it for the date of the bridge-building, this trek is worthwhile throughout the dry season.

Access. This trek can be accessed from either the city of Cuzco or the town of Sicuani, on the main road between Cuzco and Puno. Take one of the frequent buses

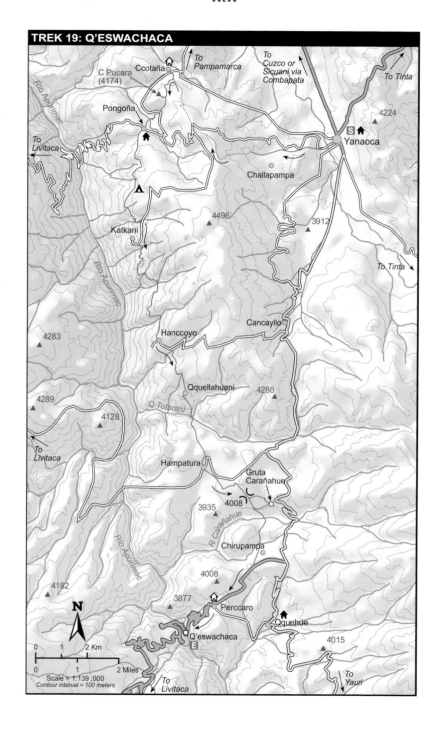

TREK 19: Q'ESWACHACA

that run between Cuzco and Sicuani—either long-distance service from the main Cuzco bus terminal to Juliaca or Puno or more economical local buses from near the Coliseo Cerrado. Get off at Combapata (100 km from Cuzco; 35 km from Sicuani). From Combapata shared taxis run throughout the day to Yanaoca, a 20-km ride.

Route. From the plaza of **Yanaoca**, follow the street by the church west, down to the cemetery. Just ahead, where the road turns north, leave it and continue west on a wide trail up the *ichu*-covered hillside ahead. Past the top of the hill are several forks; continue west at all of them, heading down into a broad valley with a few homesteads, north of **Challapampa**. The trail ends at a small stream draining this valley, 3.2 km from Yanaoca. Climb west cross-country over open slope and pastures toward the ridge ahead. At 1.7 km past the stream you again reach a fragment of trail; take it north to the ridgeline, with superb 360-degree views including the glaciers of Ausangate to the east and the deep

Putting the finishing touches on the bridge at Q'eswachaca, 2015

blue lakes of Pampamarca and Asnacocha to the north.

There are various trails and vehicle tracks ahead, but our route follows the broad ridgeline as it runs north and west amid more great views. After 1.9 km you cross the road connecting Yanaoca and the village of Pongoña. You could follow the road west (left, with a few shortcuts) to spend the first night in Pongoña and make the trek a little shorter. Our route continues 2.9 km northwest to the smaller village of **Ccotaña**, a spread-out settlement with a *tambo* where you can spend the night.

From Ccotaña a road runs to Pongoña, but our route goes up and over the ridge separating the two villages. Head south past the cemetery and climb to the top of the ridge 1.5 km from Ccotaña. A worthwhile detour goes 250 m west along the ridgeline to **Cerro Pucara** (4174 m), a rocky outcrop that is likely an ancient ceremonial site. Tear your gaze away from the wonderful scenery long enough to look at all the broken pottery scattered about. Return to where you met the ridge, head down southwest to cross the road from Ccotaña, and reach a large soccer field below **Pongoña**. Climb up to town, a total of 2 km from the ridgeline.

Head south up the hill from the Plaza of Pongoña for your first views of the great Apurímac canyon below. A vehicle track leaves the upper part of town and soon divides: right down to a bridge over the Río Apurímac and on to the mining town of Livitaca; we head left, south along a trail running high above the east side of the canyon. The trail crosses several side valleys draining down to the Apurímac. Some are dry, but there is a pleasant watered spot suitable for **camping** 2.7 km past Pongoña, and 2 km farther south is the little village of **Katkani** spread far and wide over a steep hillside.

Head 1.2 km south along a vehicle track to the *inicial* (nursery school) of Katkani, next to a large soccer field. Leave the road 1.5 km ahead, where it makes a hairpin bend right toward the center of this exceptionally diffuse village. After leaving the road, follow the middle of three trails ahead, heading south with terrific views over the Apuríac canyon. At 1.4 km from the road you ford two side streams at their confluence, a very pretty spot, and 3.2 km beyond you reach the authentic little village of **Hanccoyo**. The crumbling old church of Hanccoyo is a gem, and the nearby *mirador*, incongruously crowned with TV antennas, affords superb views over the Apurímac canyon.

From Hanccoyo, head southeast along the road to Cancayllo. Leave the road 500 m from Hanccoyo and take a good trail to the right. The trail crosses two streams on small bridges, then climbs steadily to a ridge with an old stone cemetery and commanding views, before descending gradually to the hamlet of **Qquellahuani**, 2.4 km from Hanccoyo. Qquellahuani, even more than the other communities along this route, seems utterly lost in time and well worth wandering through at leisure. Past Qquellahuani, continue south along the trail descending steeply into **Quebrada Totorani**, crossed on a concrete footbridge 1.2 km ahead.

The trail runs along the bank of Quebrada Totorani for a short distance upstream before turning south (right) to climb steadily alongside a dry ravine. Ahead, the surroundings are increasingly agricultural with a number of farmsteads scattered about. Continuing south on the trail, you reach a broad plateau and then descend to the larger village of **Hampatura**, 2.5 km past Quebrada Totorani. Navigation is tricky ahead. Leave Hampatura along the vehicle track leading to the Qquehue–Yanaoca road, and leave the vehicle track after 400 m to follow a trail southeast amid grain fields and large stone corrals. After 3 km you reach a rocky **saddle** at 4008 m with several stone structures and a fragment of ancient road. Southeast of the saddle, 450 m away, is **Gruta Carañahue**, one of several large limestone caves in the area. The cave is accessed by a precarious metal stairway but is not safe to explore beyond the entrance without spelunking equipment and experience.

From either the rocky saddle or the cave, descend 1 km to a footbridge over the **Río Carañahue**. Climb south from the bridge over the next ridge and descend into a broad flat bowl around **Chirupampa**, 1.1 km past Río Carañahue. The bowl is populated, and the first place along our route where *q'oya* cords for the rope bridge are made. Continue 1.2 km south to a narrow paved road and follow it west (right) for 2 km to the village of **Perccaro**. This is the closest place to the rope bridge where you can stay, with a *tambo* as well as family accommodations. It is 3.7 km farther west along the paved road to **Q'eswachaca**, a vertical descent of 300 m; use shortcuts to avoid the zigzags. There is no village, nor any services down below, just the rope bridge alongside a vehicle bridge over the Río Apurímac.

Return. A vehicle track runs 3 km east from Perccaro to Qquehue, a small town with minibus service to Yanaoca on most days. You can also walk back in one day from Perccaro to Yanaoca (21 km), mostly on vehicle roads.

20 QOYLLUR RIT'I
THE GREAT PILGRIMAGE

Rating: Moderately difficult 40-km, 3- to 4-day trek
Elevation: 3826 to 5020 m
Maps: IGN 1:100,000 Ocongate (28t); ESCALE Cusco (Quispicanchis)
Water: Abundant along most of the route
Hazards and annoyances: Watch your belongings wherever there are crowds, and do not leave your campsite unattended near the sanctuary. Be wary (in terms of hygiene) of food sold along the pilgrimage route. Do not climb onto the Sinakara glacier.
Permits and fees: None. Note, however, that, as an outsider, you may be asked to refrain from visiting certain sensitive areas, including the glaciers of Sinakara.
Services and provisions: Basic hotels and shops operate year-round in Tinqui, with a better selection in Ocongate. During the 2 weeks preceding Qoyllur Rit'i, numerous makeshift places offer accommodations and meals in Mahuayani, as well as horses for hire. Cuzco agencies offer trips to see the pilgrimage. Bring supplies from Cuzco or Ocongate. Except for food sold en route to the sanctuary during the pilgrimage, there is nowhere to resupply en route.

QOYLLUR RIT'I IS AT once a time, a place, an event, and a spectacularly complex object of devotion. The time is the full moon prior to Inti Raymi (the June solstice), which coincides with the appearance of the Pleiades in the Andean sky and with Trinity Sunday, eight weeks after Easter Sunday. The place is a broad valley floor at 4700 m, beneath the glaciers of Nevado Sinakara (Cinajara, 5471 m) and in the shadow of the Cordillera Vilcanota crowned by Ausangate (6384 m). The object of devotion is at once an image of Christ painted on a rock, around which a sanctuary has been built, and the *apus* (mountain gods) that surround this spectacular venue.

It all comes together once a year when over one hundred thousand pilgrims pay homage through travel, music, and dance to a multifaceted concept of divinity inherited from their heterogeneous ancestors. The pilgrims come from all walks of life, both urban and rural. They come as individuals, families, and *Pabluchas*—groups representing a fraternity or community, each with its own special attire, banner, and musicians. This infantry of pilgrims is accompanied by a veritable cavalry of horse packers and a mass of vendors hawking food, drink (alcohol is not permitted), clothing, blankets, and ceremonial items from as far afield as Bolivia. The pilgrimage gradually builds over two

Pabluchas *somewhere between devotion and exhaustion*

weeks and culminates on the Tuesday after Trinity Sunday. Be sure to confirm dates in advance in Cuzco; a second smaller pilgrimage takes place in September. Qoyllur Rit'i was declared part of UNESCO's Intangible Cultural Heritage roster in 2011.

This trek is worthwhile throughout the dry season for solitude (the sanctuary is deserted most of the year), amazing views, and authentic villages where only Quechua is spoken. It is equally worthwhile, but an entirely different experience, during the pilgrimage. Our route follows the pilgrims' progress and then ascends above the press of dancers and vendors to the ethereal realm of the *apus*, before coming down to earth in the Tinquimayo valley near Tinqui.

Access. The trek begins in the village of Mahuayani on the Carretera Interoceánica, the paved highway connecting Cuzco and Puerto Maldonado in the jungle. Ocongate is a larger, lower town 22 km west of Mahuayani on the same highway, with more services and a warmer climate. During the pilgrimage buses run frequently from the Coliseo Cerrado in Cuzco to Mahuayani, a 3- to 4-hour ride. At other times you can take a local bus from the same location in Cuzco to Ocongate (or Tinqui, 10 km farther east), and a shared taxi from there. You can also take a long-distance bus from Cuzco to Puerto Maldonado and ask to be let off in Mahuayani, although this will be more expensive.

Route. From **Mahuayani**, an unpaved road (closed to vehicles) climbs north along the east side of Quebrada Sinakara. This is the main route to the sanctuary, packed with

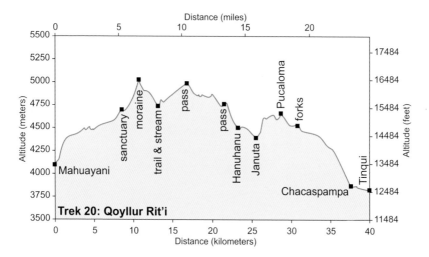

pilgrims on foot and horseback. For a less-crowded alternative, our route climbs north from the school in Mahuayani, zigzagging along a clear trail up the steep hillside above town. After the zigzags the trail turns east and then again north, to enter the canyon of **Quebrada Sinakara** 1.7 km past Mahuayani. From here the trail follows the west side of the canyon for 3 km to a small sod bridge where it crosses to join the road on the east side. A further 3.6 km of road-walking brings you to the **sanctuary** at 4700 m, where, during the pilgrimage, the *Pabluchas* perform their most devoted dances and masses are celebrated 24 hours a day. There is ample ground to **camp** in the surroundings, most of it occupied by tents and blue plastic shelters during the pilgrimage. Many *Pabluchas* jealously guard reserved camping spots year after year. Don't expect to sleep much amid the continuous music and fireworks that carry on day and night.

When you have had your fill of the blue-plastic metropolis, head northeast cross-country past the sanctuary buildings toward the glaciers and summits of Sinakara. The **moraine** at the foot of the glacier is an oasis of tranquility overlooking the frenetic scene below. Groups of *Ukukus* (literally "bears," pilgrims who guard the sacred ice and summits) patrol here and bring down blocks of ice that, when melted and blessed by a Roman Catholic priest or native Andean priest, become a treasured talisman to take home from Qoyllur Rit'i. In 2014 the snow line stood at 5020 m, 2.2 km from the sanctuary. Although some participants do so, it is best not to climb onto the glacier itself, both because of the risk of crevasses and because this may offend the *Ukukus*.

In order to avoid returning to the sanctuary, head southwest cross-country, contouring at first and then descending high above the north side of the valley. Pick up a clear trail in 2.4 km, just after you cross a small stream. The trail climbs west for 1.8 km to a boggy valley with many spots to **camp**. Continue west past several pretty ponds to reach a **pass** at 4957 m, 1.2 km beyond the boggy valley. The trail forks here: right (northwest) to the village of Anccasi and left along our route, which weaves from side to side of the ridge we follow west. Trails fade in and out along the way, but it is mostly cross-country travel

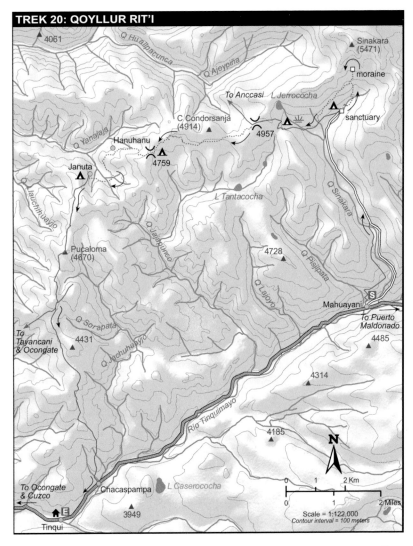

TREK 20: QOYLLUR RIT'I

ahead. Look south for amazing views of the Cordillera Vilcanota, and note the well-watered alpaca-grazed balconies with many good camping spots on either side of the ridge.

Continue west along the south slope of **Cerro Condorsanja**, with more ponds, unforgettable views, and **camping** possibilities. Continue cross-country headed west. There are various small notches along the way, and the next substantial **pass**, at 4759 m, is reached 5.4 km from the fork to Anccasi. This pass separates the drainage of Quebrada Yanajaja, to the north, from that of Quebrada Jajapunco, a tributary of the Río Tinquimayo, to the south. Head down the west side of the pass over barren ground alongside a reddish pond. Various *quebradas* open ahead and coalesce into a deep one below, crossed 1.7 km from the pass.

Continue west above the tiny hamlet of **Hanuhanu**, then climb around the next ridge for your first views of the slightly larger and exceptionally friendly village of **Januta**, surrounded by a very beautiful valley. The slopes ahead are crisscrossed by so many streams and fences that Januta is not easy to reach even though it is in plain sight. Head south and then west across several unnamed *quebradas*, to finally arrive at Januta, 2.3 km past Hanuhanu. You can ask to **camp** in Januta, and do take water here for the climb ahead; it is dry and exposed for most of the remainder of the trek.

From Januta, an increasingly clear trail climbs steeply 1 km southwest above town, then south for another 1 km to a small knob with endless 360-degree views, among the finest in all of Peru. Gathered here are all three major glaciated ranges of Cuzco: the Cordilleras Vilcanota, Urubamba, and Vilcabamba. It can be very cold and windy, but we were so enthralled that we hardly noticed. The trail contours south along the west flank of the ridge ahead, but it is well worth staying up on the ridgeline. In 1.1 km you reach **Pucaloma** (4670 m), another hill with more unforgettable vistas. Continue south for 1.9 km to a fork, and go south (right). Just 200 m ahead is another intersection; again go south (left). The right branch leads to Oconcgate via Tayancani, a potential alternate route to finish the trek.

We continue south to a broad unnamed valley with a few small mines. The miners commute here by motorcycle from Tinqui, and their bikes have made numerous trails, all of which lead south down into the valley of the **Río Tinquimayo**. It is 7 km south from the fork to Tayncani, to **Chacaspampa** on the paved highway; then a further 2 km west along the highway to **Tinqui**.

Return. See Access for bus service along the Carretera Interoceánica. Following the end of Qoyllur Rit'i on Tuesday, throngs return to Cuzco for the next festival: Corpus Christi, on Thursday. Some *Pabluchas* travel from Qoyllur Rit'i to Cuzco on foot, using parts of the route described above.

21 VILCANOTA TO CARABAYA
ODYSSEY AMONG THE APUS

Rating: Very difficult 135-km, 14-day trek
Elevation: 3800 to 5250 m
Maps: IGN 1:100,000 Ocongate (28t), Corani (28u), Ñuñoa (29u); ESCALE Cusco (Quispicanchis, Canchis), Puno (Carabaya)
Water: Abundant along most of the route
Hazards and annoyances: This route covers isolated areas and five passes near or above 5000 m. You should be self-sufficient, fit, prepared for cold, and acclimatized to altitude.
Permits and fees: Trekkers are charged a small fee at the bridge in Tinqui.
Services and provisions: There are hotels in Ocongate and Tinqui, as well as shelters in Upis, basic municipal accommodations in Phinaya, and a *tambo* in Aymaña. Take supplies from Cuzco or Ocongate and resupply in Phinaya, Quelcaya, or Aymaña. Cayetano

Crispín (see Appendix A), in Tinqui, is very knowledgeable and can organize guides and pack animals. Cuzco agencies do not routinely offer this trek but might undertake to do so with advance notice.

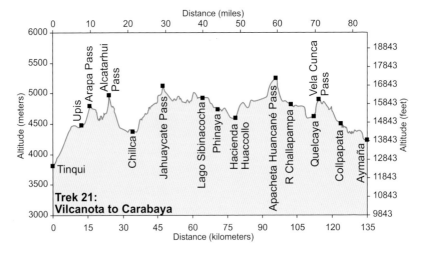

THIS TREK IS ALL about transitions. Geographic transition: from the glaciated summits, turquoise lakes, and deeply incised green valleys of the Cordillera Vilcanota, to the high flat *puna* and extensive rock formations of the Cordillera Carabaya; ethnic transition: from the Quechua heartland of Cuzco, where mortar-board *montero* hats are part of every woman's attire, to the department of Puno, where Aymara influence begins to be felt and bowlers have found their way into local head dress; and transition between dominions: from the realm of *Apu* Ausangate (6384 m) to that of Allin Capac (5780 m), both of which lord over their underling summits and vast surroundings.

The transition is long and gradual, with plenty of high hard hiking, wilderness camping, and navigational challenge along the way. The effort is amply rewarded by your proximity to the amazing 44-sq-km glacier of Quelcaya, the largest ice cap in the world's tropics; by a stroll along the shores of Laguna Sibinacocha, 1000 m higher than Titicaca and ringed by an endless crown of snowy mountains; and by the incomparable feeling of being out on your own in the backcountry of Peru. The first two days of this trek coincide with the Ausangate Circuit, a popular route that circumnavigates the great mountain. You may meet one or two groups in this section but will be on your own the rest of the way.

Access. The trek begins in the small town of Tinqui, on the Carretera Interoceánica, the paved highway connecting Cuzco and Puerto Maldonado in the jungle. Ocongate is a larger lower town, 10 km west of Tinqui on the same highway, with more services and a warmer climate. There are local buses throughout the day from the Coliseo Cerrado in Cuzco to Ocongate, a 3-hour ride; some continue to Tinqui. You can also take a long-distance bus from Cuzco to Puerto Maldonado and ask to be let off in either town, although this will be more expensive. Shared taxis run frequently between Ocongate

Apu Ausangate (6384 m)

and Tinqui. You can also take a taxi from Tinki to Upis for about US$10, to make this trek 1 day shorter.

Route: **Tinqui to Chillca.** At **Tinqui** (Tinki, Tinke) cross the vehicle bridge over the Río Tinquimayo and follow the unpaved road east for 1 km to another bridge over the **Río Pinchimuro.** Stay on the road, heading south at several forks ahead. At 2.8 km past Río Pinchimuro, leave the road and take a wide trail on your left heading southeast. The trail climbs steadily and in 4.3 km levels off amid several small ponds with many waterbirds. The north face of Ausangate is visible all along the way, radiant in the afternoon light. Follow the trail southeast as it drops into the large boggy valley around **Upis,** reached 4.4 km past the ponds. Upis is the first night's stop for trekkers on the Ausangate Circuit, with steaming hot springs, various **campsites,** and basic shelters, all commercial. You can spend a day here to enjoy the thermal baths and take a side trip up to a lake at the base of the glaciers of Ausangate.

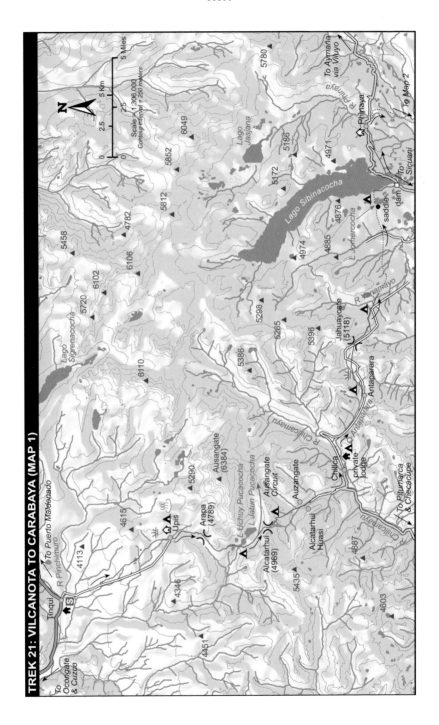

TREK 21: VILCANOTA TO CARABAYA (MAP 1)

At Upis cross the glacial river on a footbridge and follow a clear trail headed southeast, upstream above the west shore. At 1.1 km past Upis the trail turns south and you begin the steep climb to **Arapa Pass** (4789 m), 2.4 km ahead. There is a small *apacheta* here and the trail turns southwest, contouring around the west flank of the Ausangate massif. At 1.8 km beyond the pass the trail again turns south and begins to descend, at times steeply, toward a series of lakes nestled below the glaciers—an exceptionally scenic part of the trek. A further 2.4 km brings you to the outflow of **Lago Uchuy Pucacocha** ("Little Red Lake," even though it is turquoise blue) with ideal **camping** spots. Cross the outflow and climb steadily southeast along the trail above the west side of the lake. Views back to the glaciers are superb, and you might hear the odd avalanche rumbling downslope.

Follow the trail as it makes its way toward **Lago Jatun Pucacocha** ("Big Red Lake," also blue and the largest of the many in this area) and then descends past some reedy ponds. At 2.7 km past the outflow of Uchuy Pucacocha we leave the wide trail of the Ausangate Circuit to climb steeply toward the broad flat pass that separates the lakes from the large drainage of the Río Chillcamayu to the south. The trail ahead is smaller and is lost altogether near the recently deglaciated ridgetop. **Alcatarhui Pass** at 4969 m, marked by several immense *apachetas*, the largest we have ever seen, is reached 1.4 km from where you left the Ausangate Circuit trail. Head southeast down from the pass to the flat balconies above the deep valley ahead. Follow the small cairns in preference to the red arrows painted on the rocks. At 1.2 km from the pass is a stone corral, slightly east of our route, with good wind shelter for **camping** and a small spring nearby.

Follow the cairn-marked trail as it descends steadily south over open ground with fine views of the broad glacial valley ahead. At 2.4 km past the corral mentioned above you pass the tiny hamlets of **Auzangate**, on the east side of the drainage, and a little farther downstream **Alcatarhui Huasi** on the west. The trail becomes a rough vehicle track and in 4.2 km meets a larger unpaved road climbing from Pitumarca and Checacupe (on the main Cuzco–Puno Highway). Follow the larger road east (left) for 2.3 km to the village of **Chillca**. Chillca is 33 km by road from Pitumarca, but only a couple of vehicles a week (mostly trucks for Sunday market) make this journey and Chillca, in general, does not have much to offer.

Route: Chillca to Phinaya. At 1.2 km past Chillca, leave the road and cross to the south side of the **Río Chillcamayu** on a small wooden footbridge. On the far side, 500 m ahead, is a comfortable **lodge** in a lovely setting, reserved—alas—for the exclusive use of the owner's groups. You can ask to **camp** nearby. From the lodge, follow animal trails that climb ever more steeply east along the south side of the valley for 1.4 km to the impressive canyon of **Quebrada Antaparara** (also called Misquiunuj), where you turn southeast onto a clearer trail. Look north here for amazing views of Ausangate and surrounding summits. The trail climbs more gradually south as the valley floor rises from the depths of the canyon to meet it. After 1 km you meet the vehicle track from Chillca and follow it southeast for 3 km to the scattered stone houses and corrals of **Antaparara**.

Continue east from Antaparara along the broad boggy glacial valley, with several **camping** possibilities en route. The vehicle track continues too, headed in the same

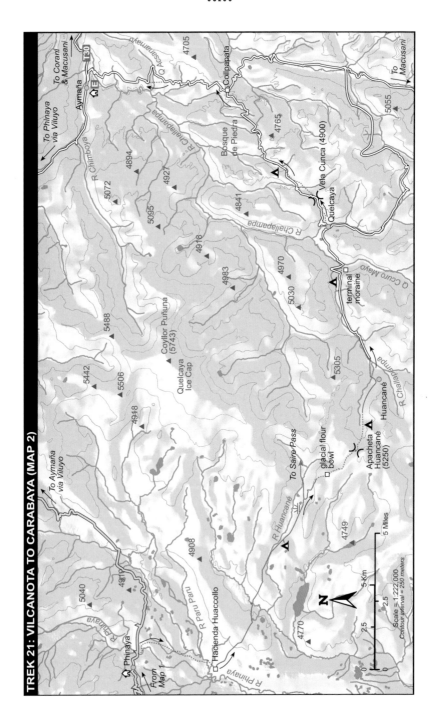

TREK 21: VILCANOTA TO CARABAYA (MAP 2)

direction, so you can use parts of it and take advantage of shortcuts when the road zig-zags. In 4.5 km you reach a large bog surrounded by craggy peaks with glacial remnants, a very pretty spot. Cross the bog carefully, as parts are soft, climbing east to **Jahuaycate Pass** (5118 m), where you again meet the road, 1.2 km past the bog. Head southeast from the pass down a broad trail. After 4 km you meet the road yet again and ford the **Río Yanamayo** (Chuamayu), where you can **camp**, although the river may be dry.

Head east cross-country from the Río Yanamayo over many open hills and through gentle valleys. Water can be scarce here in the dry season. After 6.3 km you pass through a notch between two rounded hilltops, then cross a vehicle track in the next valley and climb to a final broad **saddle**, 2.8 km past the notch. Spread out before you is a scene of unusual grandeur, wonderful in the long afternoon light: **Laguna Jomercocha** at your feet with the much larger Lago Sibinacocha beyond, its azure blue waters spread beneath the many glaciated peaks of the eastern Cordillera Vilcanota and, eastward still, the immense ice cap of Quelcaya. From the saddle descend gently to skirt the north side of Jomercocha and continue east to the shore of **Lago Sibinacocha**, 1.5 km past the saddle. Sibinacocha is inhabited by many waterfowl and very few people. **Camping** here is cold, breezy, and gorgeous.

It is a pleasant stroll south along the west shore of Sibinacocha. In 2.3 km you reach a fenced compound of the electric company by a **dam** that regulates the water level at the outflow of the lake. Call out from the fence for permission to pass. If it is getting late, then you might be able to spend the night. Here you meet an unpaved road from Sicuani. Follow it east across the spillway and 1.6 km ahead leave the road to take a wide trail 5 km northeast to **Phinaya**, a substantial shortcut of the road. Phinaya is a small town but the largest along the route, a good place to spend the night and stock up at local shops. One truck a day runs from Sicuani to Phinaya and back, 4 hours each way, so you can start or end the trek here.

Route: **Phinaya to Aymaña.** Take the road headed east from Phinaya for 1.5 km to a bridge over the **Río Phinaya**. Leave the road just after the bridge, heading south cross-country over the hills on the east side of the river. Follow a low ridge between the Río Phinaya on your right and Río Paru Paru to the left. After 2.6 km from the vehicle bridge, you pass a small pond and in another 2.8 km reach the shore of the **Río Paru Paru**. There is a pedestrian bridge here but not in plain sight; explore upstream about 150 m from where you meet the river. **Hacienda Huaccollo** is a cluster of buildings 800 m southwest of the bridge, a good place to ask permission to spend the night.

Pick up a trail just behind the buildings of the *hacienda*. It climbs southeast, steeply at first, before leveling off as you make your way into open landscape amid herds of graceful vicuñas. Continue southeast and east for 5 km to a tributary of the Río Huancané, an ankle-deep ford in the dry season. The trail is vague in the flats on the east side of the tributary but becomes clearer as you climb steadily east onto rocky terrain. In 1.5 km you reach the next height of land, with views over the wide glacial valley of the **Río Huancané**, which you ford 1.9 km farther ahead. There are a few widely scattered houses in this high valley and the occasional herd of alpacas. Try to camp as far up the valley as you can find water and start early the next morning, with full bottles, for the high pass ahead. A couple of stone corrals on the south side of the valley, 1.2 km past the ford, are good **camping** options.

The upper Huancané valley is flanked by high, craggy rock walls, crumbling into large boulder fields created by past glacial activity. The trail is faint over the boggy valley floor but not too difficult to follow. At 3 km past the corrals you reach an important fork, marked by an *apacheta*: the left branch heads east through the valley toward Saire Pass, an alternative and more difficult route; take the right branch, climbing steadily southeast over rocky terrain. At 1.6 km after the fork, the trail veers south at another *apacheta*, the climb becomes more gentle, and the ground underfoot turns to white glacial flour liberally strewn among the black boulders, adding to the surreal feeling of the place.

Navigation to the pass is difficult. Climb gently cross-country from the last *apacheta* mentioned above, following a 160-degree bearing. In 500 m you reach a large **glacial flour bowl**. Continue 1.2 km along the same bearing to the ridgeline ahead, with amazing views in all directions. Turn left to follow a 110-degree bearing for 400 m along the ridgeline to a small boggy patch, then a final 1 km bearing 135 degrees to **Apacheta Huancané Pass** at 5250 m. The top is marked by several large *apachetas* and a low stone wall. This is the border between Cuzco and Puno and, literally as well as figuratively, the high point of the trek. You stand between the Cordilleras Vilcanota and Carabaya.

From the pass follow the route on your right marked by two large and then several smaller *apachetas*. A trail again becomes evident as you descend steeply east amid rocky and then boggy terrain into the broad glacial valley below, grazed by herds of alpacas and other livestock. The first stone *choza* and **camping** possibilities are reached 2 km from the pass. Continue east along the south side of the valley at the edge of the boggy floor or the on the rocky slope slightly above it. The hamlet of **Huancané** is reached 5 km from the pass. Cross to the north side of the valley here and continue 1.4 km east, down to a ford of the **Río Challapampa**, just past its confluence with the unnamed drainage you have been following. On the other side of the ford is a vehicle track descending along the south side of the Challapampa, 5.7 km to reach the **terminal moraine** of the glacier that once filled the valley. Corrals offer shelter from the wind for **camping** before the moraine is reached.

The vehicle track turns sharply north (left) to wind its way down the moraine and cross **Quebrada Ccuro Mayo** just above its confluence with Río Challapampa, but a steep cross-country descent east is preferable; in 500 m you rejoin the road. Then it's 3.6 km of road-walking above the southeast side of Río Challapampa to the village of **Quelcaya**, tucked into an unnamed side valley. Quelcaya consists of tin-roofed houses, and only the church speaks of a more distant past. There is one truck a week, on Sunday, from Quelcaya to Macusani. Cross the cement footbridge at Quelcaya and head east into the boggy green valley ahead. It is 2.1 km, partly on a road, up to **Vela Cunca Pass** at 4900 m. This is the final high pass of the trek and the final transition. The boundless glaciers of Quelcaya are at your back, and the boundless *puna* lies ahead.

From the pass, head northeast cross-country over the wide open landscape and across a shallow *quebrada*, in order to shortcut the road and meet it again in a saddle

2.8 km ahead. Follow the road for 2.6 km northeast through another *quebrada* and then east to a gentle ridgetop with great views of Quelcaya behind and Allin Capac ahead. Continue 5 km northeast along the road to a fork called **Collpapata**, where you take the north (left) branch. From here it is 5.5 km of road-walking north to **Quebrada Acsanamayu**, where there is a useful shortcut, then another 6 km north along the road to **Aymaña**.

The road-walking at the end of the trek takes you alongside the vast and extraordinary **Bosque de Piedra** (stone forest, rock formations), which covers the ridges and valleys to the north and west of the road. Take in the amazing overview, then pull out your binoculars and give your imagination free rein to spot everything from naturally sculpted penguins and condors to extraterrestrials, while real live condors might circle overhead. Although tempting, a cross-country shortcut through the *Bosque de Piedra* is not advisable. The *bosque* is a maze, not only of wonderful otherworldly rock formations but also of convoluted ridges and plummeting ravines. Navigation is extremely difficult and water is scarce or absent. The drainages may be completely dry but are prone to flash flooding should it rain. It would be a shame to get into serious trouble here at the end of such a long and glorious trek. For additional information about this area, see the end of Trek 30.

Return. There is one bus a day from Aymaña via Corani to the regional center of Macusani, 3 hours along a spectacular hair-raising road. Buses and vans run from Macusani to the city of Juliaca (4 hours on paved roads), which in turn has an airport and bus service throughout southern Peru. Alternatively, you can resupply in Aymaña and continue on to do Trek 30, the Carabaya Traverse, in reverse, thus extending the odyssey among the *apus* all the way to Allin Capac.

22 CHOQUEQUIRAO TO HUANCACALLE
A WORLD BUILT IN THE AIR

Rating: Difficult 84-km, 8- to 12-day trek
Elevation: 1500 to 4600 m
Maps: IGN 1:100,000 Abancay (28q), Machu Picchu (27q); ESCALE Cusco (La Convención)
Water: May be scarce on the canyon slopes; tank up at every opportunity (except water from the Río Apurímac, which is unfit to drink even when purified). Water is more abundant north of the Río Yanama.
Hazards and annoyances: Hot, dusty canyon bottoms full of biting insects. When traveling between Cuzco and Cachora, avoid changing vehicles in Curahuasi for public safety reasons.
Permits and fees: A US$12.50 fee charged at Choquequirao, including site entry and camping.
Services and provisions: Comfortable hotels in Cachora include Casa de Salcantay and Casa Nostra (see Appendix A) and a hostel in Huancacalle (see Trek 23). Along

the route are various commercial campgrounds with basic amenities, most between Cachora and Choquequirao. Drinks, snacks, and meals are available at some campsites, but not at Choquequirao, and should not be relied on exclusively; bring supplies from Cuzco. Shops in Cachora and Yanama carry simple goods, and the campground in Marampata sells a few food items of particular interest to trekkers, at particularly high prices. Horses and guides can be hired in Cachora, and Cuzco agencies offer treks to Choquequirao; a few continue to Yanama, and even fewer to Huancacalle. See also Trek 23.

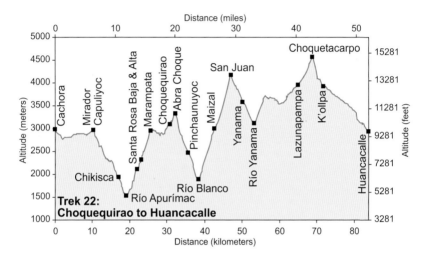

OF THE MYRIAD ARCHAEOLOGICAL sites in the department of Cuzco, two currently combine lavishly restored ruins with amazing trekking. Most famous is Machu Picchu, which receives twenty-five hundred to three thousand visitors a day, including five hundred trekkers along the Classic Inca Trail. Less known, with at most fifty trekkers a day in 2014 and fewer outside high season, Choquequirao is for now every bit as spectacular as its celebrity neighbor, without the crowds. If controversial plans to build a cable car to Choquequirao go ahead, however, then it will become another mass tourism destination. Until then, the difficulty of the trek from Cachora down to the bottom of the Apurímac canyon and almost 1400 m back up to Choquequirao are the site's best protection and greatly enhance the experience for those who wish to make the effort.

Choquequirao, however, is only the beginning of this trek, which continues through two more bottomless canyons and over three substantial passes to Yanama and Huancacalle, in the watersheds of the Ríos Vilcanota and Vilcabamba, respectively. Along the way are more modest but nonetheless impressive archaeological remains and a beautifully restored section of Inca road over Choquetacarpo Pass (4600 m). Scenery includes many glaciated summits, the rich flora ranges from austere moorland through exuberant cloud forest to dry tropical forest, orchids are abundant, and condors fly overhead. The route is very flexible: you can return to Cachora from Choquequirao, end in Yanama or Huancacalle, or connect with Trek 23 to Santa Teresa and even continue all the way to Machu Picchu. If you go for the long haul and prefer to lighten your load on the initial grunt, then consider hiring pack animals as far as Choquequirao and carrying your own pack from there.

Access. From the main terminal in Cuzco, several daily buses run to Abancay, a spectacular ride interminably down to cross the Río Apurímac into Apurímac Department. Take any Abancay-bound bus and get off at a crossroads called Ramal de Cachora, about 4 hours from Cuzco. Shared taxis wait here throughout the day and run to the town of Cachora in 30 minutes.

Route: **Cachora to Choquequirao.** From the plaza of **Cachora**, follow Av Julián Velarde north past the *puesto de salud* (health center), where it becomes a larger road. This road runs all the way to Capuliyoc (see below), and you can cut half a day from the trek by hiring a vehicle to take you there. If walking, you mostly follow the road north with a few signed shortcuts along the way. The route (too close to the road to show separately on our map) crosses a stream on a pedestrian bridge 2.1 km past Cachora. A trail climbs north from the bridge 1.7 km to a former hacienda called **La Colmena**, with an attractive **camping** area. Continue north along the trail from La Colmena to join the vehicle road 1.1 km ahead; from there it is steady road-walking north on the west side of the deepening canyon on your right, a tributary of the Río Apurímac. Along the way are increasingly spectacular views of the glaciers of Nevado Padreyoc (5771 m), towering an incredible 4200 m above the bottom of the Apurímac canyon.

The road ends at Capuliyoc, a simple **campsite**, 4.9 km after you joined it. Here a wide trail runs west high above the Apurímac for 500 m to **Mirador Capuliyoc**, a splendid viewpoint where the trail begins its 1440-m descent to the Río Apurímac. Along the way are several group **campsites** but nowhere suitable for independent camping between them. First is **Cocamasana**, 4 km past Mirador Capuliyoc, but it is well worth pressing on to **Chikisca**, 2.8 km farther. The Chikisca camping area has two levels; the upper one is especially nice. From here it is another 2 km over impressive zigzags to **Playa Rosalinas**, where there is a large ranger station (all trekkers must register here), free but very buggy camping, and a pedestrian suspension bridge over the **Río Apurímac**.

On the north side of the Apurímac canyon, the trail is less rocky than on the south. It climbs very steeply for 2.8 km to **Santa Rosa Baja**, with a pleasant **campsite**. The gradient is then a little more gentle to **Santa Rosa Alta**, with another **campsite** 1 km ahead, and on to the idyllic

"Llama terraces" on the west side of Choquequirao

TREK 22: CHOQUEQUIRAO TO HUANCACALLE

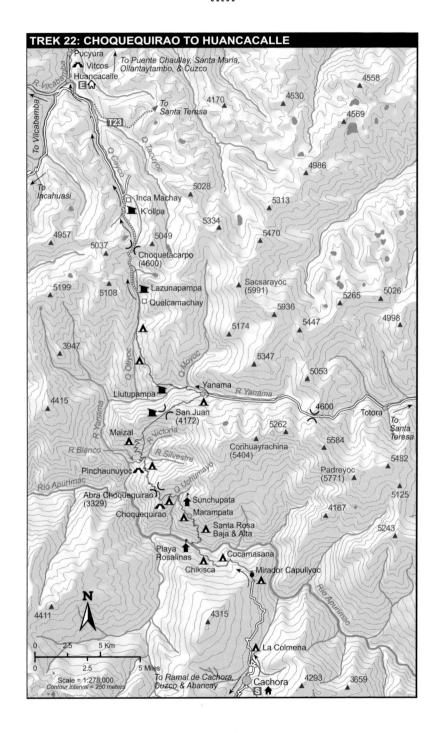

hamlet of **Marampata**, with two more **campsites**, 2.9 km farther. Here the air is refreshingly cool, the landscape is green, and the seemingly endless climb out of the Apurímac canyon is over. Choquequirao is at last in plain sight, and the trail leads 1.1 km northwest to a small ranger station at **Sunchupata**, where the entry fee is collected. Continue on if the rangers are not there; they will catch up with you at the Choquequirao campsite.

The trail continues northwest 1.4 km to a waterfall plunging through a cleft in the mountainside at **Quebrada Uchumayo**. Along the way are views west to the hanging terraces of Choquequirao, built on an impossibly vertical slope. We swore they were built in thin air! The increasingly forested trail crosses Quebrada Uchumayo on a wooden bridge and 400 m ahead reaches a signed fork: the right branch leads to the archaeological site of **Choquequirao**; the left runs 700 m to the site's ample **camping** area, beautifully situated on a terraced slope.

A detailed description of Choquequirao is beyond the scope of this book, but a few highlights are worth mentioning along with our suggestion that you give yourself a minimum of one full day, better yet two, to explore them at leisure. The extra time will allow you to immerse yourself in the exceptional atmosphere of this large spread-out site, straddling a north–south ridge at 3050 m. Only about 20 percent of its estimated 18 sq km have been excavated. The priests' lodgings at the south end of the ridge are superb, surrounded on three sides by 1500-m vertical drops into the Apurímac canyon. The elliptical hilltop *usnu* (a ceremonial or spiritual area), overlooking the large lower plaza, is awesome for sunrises and sunsets. Walls of the terraces on the west side of the ridge are inlaid with lifelike white stone figures of llamas. Most impressive of all are the vertical terraces on the east side of the ridge, which seemed to be built in the air as we approached from Marampata.

Route: Choquequirao to Yanama. From the Choquequirao camping area, signed trails mark the start of the route to Yanama. We recommend a detour, however, via the lower plaza, 1.5 km from the camping area. From the lower plaza, climb the stairs that run north alongside an impressive channel that once brought water from Quebrada Uchumayo to Choquequirao. In 300 m you reach the upper plaza. Look again for the water channel running north up the ridge, and follow it, even though there are no more stairs. The steep scramble is rewarded by great views back over most of the archaeological site. After 500 m the canal crosses a clear trail; follow it north (left). The trail climbs steadily on zigzags through pretty cloud forest for 300 m to **Abra Choquequirao**, a pass at 3329 m (Abra Choque on our elevation profile), before beginning the long descent to the Río Blanco.

Beyond Abra Choquequirao, follow the trail northwest as the cloud forest turns to scrub and there are more amazing views. After 2.4 km you reach El Pajonal with a large flat area occasionally used for camping, although there is no water. Continue north along the trail for 1.2 km to the impressive semicircular terraces of **Pinchaunuyoc**, perched on the west slope of the mountainside, once again seemingly in midair. Water continues to flow through the irrigation channels here, making it both a practical and very atmospheric place. There is a trashed **camping** area just north of Pinchaunuyoc.

ANTISEISMIC INCA TERRACES?

We had arrived early at Pinchaunuyoc on a glorious afternoon, and the temptation to spend the night was more than we could resist. After settling in, Daisy enjoyed a wash from the still-functioning Inca water channel while Robert found a sitting nook with a terrace wall for a back rest, to make notes of the day's trekking. No armchair could have been more comfortable.

The following day on reaching Maizal, we were greeted with anxious questions: "Are you okay? Where were you during yesterday's earthquake?" At the same time as we were enjoying Pinchaunuyoc, folks in Maizal, only 2 km away as the crow flies, had felt a strong tremor. With a magnitude of 6.6 on the Richter scale, the quake had been felt throughout the southern Andes of Peru. Yet even seated on the ground, we had noticed absolutely nothing.

How have Inca terraces built on impossibly steep slopes survived not only centuries of erosion but also regular earth movements? In addition to all the other remarkable features of their architecture, are they also antiseismic?

Indestructible Pinchaunuyoc with the Río Blanco far below

From Pinchaunuyoc continue to descend along the zigzagging trail as the vegetation now turns to dry tropical forest. In 2.8 km you reach the **Río Blanco** (Quebrada Yuracmayo), just below where it is formed by the confluence of the Ríos Victoria and Silvestre. There is no bridge here, and trailheads on either side of the ford, calf deep in the dry season but impassable after heavy rain, may be washed away from year to year, so it takes time to find the best place to cross. There is a buggy campsite above the north shore. Take as much water as possible here for the long, dry climb ahead.

From the Río Blanco the trail climbs steeply north, a tough slog in the hot sun, but the glacier of Nevado Corihuayrachina (5404 m) promises cooler temperatures on the higher ground ahead. After 3.6 km you reach a fork with a small homemade sign: right (north) is the main trail, left (west) the single-family community of **Maizal** with a very pleasant **campground**, 600 m past the fork. Fill all your water bottles here. There is no need to descend back to the fork from Maizal; instead climb north and then east along a small trail to meet the main trail 1 km ahead. It now climbs more gradually northeast along the slope of the ridge on your left, before starting a steep zigzag ascent to **San Juan Pass** (4172 m), 3.3 km past where you rejoined the main trail. There is a small open-sided **shelter** at the pass but no water. Views ahead to the glaciers of Nevado Sacsarayoc (5991 m) are magnificent, and the next canyon, of the Río Yanama, yawns below.

From San Juan Pass the trail continues northeast, offering more gorgeous views. The descent is gentle and spectacular as the trail passes a landslide with large boulders and then makes its way etched into a high cliff. In 1.6 km from the pass you reach a small but very welcome spring and 1.7 km farther the spread-out end-of-the-road village of **Yanama**. There are several pleasant group **campgrounds** here. The road only arrived in 2013, it is not always passable, and there is no regular transport. If you wish to end the trek here, then you can either wait (several days or longer) until a private vehicle is available or hike east along the road for 16 km over a 4600-m pass to Totora, which has transport to Santa Teresa.

Route: **Yanama to Huancacalle.** To continue on, resupply in Yanama and follow the trail west from the lower part of the village for 2 km, down to a bridge over the **Río Yanama** just downstream from its confluence with Quebrada Moyoc. Continue east, downstream along the trail on the north shore of Río Yanama for 700 m, where the trail turns away from the river. This is the start of another long ascent, fortunately less grueling than the previous two, thanks to a more gentle gradient and fresher climate. In 1 km you reach another open-sided **shelter** at a spot called **Llutupampa**. The trail continues climbing east for 1.5 km past a few homes and pastures, where it turns north into **Quebrada Otiyoc**, and 2.1 km beyond crosses above a large balcony used for grazing; this is the only flat ground suitable for **camping** in the area. The nearest water is 600 m ahead along the trail.

The trail continues north, contouring and then descending gently along the east side of Quebrada Otiyoc. In 3.6 km you reach an open grassy area by the river, good for camping. The route ahead, through lush cloud forest and past many little waterfalls, is especially pretty. After fording a few side streams and crossing Quebrada Otiyoc twice on small footbridges, the forest thins and the trail reaches a sign for **Quelcamachay**, a disappointing cave filled with trash, 3.4 km past the open grassy camping area mentioned above. A further 700 m along the trail is **Lazunapampa**, a large open area with an unused ranger station and three open-sided **shelters**.

Beyond Lazunapampa the route divides: the right branch is a large horse trail through the center of the valley; the left branch is a beautifully restored section of Inca road above the west side—highly recommended. Following the latter, you climb gently at first, along the ancient road built into the slope of the valley and supported by an impressive retaining wall. When the climb gets steeper, the road becomes a stairway, allowing you to ascend with remarkable ease. Along the way are wonderful views of glaciated peaks ahead and the Otiyoc valley behind. After 2.6 km the two branches merge and the trail beyond shows less evidence of Inca origins as it zigzags up to **Choquetacarpo Pass** at 4600 m, 1.3 km ahead. To judge by the mangled remains of a shelter here, high winds are common at the pass, so do not linger if the weather looks ominous.

Beyond the pass the route again divides: right along a horse trail; left on splendid Inca road, which is once again the path of choice. This section is truly exceptional, including long stone stairways snaking down the precipitous slope, corridors of a world built in the air. When the slope finally becomes more gentle, the stairs turn into a well-made stone roadway heading north along the west side of **Quebrada Cayco**. At 2.9 km from the pass you reach **K'ollpa**, an unused ranger station and three open-sided **shelters** like those at Lazunapampa. At 400 m past K'ollpa is **Inca Machay**, a cave where you could take shelter in bad weather, and in another 250 m you meet a vehicle road, just west of its intersection with the horse trail from Choquetacarpo. Follow the vehicle road north (left) for 11 km along the west side of the Quebrada Cayco, with a few shortcuts along the way. Don't miss the final shortcut, which leads to a pedestrian bridge over the **Río Vilcabamba**, with **Huancacalle** on the north side.

Return. For transport from Huancacalle, see Trek 23 Access, below.

23 HUANCACALLE TO MACHU PICCHU
THE MANCO INCA TRAIL

Rating: Moderately difficult 56-km, 5- to 6-day trek
Elevation: 1573 to 4567 m
Maps: IGN 1:100,000 Machu Picchu (27q); ESCALE Cusco (La Convención)
Water: Abundant throughout the route
Hazards and annoyances: Keep alert for trains if walking along the tracks from Santa Teresa to Aguas Calientes.
Permits and fees: None along our route, but all entry fees to Machu Picchu must be paid as usual if you wish to visit that site.
Services and provisions: Sixpac Manco hostel in Huancacalle is run by the Cobos family who can organize guides and pack animals for treks throughout the region. Santa Teresa has several simple hotels. Pucyura, 1.5 km north of Huancacalle by road, has reasonable shops; this is the place to resupply if connecting treks here, otherwise bring supplies from Cuzco. Shops in Huancacalle have only basic items. Yanatile and Santa Teresa, at the end of the trek, are the only places to resupply en route.

AT FIRST GLANCE, THE sleepy little village of Huancacalle may not seem like the trekking hub of the department of Cuzco. Through this area, however, have passed some of the most illustrious expeditions of Inca history and of contemporary Inca research. Around the year 1440 the Inca Pachacutec led his victorious troops

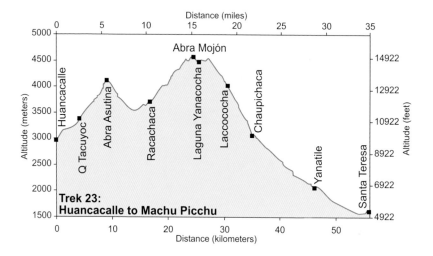

up the Río Vilcabamba, where Huancacalle is today, to conquer the first new provinces of what would become the vast empire. Less than a century later, Manco, the Inca heir who survived the initial Spanish conquest, led his loyal followers along the same route. He held court for a time at Vitcos, near Huancacalle, before retreating deeper into the hinterlands of Vilcabamba, the final stronghold of the disintegrating empire. Vilcabamba held out against the *conquistadores* for some forty years before being crushed, razed, and forgotten. Centuries later, it would become a Holy Grail for explorers like Antonio Raimondi, Hiram Bingham, Victor von Hagen, Gene Savoy, and Vincent Lee (see Chapter 1). The latter two mounted their expeditions with the assistance of the Cobos family, who remain an invaluable resource for trekkers in Huancacalle.

Today, Huancacalle stands at the intersection of several excellent trekking routes: it is the end of our Trek 22 from Choquequirao, it remains an access to ancient Vilcabamba, and it is the start of this trek. There is also good day hiking from Huancacalle to the Vitcos archaeological site and to Vilcabamba Nueva, a colonial village 5 km up the valley. Our route may not be precisely the one taken by all the Incas and famous explorers, but it is very scenic and quite seldom used, considering how close it is to the tourist mecca of Machu Picchu. It includes partly restored sections of Inca road along the way, as well as very pretty cloud forest. You can end the trek in Santa Teresa, as described below, or hike all the way to Aguas Calientes (the access to Machu Picchu) along the railway line, a popular unrestricted trekking access to that area.

Access. Huancacalle can be reached by shared taxi (three a day, a 2.5-hour ride) from the regional center of Quillabamba, which in turn has service from the Santiago district of Cuzco, 5 hours away. Although it would save some travel to get off the vehicle from Cuzco at Puente Chaullay and change to one for Huancacalle, these often come full from Quillabamba, and you could be stuck in Puente Chaullay or Santa María (see map).

Route. From the lower (south) end of **Huancacalle**, cross the footbridge over the Río Vilcabamba and follow the trail 100 m to a fork. The left branch leads to the Vitcos archeological site; we go right (southeast) past a few houses and pastures to a second fork 1 km farther along. Here the right branch goes south along a vehicle road, the reverse route of Trek 22; our route continues southeast (left). In 2.1 km past the second fork, you reach a small footbridge, and as soon as you cross, the trail shows signs of having been an ancient road. It climbs southeast steadily along the east side of the drainage, gradually moving away from the river, and in 1.2 km enters **Quebrada Tacuyoc** above its confluence with Quebrada Cayco. Here the pastures become lovely cloud forest and the Inca road has been restored.

The elevated stone roadway climbs gradually along the northeast side of Quebrada Tacuyoc for 2.1 km, then turns northeast to enter an unnamed side valley. Here are great views of the glaciated slopes of Nevado Choquetacarpo (5428 m) to the south, towering above the green valleys. As this is a wet area, many drainage canals cross the road, still perfectly functional after hundreds of years. Several of the larger canals are spanned by rough log bridges, slippery when wet. Cross the stream draining the side valley 900 m after you entered it. There are several idyllic **camping** spots nearby.

The Inca road, at times evident, at times transformed into a horse trail, climbs steadily on the south side of the valley for 1.6 km to reach the first of two saddles at a **double pass** called **Abra Asutina** (4116 m), with great views along the way. Between the two saddles the trail forks: northwest (left) into deep Quebrada Pachaco, heading back to Huancacalle, and east (right) to climb to the second saddle of Asutina Pass, reached 1 km past the first. From the second saddle the trail descends east through another unnamed and very pretty valley with various good **campsites**. After 2.4 km the trail turns south (right) as you enter the broader valley of **Quebrada Marampampa** high above the valley floor. It is a gentle descent into Quebrada Marampampa followed by a climb southeast along the west side of the valley, 4.7 km to the tiny community of **Racachaca**, with only a handful of inhabitants spread out over a large area. Views south up the valley to Nevado Sacsarayoc (5991 m) are amazing, especially in the morning light.

Several pedestrian bridges span the river near Racachaca, but some are unsafe. Cross on either an old stone bridge by the community center (on the east shore) or on a concrete bridge slightly farther upstream. Take the trail from the stone bridge, closely following the south shore of a side stream that joins Quebrada Marampampa here. Climb steadily east through the broad glacial valley ahead. After 2.4 km from the bridge at Racachaca, the gradient becomes more gentle, additional glaciers come into view, and the drainage changes from a swift tumbling stream to a shallow meandering one. Another 700 m ahead, cross to the north side of the drainage at a ford or on a wooden bridge just upstream from the ford. Follow the trail as it turns gradually northeast into yet another side valley with many ponds, climbs more steeply, and in 2.1 km from the bridge reaches two small ponds, side by side like a pair of eyeglasses, just left of the trail—a good little **camping** spot.

Continue climbing east along the trail through increasingly muddy terrain toward **Mojón Pass**. This is another multipart pass with three or four consecutive **saddles**, the

Looking up Quebrada Marampampa to Nevado Sacsarayoc (5991 m)

first of which is marked by cairns, 1.2 km from the eyeglass ponds. The highest saddle (4567 m) is 1.4 km east of the first cairns, past several small and pretty ponds with more potential **camping** spots. Past the highest saddle the trail turns briefly south to descend to a larger lake called **Laguna Yanacocha**, 900 m ahead, before climbing again for 1.6 km to a final saddle. The trail at first contours, then descends gently east into the valley ahead. At 2.2 km past the last saddle you ford a side stream with a large, somewhat trashed campsite used by groups; there are also several nicer **campsites** nearby.

Past the ford, continue to descend east along the trail, following the drainage at first, then veering south away from it. Here are great views to the glaciers of Verónica (5893 m) and surrounding peaks, a spectacular backdrop to the ridges around Machu Picchu, 22 km east as the condor flies. The trail then turns east again and passes a few tin-roofed houses in an area called **Laccococha**, 1.5 km past the ford mentioned above. To the north is a huge rounded glacial valley below Lago Coyllorcocha.

Past Laccococha the trail returns toward the river and, after 1.7 km, enters a spectacularly steep, narrow, and wooded section of the valley. Watch for flowering orchids and mixed-species flocks of birds here. Despite the rugged terrain, the descent southeast is gentle, through lovely cloud forest, as the trail zigzags toward the confluence of the valley you have been following and the Río Sacsara below. At 1.8 km after you entered the cloud forest, you cross a metal bridge over an unnamed side stream and 900 m farther a larger bridge called **Chaupichaca** over the **Río Sacsara**. Pastures before the second bridge are the only reasonably flat and dry spots for **camping** here. Temperatures are

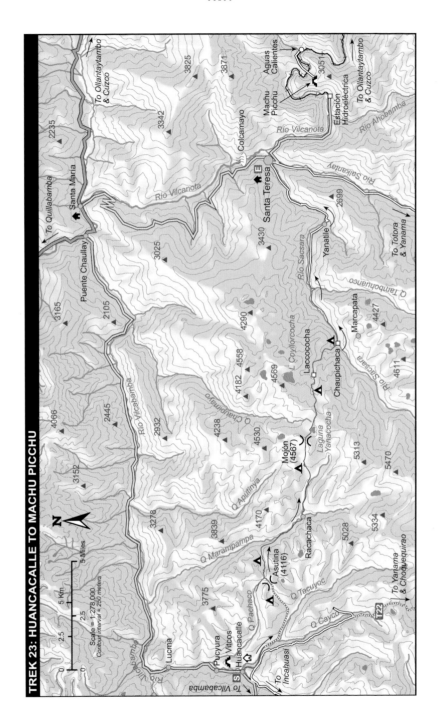

TREK 23: HUANCACALLE TO MACHU PICCHU

Scale = 1:278,000.
Contour interval = 250 meters

To Ollantaytambo & Cuzco

To Quillabamba

Santa María

Puente Chaullay

Rio Vilcanota

Colcamayo

Machu Picchu

Aguas Calientes

Estación Hidroeléctrica

To Ollantaytambo & Cuzco

Rio Ahobamba

Río Vilcanota

Santa Teresa

Río Salkantay

Yanatile

To Totora & Yanama

Q Tambohuanco

Marcapata

Rio Sacsara

Laccococha

Chaupichaca

L Coyllorcocha

Rio Chaupimayo

Mojón (4567)

Laguna Yanacocha

Q Apurimya

Q Marampampa

Racachaca

Asutina (4116)

Q Tacuyoc

Q Pachaco

Pucyura
Vitcos
Huancacalle

Lucma

Río Vilcabamba

To Vilcabamba

To Incahuasi

Q Gayco

To Yanama & Choquequirao

T22

Río Vilcabamba

3825
3871
3051
3342
2235
3165
2105
3025
3430
2699
4427
4290
4558
4182
4569
4238
4530
4611
4066
2445
2932
5313
5470
3152
3278
3839
4170
5028
5334
3775

N

5 Miles
5 Km

pleasantly mild at the bottom of the valley, but it is also humid and heavy rain can occur at any time of the year.

A very beautiful trail ran east through the forest from Chaupichaca along the south side of the Río Sacsara for 11.5 km to the village of Yanatile. Unfortunately, in 2014 it was being torn up to make way for a vehicle track just as we hiked through. Although a great shame, the obligatory road-walk will not detract from the preceding parts of the trek, which overall remains entirely worthwhile. There was also talk of restoring a section of Inca road running parallel to and above the vehicle track, from Chaupichaca to Yanatile via Marcapata, an interesting alternative if it pans out.

Yanatile is a very friendly village, divided into upper and lower sections. You can ask to camp in the soccer field or near someone's home. It is 9 km of pleasant road-walking through coffee and avocado plantations, from Yanatile to the warm relaxed town of **Santa Teresa**. A couple of vans also cover this route, early in the morning, on most days. The clean and pleasant Colcamayo thermal baths, 2 km north of Santa Teresa, downstream along the Río Vilcanota, make a nice finale to the trek. If continuing to Aguas Calientes and Machu Picchu (see below), you can resupply in Santa Teresa to avoid the tourist prices ahead.

Return. Shared taxis run from Santa Teresa throughout the day to Santa María, a 45-minute ride. Here you can catch a bus or van north to Quillabamba or east to Ollantaytambo, other cities in the Sacred Valley, and Cuzco (4 to 5 hours). For Machu Picchu, shared taxis leave Santa Teresa twice a day for the Estación Hidroeléctrica train station (10.5 km, 30 minutes away), to meet the train that runs from there to Aguas Calientes (Machu Picchu Pueblo). A popular alternative is to walk 11 km along the railway tracks to Aguas Calientes, a surprisingly pleasant 3- to 4-hour hike with great views, many birds, and butterflies.

11

AREQUIPA

Situated in the southwest of Peru, the department of Arequipa could well be a separate country. Unlike Ancash or Cuzco with their long cordilleras and gentle green valleys, Arequipa's geography is dominated by massive volcanoes up to 6425 m above sea level. Several of these volcanoes are active (the Instituto Geofísico del Perú website posts current activity levels; see Appendix A), and they tower above the world's deepest canyons. The people of Arequipa are also distinct, generally of more European stock than elsewhere in the Peruvian highlands and intensely proud of their regional identity. Even in remote areas here, villagers may speak more Spanish than Quechua.

Arequipa is a popular tourist destination and known for its regional gastronomy. Its charming colonial capital, of the same name, is Peru's second-largest city and provides all services and comforts when preparing for a trek or relaxing afterward. The city has good road connections and frequent flights to Lima, Cuzco, and Puno. Many Arequipa agencies offer trekking tours, mostly to the Colca Canyon. The Casa de Guías provides information from June to September. Another useful contact is KAT, which can help arrange guides and pack animals. See Appendix A for both of the above.

Arequipa is also home to various cultural attractions and museums, of which the Museo Santuarios Andinos (see Appendix A), may be of particular interest to trekkers. The museum features a spectacularly well-preserved frozen Inca mummy, left as a child-sacrifice on the summit of Ampato Volcano, as well as an interesting video of an expedition to uncover similar remains.

The beaten path. The south rim of the Colca Canyon, 175 km from the city of Arequipa, is one of the most visited places in Peru (see website in Appendix A). Tourists concentrate in the towns of Chivay and Cabanaconde and along the road between them. In a single morning in we counted over fifty tourist vans plying this road to Cruz del Cóndor, a bustling condor observation site above the canyon. The most heavily used trekking routes run from Cabanaconde down to Sangalle at the bottom of the canyon and back up to the south rim in 2 to 3 days. Also popular is a 1-day hike from Cabanaconde to Llahuar, where Trek 26

Arequipa is a land of volcanoes. From left to right: Hualca Hualca (6025 m), active Sabancaya (5976 m), and Ampato (6265 m).

ends, so you can join the tourist trail here if you wish, at this tiny resort known for its rustic thermal baths.

Limbering up. From Cotahuasi, the regional center that provides access to Treks 24 and 25, there are many good opportunities for day walks to get used to the vertical terrain and take in grand views. The steep 3.5-km-one-way trail from town down to the pedestrian suspension bridge over the Río Cotahuasi makes a good short introduction, and there are also various trails along the slopes above town. A moderately difficult full-day 12-km training hike runs from Alca (19 km from Cotahuasi, 1 hour by bus) up to the sleepy little village of Ayahuasi, then across the Río

Chococo and back down to the road to Cotahuasi. Closer to Cotahuasi, the pleasant little town of Tomepampa is also a good base for day hiking. From Puyca, the start of Trek 25, an easy 5-km loop, visits the Maukallacta archaeological site and a nearby viewpoint over the upper Cotahuasi Canyon. From Andagua, the start of Trek 26, a moderately difficult 13-km full-day hike takes you up to twin volcanic cones called Los Mellizos and on to a lookout over the Sankillay Waterfall on the Río Andagua.

Featured treks. Trek 24, Cotahuasi Canyon, provides a great overview of this spectacular area, descending almost 2000 m to its deepest point amid beautiful cactus forests, interesting

HOW DEEP IS THAT CANYON?

The people of the Colca Canyon were more than a little disgruntled when it was announced that neighboring Cotahuasi is slightly deeper than Colca, taking its place as the deepest in the world, a distinction many Colca guides still cling to. But is there a precise universally accepted definition of the depth of a canyon? Apparently not.

Gonzalo de Reparaz Ruiz, a French–Basque geographer, was the first to study the hydrography of southern Peru in the 1960s. He was the one to crown Colca as the deepest canyon (3270 m), perhaps overlooking its neighbor. Using Reparaz's system, the depth of Cotahuasi was later determined by measuring the height of the summit of Solimana, considered the highest point on the southeast rim, then the highest point on the northwest rim opposite Solimana. The average of these two points is 3354 m above the Río Cotahuasi at Quebrada Ushua.

These figures and the respective claims of Cotahuasi and Colca are hotly disputed around the world, with a long list of contenders in the Himalaya, Tibet, and elsewhere. Regardless of the exact depth of Cotahuasi and Colca, they are both spectacular, and trekking in either one is an unforgettable experience.

The Cotahuasi Canyon plunges 3354 m from the summit of Solimana (on the right).

archaeology, and a thundering waterfall. Trek 25, Cotahuasi to the Valley of the Volcanoes, follows a high route over the *puna* still used by a few llama caravans, to a broad valley with Arequipa's smallest and most easily accessible volcanoes. Trek 26, Valley of the Volcanoes to Colca, is a longer and more ambitious crossing from the Valley of the Volcanoes to the Colca Canyon over potentially snowbound passes. The latter two treks can be combined into a long-haul traverse between Cotahuasi and Colca, linking two of the world's deepest canyons. All three treks offer incredible scenery and good opportunities to see condors in the wild.

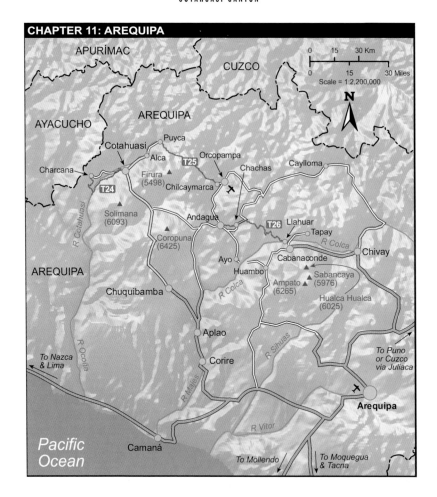

CHAPTER 11: AREQUIPA

24

COTAHUASI CANYON
EXPLORING THE ABYSS

Rating: Moderately difficult, 61-km, 3- to 4-day trek

Elevation: 1520 to 3435 m

Maps: IGN 1:100,000 Pausa (31p) and Cotahuasi (31q); ESCALE Arequipa (La Unión); a Cotahuasi orientation map may be available from the iPerú office in Arequipa or Purek Tours (see below).

Water: Scarce; tank up whenever possible, and use small side streams in preference to the Río Cotahuasi, which receives sewage from several towns and is not ideal even when purified. A few side streams, however, including the Río Picha and Quebrada Ushua, have a high mineral content (*agua jollposa*), which also makes them unfit for consumption; watch for white mineral crust along the banks.

Hazards and annoyances: High winds at the bottom of the canyon, strongest in the afternoon, hazardous on suspension bridges and precarious overlooks. Biting insects near the Río Cotahuasi and sharp cactus spines everywhere.

Permits and fees: The route runs through Reserva Paisajística Cotahuasi, a protected natural area, but no permits or fees are required.

Services and provisions: Comfortable hotels, various restaurants, and simple well-stocked shops can be found in Cotahuasi. Specialty items should be brought from Arequipa. The villages of Charcana, Quechualla, and Velinga offer community accommodations, but their small shops stock only a few essential goods. Purek Tours in Cotahuasi runs trekking tours and can help arrange community accommodations (see Appendix A).

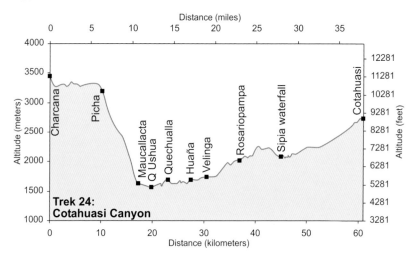

IT IS NOT EASY to get a grip on something as big as the world's deepest canyon, and taking a selfie from the rim, however glorious, does not suffice. You need to observe it from different angles, from above and below. You need to experience its chilly heights and its hot, dry depths. Only as you gingerly make your way down or grunt up the steep cactus-covered slopes and watch the Río Cotahuasi roaring over the rainbow-crowned 150-m Sipia waterfall, do you gradually come to appreciate the immensity and wonder of it all.

This trek offers all these opportunities, mostly along good trails and narrow vehicle tracks, as it takes you from a little village perched below the northwest rim down, down, down to the deepest point in the canyon. The route then heads more gradually upriver along the Río Cotahuasi, crossing it three times on memorable bridges and making its way through increasingly populated agricultural areas. There are striking differences between the climate and vegetation in the upper and lower sections. Typical Andean

Pedestrian bridge below Quechualla

crops like corn and potatoes thrive above and luscious fruit orchards below. All depend on irrigation, and the rest of the canyon is very dry. Condors may be seen along the route, as well as several species of cacti.

Access. A couple of daily buses run from Arequipa to Cotahuasi. In the past they've run overnight, but check to see if there are any daytime trips: it is a gorgeous ride in the day. From Cotahuasi, one mini-bus a day (around 2:00 PM) goes to the little village of Charcana, a breathtaking 3-hour ride; sit on the left for best views. You'll arrive around nightfall, so it is best to spend the night in Charcana and head out early the following morning.

Route. In **Charcana** (3435 m), head downhill along steep cobbled streets to the school and turn right to make your way around its wall. Past the school you will see three trails ahead: lower, middle, and upper. Take the middle trail, contouring southwest along the slope through agricultural terraces, their green crops a pleasant contrast with the dry surroundings. Cross three substantial *quebradas*, headwaters of the Río Chuquibamba, beyond which the trail veers southeast. At 4.3 km from Charcana, turn southwest (right) on the slopes of **Cerro Toicca**. Here you have the first amazing views of the Cotahuasi Canyon below, with the snows of Solimana (6093 m) gleaming above to the south. The trail continues almost level for 3.9 km through cactus forest to a notch with a fork. Take the right branch and descend northwest 2.1 km to the tiny, almost abandoned, village of **Picha**.

There is nowhere to stay or camp in Picha. Turn south here to enter the rapidly deepening valley of **Quebrada Picha**, 1.8 km to a turnoff for **Hacienda Pucará** surrounded

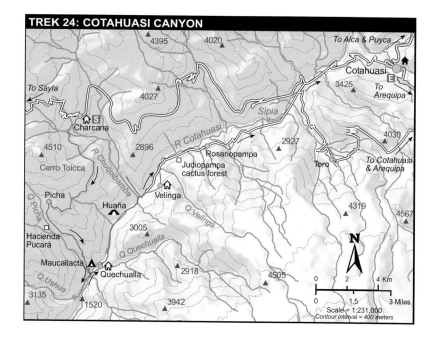

TREK 24: COTAHUASI CANYON

by green fields grazed by cattle. This is the last water until the bottom of the canyon and a potential camping spot if it is getting late. Beyond the *hacienda* the trail is increasingly narrow and rocky, tricky going in a few places, as it snakes its way down to the seemingly bottomless depths of the Cotahuasi Canyon, still 5.6 knee-jarring km ahead. There is no village at the bottom, just a few scattered homesteads in an area known as **Maucallacta** where you can ask for water and permission to camp. The 1800-m descent makes for a long first day.

A worthwhile side trip from Maucallacta follows the northwest side of the Río Cotahuasi downstream to **Quebrada Ushua**, the deepest point in the canyon at 1520 m above sea level. There are two pretty little waterfalls in the *quebrada*, just upstream from its confluence with the Río Cotahuasi. It is a hot but gentle 5-km round-trip from Maucallacta, leaving time to continue on the same day. Cross the **Río Cotahuasi** at the nearby pedestrian bridge and proceed 1.2 km northeast to **Quechualla**. This delightful little place, almost without inhabitants, is a plausible vision of paradise. Surrounded by a well-watered oasis of fruit orchards, the village streets are shaded by overhanging grapevines. Alas, it will likely change when a proposed road arrives from Cotahuasi.

Leave Quechualla along a steep trail starting behind the "plaza," and zigzag down toward the fields and orchards below. Soon you join a larger trail heading northeast to cross **Quebrada Quechualla**, which bears meltwater from the glaciers of Solimana to bring the little Garden of Eden to life. There are spectacular views at every turn ahead as you make your way north over sandy terrain amid *molle* (Peruvian pepper) trees to another pedestrian bridge over the Río Cotahuasi, 3.9 km from Quechualla. Then, in 700 m you reach the terraces of the **Huaña** archaeological site. Long abandoned, the terraces were once richly irrigated and supported extensive agriculture. At 2.6 km past Huaña, you again cross the Río Cotahuasi where, just at the bridge called Niño Chaca, a trail branches north to climb steeply back up toward Charcana. Beyond the bridge the trail again divides, right up to the village of **Velinga** and left along our route ahead. In 2016 the roadhead was 800 m past the bridge, below Velinga, with plans to eventually continue construction to Quechualla. Inquire locally about the resulting changes to our trekking route.

A minibus runs daily to Cotahuasi, so you could end the trek here, but it is well worth continuing on. Walking the narrow road, at times perched high above the rushing river, is very beautiful and seems safer than riding it on the bus. After climbing 3.9 km from Velinga, you reach a large cactus forest in an uninhabited area called **Judiopampa** and, 2.6 km farther, **Rosariopampa**, an agricultural zone with a few homes. Beyond, the road climbs high above the river with more amazing views, including your first glimpse of the **Sipia waterfall**.

The turnoff for Sipia is 7 km past Rosariopampa. Follow the well-signed trail 2 km west to reach a series of lookouts over this splendid cascade, plunging 150 m in three tiers. The best light is from around noon to 3:00 PM, depending on the time of year. Beyond the turnoff for Sipia the canyon is wider and views, although still nice, are less awe-inspiring.

Return. You can catch the bus to **Cotahuasi** at the Sipia turnoff; it passes daily around 10:00 AM and Monday and Friday also around 5:30 PM. If you miss it, then you can ask to camp in the agricultural area also known as Sipia, 700 m east along the road. If you prefer to walk the road all the way back to Cotahuasi, it is a further 13 km of gradual uphill travel.

25 COTAHUASI TO VALLEY OF THE VOLCANOES
LLAMEROS ROUTE

Rating: Difficult, 52-km, 3- to 4-day trek
Elevation: 3475 to 4943 m
Maps: IGN 1:100,000 Cotahuasi (31q), Orcopampa (31r); ESCALE Arequipa (La Unión)
Water: Available at various *quebradas* en route
Hazards and annoyances: Intense cold (to about −10°C) at night in June and July. Sharp cactus spines and other spiky vegetation in lower areas.
Permits and fees: None
Services and provisions: You can purchase simple supplies in Cotahuasi, specialty items in Arequipa. Puyca at the start of the trek and Chilcaymarca, at the end, both have community accommodations and basic shops. There is nowhere to stay or resupply along the route.

One of the few llama caravans that still cross the puna

THIS TREK IS IDEAL for those who enjoy wide open country, crossing the high plateau that separates the Cotahuasi canyon from the Orcopampa valley, also known as the Valley of the Volcanoes. The unobstructed vantage points and clear air provide endless and unsurpassed views of many giant glaciated peaks. Coropuna (6425 m, the highest volcano in Peru and its third-highest mountain) and Firura (5498 m) are but two of your constant companions. Toward the end of the trek, the Valley of the Volcanoes offers an entirely different landscape: eighty-five relatively small volcanic cones, only a few hundred meters from their base, poking up through the broad, flat valley floor below.

Navigation is what makes this trek difficult. Trails fade in and out on the bare terrain of low, dry ridges separated by shallow rivers and *quebradas* draining large *bofedales*. A few vehicle tracks encountered en route lead tantalizingly in unknown directions, and it's basically cross-country travel most of the way. There is not much population along the route, only a few herdsmen living on isolated *estancias*, tending to large flocks of brightly tasseled llamas and alpacas that graze the *bofedales*. A special treat would be to meet one of the few *llameros* who still drive their llama caravans across the *puna*, carrying agricultural products for barter, as their ancestors have done since time immemorial. They cover the route with their laden animals in half the time it took us. Their friendliness is genuine, but their time estimates should be taken with a grain of salt.

Access. If coming directly from Arequipa, take the bus to the end of the line at Alca. It arrives in the small hours of the morning, and a local bus waits for it before departing for Puyca, a spectacular 90-minute ride, although some of it is in the dark. If coming from Cotahuasi, you can either catch a bus passing through from Arequipa around 3:00 AM or take a local bus to Alca during the day and spend the night there before continuing on to Puyca. There are two buses a day from Alca to Puyca, at 5:30 AM and 4:30 PM.

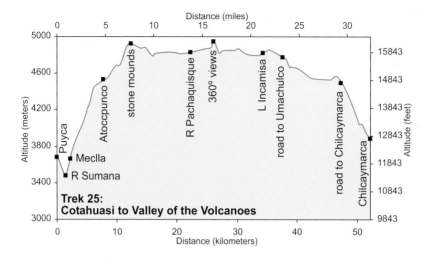

Route. From the crumbling old church of **Puyca** and the adjacent bull ring, head east down into the valley of the **Río Sumana**. Follow either the zigzagging vehicle track or a trail that shortcuts it; they meet at a bridge over the river. Leave the track about 70 m after crossing the bridge and climb southwest along a trail to the village of **Meclla**, 2.3 km from Puyca. Take water from the irrigation canal above Meclla and climb southeast past a shrine to a flat area with a *cobertizo*. There are various forks and side trails here. Continue southeast to cross a larger trail 1.7 km past Meclla, then turn southwest 500 m ahead to climb to a broad **saddle** 560 m farther. Here are great views back to Puyca and the upper Cotahuasi Canyon against a backdrop of high mountains, as well as down to the deep Quebrada Achisca to the west.

Turn southeast again at the saddle and climb steadily on a small clear trail over white sandy soil toward rocky outcrops ahead. The trail skirts to the right of the outcrops and then climbs more gently southeast, crossing a small stream 2 km past the saddle. The climb is now gradual as the trail continues 1 km east to a low **saddle** with a few stone corrals. This is **Atoccpunco** (4530), "fox gate," not to be confused with Cerro Atoccpunco (4793 m) towering above. Atoccpunco is 1050 m above the bridge over the Río Sumana, a good first day's climb. There is an *estancia* 700 m east of Atoccpunco, down in the first of three *quebradas* ahead; all have flat ground suitable for **camping**.

The trail ends near Atoccpunco. Head south and east cross-country to the last and deepest of the *quebradas*, then climb to the top of this pretty valley, where the terrain levels off and you meet a trail coming from Ayahuasi and Alca. This spot is 3.9 km from Atoccpunco. The trail goes west and our route east over open country and past large areas of little **stone mounds** (*jamajañi*) placed by countless generations of travelers to propitiate good luck along their journeys. They look like *apacheta* "forests" full of seedlings. Continue east cross-country past **Quebrada Ñacchui** and **Quebrada Morrocuchiyocc** to **Quebrada Pilluni**, 8.5 km past the top of the valley described above. Camping possibilities abound throughout the area, but most are quite exposed.

TREK 25: COTAHUASI TO VALLEY OF THE VOLCANOES

Scale = 1:278,000
(Contour interval = 200 meters)

Ignore the vehicle track at Quebrada Pilluni, as well as several others that follow, and continue past the base of a rocky hill, 1.9 km to ford the upper **Río Pachaquisque**. Another 2.9 km brings you to a broad **saddle** at 4877 m with a small but very welcome stone wind shelter. A vehicle track descends from the saddle to Quebrada Inohamisa and the valley of Río Kelluya, but we suggest a small cross-country detour climbing south from the saddle, then east to reach the highest point of the trek (4943 m) with amazing 360-degree views of countless *nevados*. From this high point, head 900 m east down into **Quebrada Inohamisa** to meet the trail coming from the saddle. Ford the *quebrada* and head southeast, climbing gently along the south side of **Río Kelluya**, to yet another gentle **saddle** at 4861 m. Below the pass and 4 km past Quebrada Inohamisa is a **stone corral** with good wind shelter for **camping**.

After the corral, cross to the north side of **Quebrada Incamisa** and follow it southeast, at first down along the *quebrada*, then climbing steadily away from it to reach **Laguna Incamisa**, 3.3 km past the corral. At the lake the trail forks: left to the village of Umachulco (15 km, mostly road-walking with very little traffic), an easier alternate way to finish the trek, and right along our route. Follow the south shore of the lake, then head southeast for 3 km, to reach a large powerline and in 300 m farther the road from Umachulco.

Cross the road and continue southeast down into **Quebrada Chapi**, a pretty valley with a few scattered *estancias* amid impressive rock formations. The trail in Quebrada Chapi at first follows the southwest side of the drainage, then crosses it and soon divides again, 5.3 km past the road. The left branch heads into steep, difficult terrain up toward Umachulco; we follow the right branch down to cross Quebrada Chapi and then climb steadily past a few scattered stone houses to a final saddle at 4572 m, 3.7 km past the fork to Umachulco.

Here begins the scenic descent to Chilcaymarca, either along a zigzagging vehicle track reached 700 m ahead or through **Quebrada Ocoruro**. Both options are about 5 km long and offer intriguing glimpses of the broad, flat Orcopampa valley ahead, sporting its characteristic assortment of volcanic cones. The route through Quebrada Ocoruro follows a combination of badly deteriorated ancient road fragments (parts are washed away), some newer trails, and cross-country travel, with a very steep and difficult descent at the end.

Chilcaymarca is particularly charming, a delightful place to finish the trek amid steep stone streets and timeless stone and adobe houses. Community tourism here is off to an enthusiastic start. Orcopampa, 5 km (10 minutes by shared taxi) away, is larger and more modern; a somewhat drab mining supply town with hotels, restaurants, and well-stocked shops. The attractive Huancarama thermal baths are 7 km north of Orcopampa, and a warm soak here is especially welcome after several nights up in the cold *puna*.

Return. From Orcopampa there are buses to Arequipa. Most run overnight via Caylloma; one around midday goes via Andagua at the start of Trek 26. There is an airstrip at Orcopampa but no scheduled commercial flights.

26 VALLEY OF THE VOLCANOES TO COLCA

THE VERTICAL LIFE

Rating: Very difficult, 79-km, 6- to 8-day trek

Elevation: 2065 to 5171 m

Maps: IGN 1:100,000 Orcopampa (31r), Huambo (32r), Chivay (32s); ESCALE Arequipa (Caylloma 1)

Water: Available mostly in the valleys. Many of the steep slopes, especially the lower ones, are completely dry.

Hazards and annoyances: There may be snow at Paso Cerani, even in the dry season. Expect sharp cactus spines and other spiky vegetation, as well as some biting insects in lower areas.

Permits and fees: Local authorities in the Colca Canyon charge US$23 per visitor. Keep your ticket handy to show inspectors.

Services and provisions: Andagua and Chachas offer a variety of accommodations as well as simple shops and eateries. Grupo GEA (see Appendix A) coordinates community tourism and is very helpful; visit their office in Andagua. If coming from Arequipa, bring most of your supplies from the city. If continuing from Trek 25, Orcopampa has the best-stocked shops. Villagers along the route subsist mostly from what they grow and may not have anything to spare, so don't count on resupplying as you go. Miña, Ucuchachas, and Llanca offer basic accommodations in a communal building, but this is also not to be relied on.

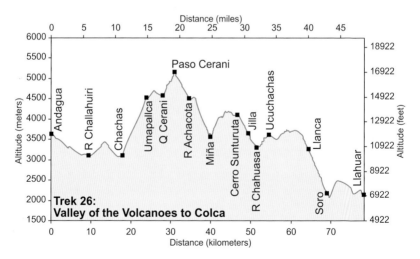

WHILE TREKKING THIS ROUTE the dominant words in your vocabulary become "up" and "down," for you are always walking and looking, even dreaming, in one of these two directions. The steep gradients are partly mitigated by good trails, but there is

Many tributaries of the Río Colca are mighty canyons in their own right.

enough cross-country travel to test both your physical endurance and navigation skills. On more than one occasion we wished we had the wings of the condors circling overhead, to take in the boundless beauty by gliding through it. Yet the hard work required to complete this trek is amply rewarded by a wealth of unforgettable experiences.

The bonsai volcanoes around Andagua make a fitting starting point as you set off in the direction of their snow-capped big brothers: Ampato (6265 m), Hualca Hualca (6025 m), and smoking Sabancaya (5976 m). These big three look down on you from afar throughout the trek, while beneath them yawn the depths of the great Colca Canyon to which you are headed. Understandably, you rapidly come to appreciate the immense geological forces that continue to shape this dramatic landscape. No less impressive, however, are the people who live hidden behind its walls, thriving in the isolation wrought by such formidable geographic barriers.

Access. One bus a day from Arequipa to Andagua, 10 hours mostly on poor roads. If continuing from Trek 25, there is one daily bus from Orcopampa to Andagua, 35 km, 1.5 hours, a rough but beautiful ride. If you prefer to skip the long first day of trekking from Andagua to Chachas, there is bus or minivan service four days a week, or hire a local vehicle. A vehicle can also be taken from Chachas to Umapallca; see route description below.

Route. Leave **Andagua** at first light and take plenty of water from town. From the southeast corner of the plaza, head east downhill. The street soon becomes a rough

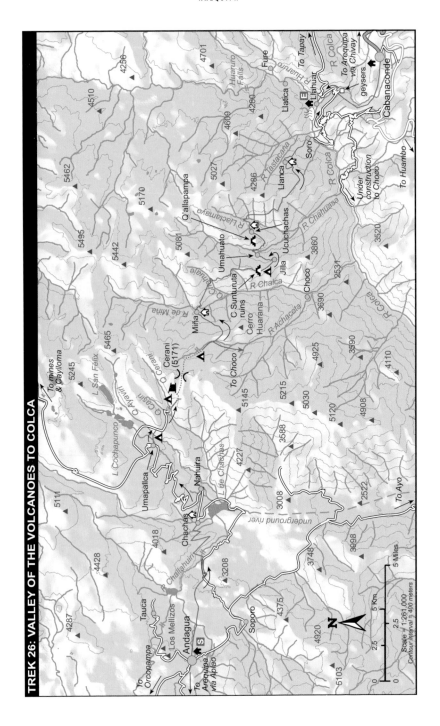

TREK 26: VALLEY OF THE VOLCANOES TO COLCA

Scale = 1:261,000
Contour interval: 400 meters

track and turns right. At the first corner after the curve, turn left and continue east down along the little-used old trail to Chachas. Where you reach a vehicle track and cross a small stream, follow the track east, staying left at each of the two forks ahead. At the second fork you cross an irrigation canal and the vehicle track becomes a trail.

Continue descending gradually east to a large flat area, 3 km from Andagua. Look for a wooden gate in the middle of the valley and go through it; do not climb up into the unstable boulder field above the gate on the right. Continue east to the end of the flats; here climb slightly right into the boulder field to pick up a trail headed east to a notch between the hill on your right and a large black lava flow on your left. At the notch the trail forks; take the left branch, which drops east through a lunar landscape of brittle volcanic rock and black sand, hot underfoot in the strong sun.

The trail fades in and out, but our route continues east above a deep gully on the left. At 2.8 km past the gate the gully turns southeast, and we do likewise to meet a road 800 m ahead. Follow the road east for 2 km to a sign marking the start of the trail to a waterfall in the **Río Challahuiri**, 500 m farther east. Enjoy the view of this impressive cascade before heading northwest down to the river's edge, at least 250 m upstream from the falls, to attempt to ford. This is safe when the water is low, but count on it being at least knee-deep, and don't take chances if the current seems too strong (note the washed-out bridge by the falls). If it is too risky to ford, return to the road, which also leads to Chachas in 11 km, a substantial but safe detour. The Río Challahuiri contains mine effluent including cyanide and is not safe to drink even when purified.

More challenging than the ford itself is reaching the abandoned road that lazily zig-zags its way up the slope on the east side of the river. The bottom of the road is only 100 m from the water's edge, but the rocky terrain is badly overgrown with spiny vegetation. The lower parts of the road are also strewn with stones, at times almost blocked by them, but the going improves as you make your way uphill. There is one long, clear shortcut along the way. At 3.8 km past the ford you reach a notch with great views back to the Valley of the Volcanoes. The old road is much improved past the notch and gradually drops over more zigzags with a few shortcuts. The views ahead to Chachas and its lake surrounded by terraced fields are lovely, but the remaining 4.7 km feel longer than they are at the end of a full day.

The friendly people, warm climate, and delightful setting of **Chachas** make it well worth spending a day or two to explore the surroundings and consider your three options for moving on. You can climb the 1400 m to Umapallca, which is 20 km along the road via Nahuira, less with shortcuts, but there is no water along the way. You can try to hire pack animals and a muleteer for the day, in either Chachas or Nahuira, to help you over the hump, but there are not many to be found as most of the young men work as miners in the mountains above town. Or you can look for a pickup truck heading up to the mines (no schedule, so ask around in advance; most leave Chachas between 4:00 AM and 6:00 AM), a very helpful elevator ride if you are already acclimatized to altitude.

Umapallca itself is entirely abandoned, just a few collapsed adobe houses at 4530 m, trash, and one *calamina* structure that provides a bit of wind shelter. Leave the road here and head east, crossing a concrete irrigation canal before descending into **Quebrada Ayaviri**. Cross the two branches of the *quebrada* just upstream from their confluence, then climb south cross-country to an area of stone corrals suitable for **camping**. Continue climbing to meet a vehicle track (coming from the road through Umapallca) and follow it south through a broad saddle as it turns east and drops gently into the next drainage called **Quebrada Casiri**, with great views along the way. After crossing Quebrada Casiri and climbing the next ridge, the track drops to **Quebrada Cerani**, where it ends 4.2 km past Umapallca. This is a lovely spot with more good **camping** possibilities.

Cross Quebrada Cerani and head south cross-country to an unnamed side stream 250 m ahead. Climb steeply southeast along the north side of the stream until it turns south. Head east here, climbing to the first of several notches marked by small cairns, as you make your way toward Paso Cerani, which becomes visible ahead. At 1.2 km after the start of the steep climb along the side stream, you reach a wind-sheltered spot with a stone **shelter**, water, and plenty of room to camp. This is a cold but inspirational place at 4890 m, beneath beautiful towering crags.

Beyond the shelter climb steeply east along the south side of the valley, past two ponds on your left, the last water before the pass. Cross an impressive boulder field, staying right of the narrow valley. The route is marked only by a few small cairns and would be difficult to follow with snow on the ground. **Paso Cerani** (5171 m) is reached 1.4 km past the stone shelter amid breathtaking views in every direction. All the mountains are gathered to greet you (or bid you farewell) as you cross from the realm of Solimana, Firura, and Coropuna towering above the Cotahuasi Canyon, to that of Ampato, Sabancaya, and Hualca Hualca dominating the Colca Canyon (see orientation map at the beginning of this chapter). This is truly a wow moment!

The descent east from the pass is steep at first over rocky terrain, following the south (right) side of the valley. At 1 km from the pass is a flat area where you could camp in a pinch but no water. Continue east and then south above the upper **Río Achacota**, descending steadily on the west side of its broad boggy valley. Look north for the frozen waterfalls (June to August) beneath the snowy cirque at the head of the valley. There are several potential **camping** spots ahead as you make your way south, and the cross-country route encounters an increasingly clear trail. At 1.8 km past the flat spot mentioned above, the trail reaches an old terminal moraine where the river tumbles down another pretty waterfall, all the more impressive when it too is frozen.

Continue 1.8 km south from the waterfall to reach a fork: go left to follow our route; or right to the village of Choco, 7.5 km south and almost 2000 m down along the Río Achacota. Choco is not far from the roadhead at the bottom of the Colca Canyon, with plans to extend the road all the way to the village, so it is an option to end the trek early. There are two minivans per week from the roadhead to Cabanaconde. We ford the Río Achacota and climb southeast to reach a ridge on **Cerro Huarana** 400 m past the fork. The ridge has more impressive views as well as an incongruously large stone wall to keep cattle from respective sides where they should be. Cross this "great wall of Huarana" through a *calamina* gate and descend east and then northeast along a zigzagging trail headed to the village of **Miña** visible 4.1 km and 1000 m below.

Cross the **Río de Miña** at the edge of the village and climb steeply southeast on a clear trail to a cross and powerline above. There are many branching trails ahead; stay to your left at the forks, aiming for the highest route. The steep gradient is mitigated by many zigzags, but it's best to start early in order to climb in the shade and take plenty of water from Miña, as the streams and springs ahead cannot be relied on during the dry season. In 3 km you cross the large steep **Quebrada Chahuaje**. There are two trails at the entrance to the *quebrada*; the lower (right) one is safer, and they soon merge.

At 1.8 km from Quebrada Chahuaje you reach a notch with glorious views of the Río Chalca to the west, a mighty canyon in its own right, bound for the even mightier Colca Canyon ahead. Here is a beautiful polylepis forest (see A Tree of Many Skins, Trek 5). The trail turns east to cross the next drainage and then south again to reach a saddle 1 km past the notch. At the saddle a trail branches east to drop steeply into the upper Río Chahuasa valley, a potentially more direct route to Ucuchachas where we are headed, but reported unsafe due to a landslide, so it is best to continue south along the top of **Cerro Sunturuta**. There are ancient stone **ruins** along the top and, 1.7 km past the saddle, more recent stone corrals and abandoned houses that make a good **camping** spot but unfortunately without water. Some 350 m farther south is another saddle where various trails intersect. Follow the one that leads southeast along the steep slope, high above the Río Chahuasa, 1.5 km to the tiny hamlet of **Jilla** where at last there is water, the first you can count on after Miña.

From Jilla, follow a larger trail northeast past **Umahuato**, another small village but with a more spread-out group of dwellings. At 2.1 km past Jilla you ford the **Río Chahuasa** and turn southeast to climb steadily on a good trail to a cross on the ridge, then northeast again to reach the **Q'allapampa ruins** and the village of **Ucuchachas**, 3.1 km past the ford. Ucuchachas is beautifully situated between the snowy summits above and the bottomless Colca Canyon below.

From Ucuchachas head northeast to ford two branches of the **Río Llactamayo** in an impressively steep gorge. Take water here for the long dry climb ahead. The trail, narrow between the fords but otherwise wide and clear, turns southeast and climbs steadily 3.3 km to a flat overlook where you get your first glimpse of the green waters of the Río Colca, still over 1800 m below. This spot has all the views imaginable, from Paso Cerani, over the entire route you have followed, to Ampato, Sabancaya, and Hualca Hualca above the Colca Canyon—another wow moment. The trail then climbs more gently for 3.9 km to a cairn on the ridgeline separating the Río Chahuasa from the Río Tastacana. Turn northeast here and continue 2.4 km steadily down to **Llanca**, a slightly larger village that feels like a metropolis after the places you have come from, even though it only has a few small shops and a very basic municipal hostel.

From Llanca a road cut descends to a pedestrian bridge over the Río Colca by Soro. A vehicle road is planned, but in 2015 the road cut was not yet passable to vehicles. For walking, the best bet is to follow the trail that intersects and shortcuts the road in several places, reaching the hamlet of Soro in 5 km. **Soro** is perched above irrigated terraces, and its residents are as friendly as their fields are productive. A 2 km route from Soro to Llahuar along the north side of the Río Colca is tempting, but parts have been swept away by landslides and the bare slopes are very steep, unstable, and dangerous. Instead, cross the **Río Colca** at the pedestrian bridge 600 m from Soro. At 2050 m above sea level it is 3121 m below Paso Cerani. Here is the roadhead and one of several options to end the trek (see Return, below). You can also continue walking, mostly along the roads, 10 km to Llahuar or 20 km to Cabanaconde, 1250 m above the bridge.

Our preferred finale starts with a 1.5-km shortcut up from the bridge to the road. Where the shortcut ends, follow the road 350 m east to a fork. The right branch climbs to Cabanaconde; for Llahuar, take the left that contours and then descends along the steep south side of the Colca Canyon with excellent views. In 3.4 km, by some hairpin bends with more shortcuts, you meet a trail from Cabanaconde and a steady stream of hikers making their way to the popular lodge and thermal baths at Llahuar or the impressive Huaruro waterfall beyond. Join the pack and continue 1.1 km to a vehicle bridge and an older pedestrian bridge that cross the Río Colca side by side. A trail from the west side of the pedestrian bridge leads 350 m upstream to a good view of geysers by the river's edge.

After crossing one of the bridges, head northwest along the road for 1.3 km to where it turns northeast and a large trail continues northwest 700 m down to a pedestrian bridge over the **Río Huaruro**, a tributary of the Río Colca. **Llahuar** is 400 m ahead.

Return. On Sunday, Tuesday, and Friday mornings (confirm details in Soro), vans run from the bridge below Soro to Cabanaconde in about 2 hours. Vans run daily from Tapay to Cabanaconde, passing the Llahuar turnoff around 5:00 AM and noon (be there early), also 2 hours. Or, if you have not yet had your fill of the vertical life, you can take the popular trail that climbs 1200 m in 12 km from Llahuar to Cabanaconde. Several daily buses run from Cabanaconde to Arequipa, 6 hours via Chivay on a scenic paved road.

12

LAKE TITICACA AND CORDILLERA CARABAYA

Lake Titicaca is an icon of South America. At 3810 m above sea level, the highest navigable lake in the world occupies 8562 sq km, straddling the border between Peru and Bolivia. This natural lake is a major tourist destination, especially along the south shore. The less-visited north side of the lake is gently hilly with many rocky promontories, beaches, and sheltered bays rich in birdlife. Scattered about the lake are seventy-two islands. The flat areas around the lake are known as *punas*.

Clear most of the year, the sky in the Titicaca area has a unique luminescent quality. Intense solar radiation is both absorbed and reflected by the deep blue waters of the lake, which tempers the climate of the surrounding *punas*, creating micro-climates that allow the cultivation of crops and flowers typical of lower, warmer, elevations.

Ancient roads, archaeological sites, and agricultural terraces attest to human presence going back many centuries—

Lake Titicaca and Allin Capac (5780 m, highest summit of the Cordillera Carabaya) both dominate the southern highlands of Peru.

BULLS ON THE ROOF

Look up as you trek through towns and villages of southern Peru. Can you spot two clay bulls on the roofs? What are they doing there and on the cover of this book? These are Toritos de Pucará placed with a cross to protect the home and bring well-being, happiness, and prosperity to its inhabitants. What better way to wish our readers and trekkers a safe and happy journey!

These curious figures stem from a millenary tradition. The Pucará culture (500 BC–AD 500), the first urban society of the northern Lake Titicaca basin, excelled in making ceramics. Today, potters of the districts of Santiago de Pupuja and Choquehuanca, in the Province of Azángaro, north of Puno, continue to shape clay, extracted from the same cliffs, into pots, vases, and the well-known toritos.

There are legends and much speculation regarding the origins of the torito tradition. The most credible versions suggest that they are a modern equivalent of the pre-Hispanic *qonopas* (Quechua) and *illas* (Aymara), stone or clay amulets in the shape of animals (often llamas or alpacas) or ears of corn. The amulets were venerated, passed on in families from one generation to the next, and used in ceremonies to propitiate fertile herds and abundant crops. When the Spanish banned and punished idolatry, the bull, a symbol of the powerful conquerors, replaced the native amulets.

Toritos represent a strong bull with bulging eyes, its tongue protruding upwards, decorations on its back, and a coiled tail suggestive of an angry animal. Filled with *chicha* laced with bull's blood, they are used in the *señalacuy* cattle marking ceremonies such as the Fiesta de Santiago (see Chapter 9). In the torito-producing area, during special festivities, they are also buried as an offering to *Pachamama*.

Over time, the amulets of fertility and abundance evolved into a more general symbol of well-being and protection. First sold at the Pucará Station along the Cuzco–Puno railway, they became known as Toritos de Pucará. In addition to the original terracotta and white design they are now available in many different colors with more elaborate decorations and they have become one of Peru's unique crafts.

from the Pucará to the Incas. Titicaca is considered a sacred lake from which emerged the founders of the Inca Empire. The great Inca Road or Capac Ñan had two branches following the northern and southern shores of the lake. Today, *altiplano* inhabitants belong to two distinct linguistic and cultural groups: Quechua and Aymara, with a predominance of Aymara people around the shore.

This is the perfect place for easy to moderately difficult hiking amid the broadest horizons in Peru. One of the only tourist establishments on the north side of the lake is the upmarket hotel on Isla Suasi (see Appendix A), a great place to pamper yourself before or after trekking in the area.

To the north and west of the lake is the remote and isolated Cordillera Carabaya, the watershed between the Titicaca and Amazon basins, connecting the Cordillera Vilcanota in Cuzco with the Cordillera Apolobamba in Bolivia. This region has beautiful glaciated mountains crowned by Allin Capac (5780 m), spectacular lakes, undeveloped archaeological sites, ancient roads, rock forests, and rock art. It has been a mining area since at least Inca times and is Peru's largest alpaca producer with huge herds grazing the *punas*. Trekking here requires strong navigation skills, good Spanish, and patient cross-cultural communication. Most Carabaya residents are unfamiliar with trekking and will assume you are a prospector or up to some sort of mischief. It is well worth the time and effort required to break the ice.

Both Titicaca and Carabaya are in the department of Puno. The city of Puno is the departmental capital and main tourist center. Puno offers bus links throughout southern Peru and into Bolivia. From the airport at Juliaca, 44 km north of Puno, there are several daily flights to Lima, Cuzco, and Arequipa. Juliaca itself is a bustling, dirty, and unsafe commercial city; mind your belongings here. It might be best avoided altogether were it not for the fact that transport to trekking areas departs from Juliaca: to Moho for the north shore of Titicaca and to

Macusani for the Cordillera Carabaya. Both are small pleasant towns with basic services. Richar Cáceres in Macusani (see Appendix A) is knowledgeable about trekking in Carabaya and a helpful contact, but he is not always around. Macusani, at an altitude of 4320 m, is always cold.

The beaten path. Most tourists in Puno visit the floating Uros islands in Puno Bay and the *chullpas* (funeral towers) of Sillustani, 32 km from the city. Some venture farther afield to the islands of Taquile or Amantaní, or the agricultural villages of the Capachica peninsula. The north shore of Titicaca is less visited, and the very few foreign travelers to reach the Carabaya are usually en route between the *altiplano* and the jungle along the Carretera Interoceánica.

Limbering up. An easy 15-km day hike through hills above the lake, from Chucuito to the outskirts of Puno, is a good start. Do not, however, venture into the hills directly above Puno, such as Huajsapata or Kuntur Wasi, without first inquiring about public safety. An easy 17-km fragment of the Great Inca Road between the towns of Juli and Pomata, east of Puno along the south shore of the lake, is also a good option. More remote and very beautiful is an easy day walk around the Huatasani peninsula, 12 km roundtrip from Tilali at the end of Trek 28. If you wish to stop for a few days en route between Puno and Cuzco, there are good day hikes out of Ayaviri, 135 km north of Puno. These include hiking through the Tinajani Canyon, with its interesting rock formations and *chullpas*, as well as visiting a large stand of *Puyas raimondii* (see Queen of the Andes, Chapter 2) at Huayatani. Both hikes are some distance from Ayaviri and require motorized transport.

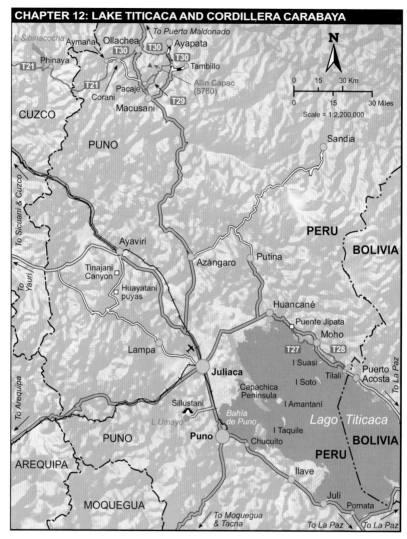

CHAPTER 12: LAKE TITICACA AND CORDILLERA CARABAYA

Featured treks. Trek 27, Puente Jipata to Moho, and Trek 28, Moho to Tilali, both follow ancient roads above the north shore of Lake Titicaca, offering endless vistas and a glimpse of traditional life along the way. They can be combined into a longer trek, easy at the beginning and gradually more challenging as you go along, almost to the Bolivian border. In the Cordillera Carabaya, Trek 29, Allin

Capac Lakes, is a very scenic loop through the heart of alpaca country, beneath the region's highest and most beautiful mountain. Trek 30, Carabaya Traverse, continues beyond Trek 29 for a longer and more difficult circumnavigation of Allin Capac. Combining Treks 20 and 21 from Cuzco with Trek 30 (in reverse) adds up to over 280 km of tough and spectacular trekking.

27 PUENTE JIPATA TO MOHO
GENTLE OMASUYO

Rating: Easy 30-km, 2- to 3-day trek
Elevation: 3850 to 4190 m
Maps: IGN 1:100,000 Huancané (31x); ESCALE Puno (Moho)
Water: Surprisingly scarce; request from homes along the route
Hazards and annoyances: Nighttime temperatures in July and August dip to -10°C. Thunderstorms can build up quickly, year-round.
Permits and fees: None
Services and provisions: Moho has a basic *hospedaje municipal* and simple well-stocked shops; bring specialty items from Puno or Juliaca. A few basic items are available from villages along the route.

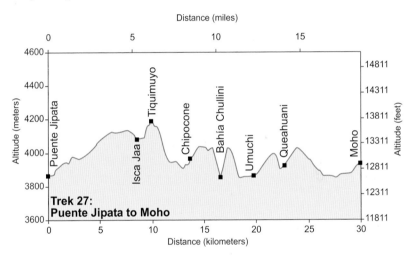

THE NORTH SHORE OF Lake Titicaca was the Omasuyo region of the Incas. It has many ancient roads and the remains of several pre-Inca settlements. Following these roads through the terraced slopes above the lakeshore, this gentle trek offers a glimpse into the traditional lives of the rural Aymara people, closely tied to the land and water. The humidity released by evaporation from the lake and the fact that the water absorbs heat and releases it at night, tempers the harsh climate of the surrounding *altiplano*. This creates micro-climates that allow the cultivation of fruits, vegetables, and flowers typical of lower, warmer elevations. Moho, the regional center at the end of this trek, proudly calls itself *el jardín del altiplano*, "the garden of the altiplano". Floating trout farms are common offshore, and in October or November you might see small boats going out at night to fish the schools of tiny endemic *ispi*, with traditional reed fishing baskets now replaced by nylon nets.

Extensive stone terracing past Chipocone

Access. From Jr Moquegua and Av El Maestro, north of Mercado Túpac Amaru in Juliaca, vans run to Moho; they can drop you off at Puente Jipata, a 1-hour ride. From Moho to Puente Jipata, the same vans take 30 minutes.

Route. This trek begins at **Puente Jipata**, a small bridge over the Río Litira Cuyo, 20.5 km northwest of Moho on the main paved road to Huancané and Juliaca. At the bridge an unpaved road heads south toward Lake Titicaca through marshes filled with *totora* reeds, waterfowl, and, unfortunately, a bit of trash. Follow the road for 500 m and look on your left for a stone-paved trail that climbs southeast. Take the trail for 350 m to a fork: the left branch heads back to the paved road; continue south along the right. Another 700 m ahead is a second fork: to the left an impressive stone stairway climbs steeply toward the ridgeline; continue along the right branch, which contours between the lakeshore and the ridge.

Squares of harvested *totora* reeds give the lakeshore a patchwork quilt appearance. Since the modern road is not far, the trail gets little use, and parts are a bit rough. Watch for small cacti between the rocks; they have beautiful flowers and nasty spines. On a prominence on top of the ridge are the undeveloped **Queñalata** ruins, visible with binoculars. Continue southeast between tilled fields framed by ancient stone walls. There are lovely views over the lake to several peninsulas and islands. Gradually, the village of **Jacantaya** comes into view at the head of the bay below.

Another fork is reached 1.3 km beyond the stone stairway: the right branch drops steeply and then heads southeast to Isca Jaa; take the upper (left) branch, which climbs gently to the southeast between terraced potato fields. Ask at a house in this area for water; there is none available beyond. Continue contouring southeast to reach a **broad saddle** 4 km ahead. Climb the low, stony ridge to the south for views of the valley below and the lake beyond. Past this point there are no more houses or worked fields; the trail deteriorates, and at times you travel cross-country. The direction of travel is southeast, descending gently and then contouring along the south flank of the ridge.

POTATOES FOR ALL SEASONS

There is nothing more Andean than the potato. This South American tuber was first domesticated in the Lake Titicaca area around 7000 BC and continues to be the main food staple of the region. Potatoes are the third most important food in the world after rice and wheat. There are over four thousand edible varieties, mostly in the Andes, where hundreds of commercial varieties are produced.

Not only did the inhabitants of the *altiplano* domesticate the potato; they also developed ways of dehydrating and preserving it. These practices are still in use, and many local dishes include dehydrated potatoes such as *chuño, tunta* (*moraya, chuño blanco*), and *papa seca*. Their preparation requires elaborate processes and special climatic conditions, with below-freezing temperatures at night and bright sunny days. *Tunta* is prepared in the Titicaca area between May and the end of July. It is first left out to freeze for three or four nights. Next it is placed in running water, a river or stream, for three to four weeks. Then it is left out to freeze again

for a night, after which it is stepped on to remove the peel and the last bit of humidity. Finally it is dried for a week in the sun. For more information, see Centro Internacional de la Papa in Appendix A.

Although the potato is an important ingredient in the cuisine of countries throughout the world, nowhere does it taste better than on its home turf. Enjoy!

In 1.6 km you reach a large trail: to the north (left) it heads for the paved road; follow it south, to the right. In 800 m you meet the lower trail that split off above Jacantaya and, 200 m beyond, the village of **Isca Jaa**. You can ask for permission to pitch your tent in the soccer field or school grounds.

At Isca Jaa a vehicle track runs west to Jacantaya and Jipata, east to Umuchi, and on to Moho. Our route goes south along a broad stone path that zigzags up to the ridgeline, 500 m from the village. Extending east along the ridge are the **Tiquimuyo** ruins with deteriorated stone structures and looted burial sites. There are great views south to the lake and Isla Uspique. Descend along the south side of the ridge past a cluster of tin-roofed houses to the village of **Milicuyo**, 1 km ahead, where the trail crosses a road. Continue south along the trail for 200 m to a second road just before it crosses a stream on a concrete bridge. Cross the bridge and follow the road, which soon divides; take the left branch, which climbs southeast 1.3 km to the larger village of **Chipocone**.

Chipocone has a lovely setting on a terraced hillside overlooking the lake. Its stone houses are surrounded by plots where potatoes, broad beans, and even peas and corn

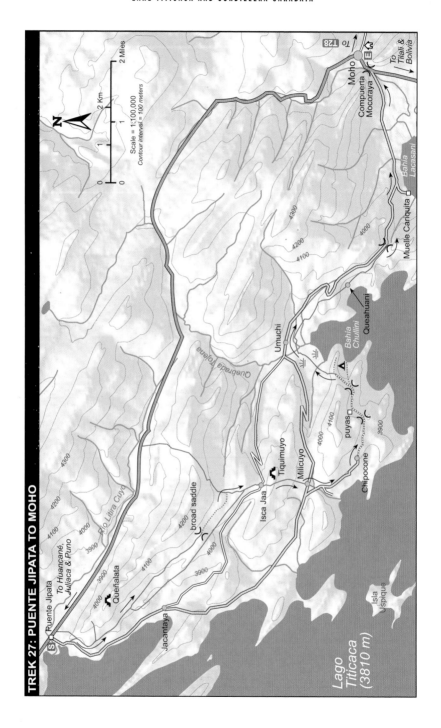

TREK 27: PUENTE JIPATA TO MOHO

Scale = 1:100,000
Contour interval = 100 meters

N

Lago
Titicaca
(3810 m)

grow—unusual crops for this altitude and a fine example of how the proximity of the lake moderates the cold climate. The streets are narrow stone-cobbled lanes between the terraces. Make your way through the village, going uphill and east, and ask for the trail to Umuchi, as it is indistinguishable from any of the other stone lanes.

Past Chipocone begins a truly spectacular section of the route. The trail that contours ahead is superbly paved with large flagstones, the hillside displays extensive and excellent stone terracing, a beautiful bay comes into view on the right, and several *Puya raimondii* plants (see Queen of the Andes, Chapter 2) can be seen on the slope to the left. In the afternoon light, this is a magical stretch of restored ancient road. In 1 km you reach a wide **saddle**, the *puyas* are just beyond, and in another 1 km is a second **saddle**.

If you wish to get closer to the lakeshore, a recommended detour is to visit secluded **Bahía Chullini**, below the second saddle. A faint track descends east along a drainage for 800 m from this saddle to terraced fields, where potatoes are grown near the shore. Some of the fallow terraces above the crops are good for **camping**. The lakeshore is swampy, so you'd best get water from a small stream at the south side of the bay. There are waterbirds among the *totora* reeds offshore and small songbirds in a patch of eucalyptus forest nearby. Cliffs make it impossible to continue east along the lakeshore, so the best route is back up the trail, the same way you came.

Back on the main route, from the second saddle the trail veers northeast to reach a notch on the ridge, 500 m ahead, and a fork. One branch heads east along the ridgeline and later fades. Follow the branch that turns left at the notch and drops steeply north on stony zigzags to the broad Umuchi valley below. In 350 m you reach some trees and a house. The route continues to the northeast across a large swampy floodplain. Be sure to stay on the trail, which becomes a causeway with bridges over several small streams and the larger **Quebrada Tojena**. Watch for buff-necked ibis and black puna ibis, as well as other waterfowl. In 1.3 km you reach a small church, and 200 m beyond to the north you can see the Puesto de Salud (public health center) of **Umuchi**, on the vehicle road. Umuchi is very spread out. Several trails go north to the main paved road, and a vehicle road north was under construction in 2014.

From Umuchi you could follow a dirt road southeast for 4.5 km, as it climbs to a saddle offering great views over the lake and a set of five promontories known as Los Cinco Dedos (The Five Fingers). If, like us, you prefer to avoid the road, ask for the cemetery and the trail to Queahuani. Also ask for water; it is scarce ahead. **Queahuani** is a tiny hamlet set above a broad beach on a lovely horseshoe bay. From here a trail climbs gradually southeast for 1.8 km between terraces, to meet the dirt road at the **saddle** mentioned above.

Continue along the road and a few shortcuts, descending toward Moho with fine views of **Bahía Lacasani** along the way. The flats by the bay and a fork are 2.4 km from the saddle. The road to the right leads to the stone pier called **Muelle Cariquita**. Follow the left branch 2.6 km to the paved Moho–Tilali road. Turn left to go through a gap in the hills known as **Compuerta Mocoraya**. You can see a section of the old trail next to the road on the left. **Moho**, a pleasant town with a nice plaza and an imposing

19th-century church, is 700 m ahead. It can be the end of the trek or a place to resupply and continue on along Trek 28.

Return. Vans leave as they fill from the plaza in Moho, bound for Juliaca. There are also vans passing through on their way east to Conima and Tilali.

28 MOHO TO TILALI
TAURANI TREK

Rating: Moderately difficult 32-km, 3-day trek
Elevation: 3860 to 4355 m
Maps: IGN 1:100,000 Moho (31y); ESCALE Puno (Moho)
Water: Except for a couple of rivers, water is scarce; request from homes along the route
Hazards and annoyances: See Trek 27
Permits and fees: None
Services and provisions: For Moho, see Trek 27. Conima and Tilali have basic places to stay and eat, and several small shops.

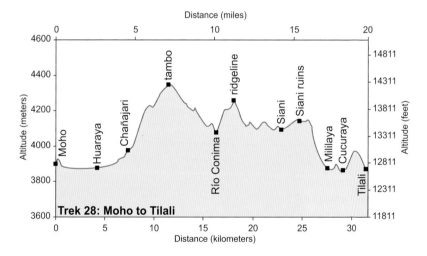

AT FIRST GLANCE, HIKING the gently rolling hills along the shore of Lake Titicaca might seem very easy. This trek, however, follows not only ancient and modern roads through Aymara villages scattered over the wide open landscape, it also heads cross-country along surprisingly steep ridgelines and across deep *quebradas*. Substantial navigational challenge likewise makes this route more difficult than you might expect.

The trek runs from the regional center of Moho to Tilali near the Bolivian border, with a couple of alternatives along the way. Roads and side trails lead to Conima and Cambria, access for Isla Suasi offshore. A day walk around the Huatasani peninsula, to the west of Tilali, is recommended as either an acclimatization hike or a gentle finale after completing this trek. Views over the lake from Huatasani are inspiring even after all you have seen along the main route. On a clear day, you can see the islands of Amantaní and Taquile off the south shore and even as far as Isla del Sol and Copacabana in Bolivia, some 80 km away.

Access. For transport between Juliaca and Moho, see Trek 27. If you wish to do this trek in reverse, from Tilali to Moho, take a van from Jr Lambayeque and Av Circunvalación Este, near Mercado Túpac Amaru in Juliaca, to Tilali, 3 hours.

Route. From the Plaza de Armas in **Moho**, follow Jirón Lima downhill to the southeast. Continue along the unpaved road; in 1.5 km you reach a three-way intersection, just before a large covered sports complex. Take the rightmost branch to the south, toward the village of Huaraya. It is all level walking here; the perfect flatness of the *puna*, stretching south to the lake, contrasts with the surrounding hillsides. **Huaraya** is 2.5 km from the triple fork, and 500 m ahead is another intersection. The right branch leads to the paved road along the lakeshore. Follow the left branch for 1 km to reach the **Río Sico** and another fork. Here, the left branch leads to Sico. Take the right branch and ford the ankle-deep river. Continue on the road, climbing gradually southeast past homes and fields to the spread-out village of **Chañajari**. Ask for water here, as it may be scarce ahead, especially in the dry season. The road ends by the school, 2 km from the river crossing.

Where the vehicle road ends, a very nice 2 km stretch of ancient stone road begins. This was part of the Omasuyo branch of the Capac Ñan (see Chapter 1), about 6 m wide and beautifully paved with flagstones except where water erosion has taken its toll. It climbs gradually to the southeast and, about 300 m from the school, crosses a deep gully on a modern cement bridge, then begins to climb more steeply. Ahead, the terrain becomes more level and the waters of the lake come into better view on the right. Here the trail gradually deteriorates and in a surprisingly short distance becomes indistinct, lost amid the straw. Continue climbing cross-country, southeast to a **broad saddle** at 4310 m with long stone walls and a modest cairn, 3.5 km past the Chañajari school. You will find a faint trail running northeast–southwest 100 m beyond the cairn. To the right this trail drops to the Río Camjata and beyond toward Conima; our route continues southeast.

Stone ruins are scattered about the hilltops around the pass, and a small detour takes you to an impressive cluster of structures. To reach them, follow the faint trail northeast (left). In 100 m this trail splits; the right branch heads northeast toward the ridge ahead. Continue on the left branch for another 300 m to the corner of a large stone corral. The **ruins**, uphill inside the corral, might have been a *tambo*, and offer great views in all directions. There is a second, smaller cluster of structures to the southeast.

Return to the broad pass and descend southeast cross-country along the south side of the valley. This drainage is one of the headwaters of the Río Conima. It is easy going over the open straw-covered terrain. Aim for Cerro Ticalacca, rising from the bottom of the valley ahead. Along the way are more stone structures, including large corrals. As you descend, the valley widens, and there are tilled fields and a couple of seasonally

A stroll around the Huatasani Peninsula, near Tilali, is a delightful finale to this trek.

occupied houses. There is ample flat ground for **camping**, and many stone walls provide wind shelter.

As the valley widens, a trail gradually becomes evident. Faint at first and interrupted by numerous stone fences, it progressively becomes wider and clearer, so that by the time the drainage turns sharply southwest at the base of Cerro Ticalacca you are on a wide stone trail. The trail contours around the ridge on the south side of the drainage, then turns southwest to run high above the west side of the **Río Conima**, before dropping to cross the river and join a road to Conima.

Navigation is tricky ahead. To continue to Tilali along our route, leave the trail just before it turns southwest, 3.5 km east of the broad saddle mentioned above. Head southeast to the river here, ford it, and continue east to cross a much smaller stream, 200 m from where you left the trail. On the far side of this stream are a couple of stone houses. Head south along the edge of the lowest wall. Pick up a faint trail that gradually becomes wider and clearer, complete with flagstones and steps. It climbs gently and in 300 m joins a larger trail running along the east side of Río Conima. Follow this larger cobbled trail south (right) for 1.2 km, until you meet a side stream flowing in from the southeast. There are fine views of the deep Conima valley running south all the way to the lake.

The stone trail continues toward Conima, but we leave it just before it crosses the stream and climb cross-country, heading southeast along the north side of the valley which separates **Cerro Ticalacca** (4295 m) from **Cerro Omospalla** to the south. Pick up a few fragments of trails along the way, skirt around the tops of some deep *quebradas*,

and in 1 km reach a broad **saddle** at 4200 m. The area nearby has signs of old mining. The saddle offers nice views southeast over the broad valley that forms ahead but also teases you: Where is Lake Titicaca?

Although you could descend gently east along the valley ahead to reach the town of Queallani and follow a dirt road from there to Tilali, it is more satisfying to take to the ridgetops in good weather. Cross the ridge directly to the south and descend to another saddle (not shown on our map) 150 m ahead. Continue southeast along a faint trail that climbs the next ridge by some rocky outcrops. In 600 m you reach a ridgeline running northwest–southeast above the **Río Parihuati** to the south. Here you are rewarded with the first of countless splendid views over the intricate array of peninsulas, islands, and bays to the south and the great open expanse of **Lake Titicaca** beyond, an unforgettable sight.

Our route would follow this rocky ridgeline southeast, but it is not safe in high winds or thunderstorms. We were forced by weather to descend south and then contour southeast along the south slope of the ridge, slow going along trail fragments interrupted by numerous stone walls. After 2.5 km on either the ridgeline or the slope, you meet a trail running from Conima to Queallani. Cross this trail and continue southeast along the ridge. The next landmark is a large water tank 700 m ahead, from where the village of Siani (Sillani) is visible in its picturesque hillside setting. Just 200 m past the tank you cross another perpendicular trail; look here on the left for a stone resembling a bull, decorated with streamers. This is **Taurani**, a curious local object of worship (see Syncretism, Chapter 2). Another 300 m ahead you meet an unpaved road; follow it right 200 m to **Siani**.

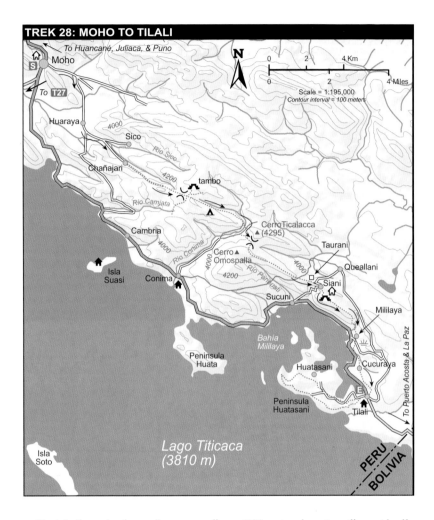

TREK 28: MOHO TO TILALI

Siani, built on the slopes of a narrow valley at 4100 m, is a charming village with effusively friendly people, working hard to develop community tourism. They offer basic lodging and meals for visitors. An ancient stone trail, referred to by locals as *Camino del Inca*, climbs southeast through the valley above Siani. It is unused, in rough shape, and crossed by stone fences in several places. This route might be an alternative if weather precludes following the ridgeline as described below, but we did not explore beyond the pass at the head of the valley.

On the ridge 250 m south of Siani is an extensive archaeological site with amazing views. A stone stairway, complete with banister, has been built from Siani to the ridge. The **ruins** appear to have been a combination of dwellings, storehouses, and tombs—a large pre-Inca center. The town's people are happy to guide you, and they have restored some of the structures west of the stairs.

Hike southeast through the ruins along the ridgetop. About 1.5 km from the stairs, the ridgeline drops steeply toward the floodplain around Mililaya. Leave the ridge where it becomes too steep to follow, making your way south by zigzagging carefully along the steep, stone-strewn slope. The view of **Bahía Mililaya** below is beautiful. About 850 m ahead and 200 m below the ridgetop, the ground begins to level off and, before you reach a line of trees, you meet a faint trail. Follow it to the northeast for 300 m to a larger stony trail that runs southwest along the west side of a deep *quebrada* with eucalyptus trees. Follow the larger trail downhill; in 500 m you cross the stream on a concrete footbridge. The pretty village of **Mililaya**, with nicely painted houses and rose gardens, is 250 m ahead.

The paved road from Juliaca to Tilali runs near the shore here. A nicer finale to the trek, however, is to follow a series of small trails south across the floodplain, over a low ridge to the next village of **Cucuraya**, 2 km from Mililaya, then over one final ridge (aim for the antenna tower where you meet an unpaved road) to **Tilali,** 2.5 km from Cucuraya. Tilali is a small town just 3 km from the Bolivian border. You can finish here or resupply and trek on into Bolivia. Puerto Acosta, 10 km past the frontier, has bus service to La Paz. There is no Peruvian immigration office at the border. You must get your Peruvian exit stamp in advance in Puno. There is a Bolivian immigration office along the vehicle track from Mililaya to Puerto Acosta. Confirm details locally.

Return. For transport between Tilali and Juliaca, see Access above.

29 ALLIN CAPAC LAKES
TARUCA TREK

Rating: Difficult 27-km, 3- to 4-day trek
Elevation: 4300 to 5080 m
Maps: IGN 1:100,000 Macusani (29v), Ayapata (28v); ESCALE Puno (Carabaya)
Water: Abundant along most of the route
Hazards and annoyances: None
Permits and fees: None
Services and provisions: Macusani has simple places to stay and eat and well-stocked shops; bring specialty items from Puno or Juliaca. No supplies are available along the route, and there is nowhere to spend the night in Pacaje at the end.

THE TWO MOST EMBLEMATIC summits of the Cordillera Carabaya are Allin Capac (Allinccapac, Allinjapac, 5780 m) and Chichi Capac (Chichiccapac, 5614 m), striking features of both the landscape and local mythology. For many people they remain venerated *apus*, mountain deities to which tributes are offered in order to propitiate a bountiful harvest or multiplication of the alpaca herd. At the foot of these two giants lies a chain of particularly beautiful lakes in a glacial valley flowing from vertical rock faces to the flat *puna*.

Outflow of Laguna Suirococha fed by the snows of Allin Capac

This trek is a short but challenging loop, climbing alongside the lakes and returning over a high pass and ridge separating their valley from a neighbouring drainage to the west. The gorgeous scenery is complemented by a rich variety of fauna, including many water birds and large mammals ranging from large herds of domestic llamas and alpacas, through shy wild vicuñas, to taruca (*Hippocamelus antisensis*)—the stately high-altitude Andean deer. Since the route is shared with the first part of Trek 30, you can make an extension along part of that more difficult trek and still return via Trek 29.

Access. From the district called El Triángulo, or Salida a Cuzco, in Juliaca, several bus and van companies have service to Macusani, a 3-hour ride. A *combi* runs from Macusani to Pacaje (Huanutuyo) on Monday to Friday around 7:00 AM and noon, 20 minutes. The van or a taxi, or any transport heading north along the Carretera Interoceánica, can drop you off at Cruce de Pacaje, the turnoff for Pacaje on the right.

Route. From **Cruce de Pacaje,** follow the unpaved road toward Pacaje for 550 m to a fork. Take the right branch east along the south side of the drainage, outflow of the chain of lakes for which you are headed. The wide glacial valley has a few houses and corrals, herds of alpacas and llamas, and large flocks of *huayatas* (Andean geese) that share the pasture. The first three lakes in the valley (**Lagunas Pauchinta** or Ttojacocha, Isicocha, and Chaupicocha, respectively) all have dams at their outflows. After 5.4 km

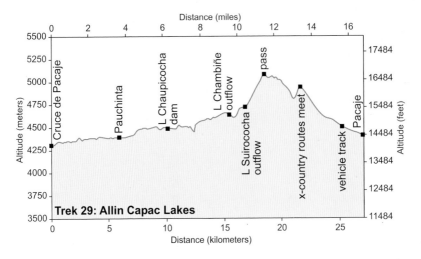

Trek 29: Allin Capac Lakes

of easy pleasant road-walking through this pastoral landscape, you pass the tiny hamlet of **Pauchinta**, with views of a pretty waterfall in the outflow of Isicocha.

The road climbs more steeply ahead (take shortcuts to avoid the zigzags), and then levels off again as you make you way around the east shore of **Laguna Isicocha**. At 4.2 km from Pauchinta the road ends at a large dam on the outflow of **Laguna Chaupicocha**. From the base of the dam, climb the steep concrete stairway and take the trail that contours along the slope above the lakeshore. Be careful here, as the bank is steep and the water is very cold. Follow the trail north along the east side of Chaupicocha for 2 km to a stone hut and corrals, then 650 m farther to a flat spot suitable for **camping**.

The next three lakes ahead are smaller, very scenic, and collectively known as **Lagunas Huascanipampa**. They have peninsulas, coves, and a few islands in the deep blue water, home to many birds. The trail continues north on the east side of the drainage, and beyond the three lakes it climbs more steeply to reach a notch, 2.2 km past the camping spot mentioned above. The notch has superb views over Laguna Chambiñe, the highest large lake of the valley, and the glaciated summits beyond.

This is a perfect spot for a break to consider your options, as here Treks 29 and 30 divide. Even if you would like to continue on Trek 29, you may wish to follow the very difficult and beautiful route of Trek 30 along the southeast shore of Laguna Chambiñe as far as the next campsite. From this camp you could make a day trip to the pass, see Trek 30 for details. You must return the same way you went in order to resume Trek 29 as described below.

Descend northwest cross-country from the notch to the outflow of **Laguna Chambiñe**, 300 m away. Ford the ankle-deep outflow and head southwest along animal tracks on the north side of the drainage. Climb steeply southwest on the rocky slope to cross a ridge 1.2 km ahead. There are **camping** possibilities near an irrigation canal nearby. Follow the canal upstream to its intake from the unnamed stream that is the outflow of **Laguna Suirococha**. The intake is 400 m past the ridge and 1.5 km southeast of Suirococha. Here begins a steep climb west to a high pass, not clearly visible until

SOUTH AMERICAN CAMELIDS

No picture of Peru's highlands would be complete without them. Llamas and alpacas are domestic, they are a source of meat and wool, their excrement is used for fuel, and llamas are pack animals. Vicuñas and guanacos are wild; in some communities vicuñas are captured, shorn, and released. As their name suggests, Andean camelids are related to camels and dromedaries. They graze, chew their cud, and are said to spit with impressive accuracy when threatened. They have a split upper lip which prevents them from destroying the roots of fragile plants they feed on, and they walk on a callus pad, which also protects the vegetation. Camelids defecate in communal dung piles, which they carefully avoid when grazing, thus limiting parasite infestation. They are social animals usually seen in herds and communicate with each other using humming sounds and body movements.

The largest and toughest of the Andean camelids is the llama (*Lama glama*), weighing up to 140 kg. The tips of its ears are bent inward, giving it a characteristic appearance. Llamas feed on even the roughest pasture and can carry loads of up to 45 kg. Their long, thick coat can be shorn every two years, yielding 4 kg of rough wool used to make clothing and blankets. The alpaca (*Vicugna pacos*) weighs up to 80 kg and has longer, finer wool than the llama. It also has a woollier face, flatter snout, and rounder rump. Alpacas are more particular about their diet, grazing mostly around boggy *bofedales*. There are two types of alpaca: the more common *huacaya*, with curly wool ideal for spinning, and the *suri*, with longer silky hair used for high-quality knits. Alpacas are shorn every two years and yield about 5 kg of fine wool. Llamas and alpacas can interbreed to produce a *huarizo*, although this is not common.

The smallest of the Andean camelids is the vicuña (*Vicugna vicugna*), Peru's national animal, found on the country's coat of arms. An adult weighs about 55 kg. Vicuñas are very graceful and delicate, with long, slender necks and legs. Their coat is reddish brown on the back, and they have fluffy white bibs and undersides. Vicuñas have resisted repeated efforts to domesticate them. They live in herds of one male and its harem of females, grazing in dry as well as boggy areas. Vicuña wool is extremely soft and warm. During the Inca Empire it was reserved for the emperor's exclusive use. Since colonial times vicuñas were hunted

Vicuña

Llamas

for their hides and came to the verge of extinction in the 1960s but were subsequently protected. A 2012 census counted 208,000 vicuñas in Peru, a forty-fold increase since 1964; Ayacucho and Puno have the largest numbers. Many highland communities have revived the ancient tradition of *chaku*, an annual vicuña roundup using human chains. The vicuñas are captured and shorn (each animal once every three years) and yield 200 g of wool priced at US$500 per kilo. Unfortunately, the increase in numbers, contact with other camelids, and the *chaku* have all fostered proliferation of vicuña diseases. Of particular concern is *sarna* (scabies), a skin disease that can debilitate a vicuña to the point that it stops eating. The mortality rate may be as high as 10 percent.

The largest of the wild Andean camelids is the guanaco (*Lama guani-coe*). It looks like an oversized vicuña, weighing about 90 kg. Guanacos are good swimmers and runners, reaching 55 km/hr. They are nonetheless easy prey for their natural predators and human hunters. This predation and habitat loss threatens the survival of the species. In 2005 there were fewer than four thousand guanacos in Peru, mostly in the departments of La Libertad, Arequipa, and Ayacucho.

Alpacas

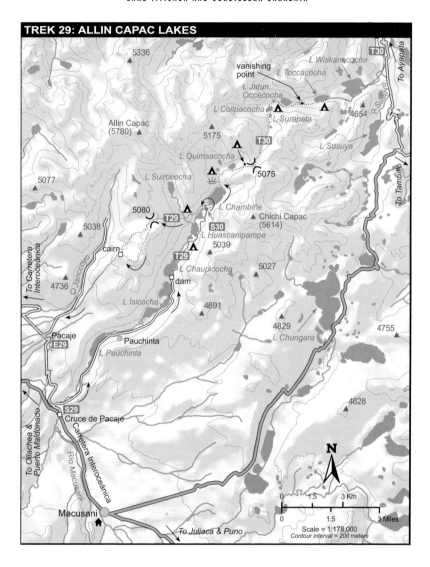

you are quite close to it. Follow livestock trails and your compass cross-country over grazed slope and then rocky terrain to the multiple *apachetas* at the 5080-m-high **pass**, with great views of both Allin Capac and Chichi Capac. Keep an eye out for vicuña and taruca in this area.

There are two possible cross-country routes ahead, both requiring about the same amount of time and effort. One goes southwest (bearing 200 degrees) along the ridge that divides the drainage of the lakes to the east from that of Quebrada Janccoyo (Janjoyo) to the west, then turns west (295 degrees) after 3 km to descend steeply along a perpendicular ridge for 1 km toward Quebrada Janccoyo. The other route is more direct, heading farther west of south (225 degrees) along the slope of the same ridge, but it climbs in and out of various deep side valleys along the way. It meets the first route in 3.5 km by a **cairn** at an elevation of 4940 m. The second option is shown in the elevation profile.

Continue descending southwest above the south side of **Quebrada Janccoyo**, looking back from time to time for views of the spectacular southeast face of Allin Capac, in all its glory at the head of the *quebrada*. Some 45 km to the east, you can also see the immense glacier of Quelcaya described in Trek 21. You gradually pick up a trail and after 3.7 km join a vehicle track. Follow the track southwest to **Pacaje**, 1.8 km ahead. Unfortunately, Pacaje is not the most hospitable town in Peru, and it would be ideal to arrive in time to catch the 1:00 PM *combi* to Macusani. This is not feasible starting from the campsite by the outflow of Suirococha, so you could either camp in Quebrada Janccoyo well above Pacaje (ask permission near homes) or hope to catch private transport later in the day even though there is not much traffic.

Return. Combis leave Pacaje for Macusani on Monday to Friday at 6:00 AM and 1:00 PM. Otherwise it is 4.7 km of road-walking with shortcuts from Pacaje to the paved highway and another 5.4 km from there to Macusani.

30 CARABAYA TRAVERSE
ALL AROUND ALLIN CAPAC

Rating: Very difficult 103-km, 12- to 14-day trek
Elevation: 2680 to 5075 m
Maps: IGN 1:100,000 Macusani (29v), Ayapata (28v), Corani (28u); ESCALE Puno (Carabaya)
Water: Abundant along most of the route
Hazards and annoyances: Fog, rain, and snow (more common here than on other highland trekking routes, due to proximity to the Amazon jungle). Fighting bulls graze near a small section of the trail between Ollachea and Corani.
Permits and fees: None
Services and provisions: Simple accommodations, meals, and well-stocked shops are found in Ayapata, Ollachea, and Aymaña. Shops in smaller villages along the route may stock a few essential items. Bring specialty items from Puno or Juliaca.

YOU CANNOT TREK MUCH farther off the tourist trail in Peru than this route. It takes in a cross-section of real life in the Cordillera Carabaya ranging from the sublime to the squalid, from views of the immense glaciers of Quelcaya to the mine-marred landscape around Ollachea. Along the way are a long list of natural and man-made wonders, as well as a few disappointments. A river vanishes before your eyes while another divides straddling a ridge. You travel difficult cross-country routes along seemingly endless chains of lakes, ancient roads that once led to the Inca's own mines, wide trails

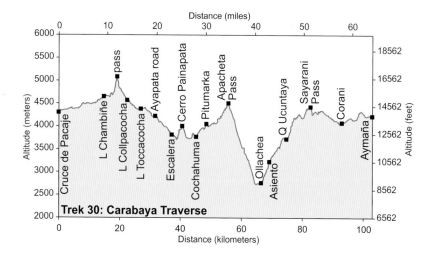

marked with milestones, and brand-new vehicle tracks that have just wrecked one of the above. A highlight is the pre-Inca Pitumarka archaeological site, reached by a stone stairway through a waterfall. All the while you are making a wide circumnavigation of Allin Capac (5780 m), the senior *apu* of Carabaya.

Access. See Trek 29.

Route: **Macusani to Escalera.** Follow **Trek 29** from either Cruce de Pacaje or in reverse from Pacaje village, to the outflow of Laguna Chambiñe. The Trek 29 map covers the route as far as Laguna Wiskanacocha in greater detail than the Trek 30 map.

From the notch above the outflow of **Laguna Chambiñe**, a clear trail heads north along the east shore of the lake but deteriorates rapidly after reaching a boulder field, 350 m ahead. Just beyond is a short hazardous section where you cross a bare rock face on a narrow ledge, ending in a steep ravine that might run with water after rain. The trail is vague ahead, making for difficult cross-country travel over tussock-covered slopes alternating with scree and boulder fields. In 1.1 km you reach an inflow at the northeast corner of the lake. Superb views of glaciated summits behind the azure blue water make the effort worthwhile.

Beyond the inflow the trail is again clearer as it turns northwest to climb above the north shore, 500 m to a second inflow. Follow the trail upstream along this inflow, north to a large flat bog. The trail contours north, skirting the bog on its east side, and reaches a very pretty little pond, 700 m after you met the second inflow. In addition to this pond, there are three larger ones in the area known as **Lagunas Quimsacocha** (Three Lakes), with many **camping** opportunities. Head northeast to cross the outflow of the largest lake and climb steeply over a rock promontory, then continue east toward the pass clearly visible ahead. One km beyond the outflow is a small stream and flat ground at 4835 m, the last potential **camping** spot before the pass.

From either Quimsacocha or the high camp, get an early start for the pass, as the going is difficult and weather is unpredictable. Climb east cross-country, first over *ichu*, then rocky terrain toward a large black rock face marking the right edge of the couloir leading up to the unnamed **pass**. After the black face, stay on the right side of the couloir all the way to the top at 5075 m, 1.1 km beyond the high camp. The pass, marked with a couple of scattered cairns, is quite broad and invites exploration for great views on both sides. Head north for about 150 m over rocks and pink glacial flour, and look for a couloir descending north into a deep valley with several lakes.

The steep descent begins at longitude 70.36409 degrees west (WGS84), latitude 13.92016 south, altitude 5048 m. Head north, then northeast, down over scree and flour toward a seasonal pond that marks the top of a short, narrow ravine flanked by black rock walls, 450 m from the start of the descent. Beyond the ravine the valley again widens and the gradient is more gentle. Continue northeast cross-country over a series of platforms with ponds (some seasonal, not all shown on the maps) separated by former terminal moraines. Despite all the flat ground, it is too stony to camp comfortably until you reach **Laguna Surapata** at 4600 m, 2.6 km past the ravine. The entire valley speaks eloquently of ancient glaciation and recent meltdown.

The next moraine separates Surapata from **Laguna Collpacocha** below. Make your way down 700 m past Surapata and around the east shore of Collpacocha, where there are more potential **camping** spots and great views of the east side of Allin Capac. Continue north to an unnamed little lake 600 m from Collpacocha, the last of the valley you have been descending from the pass. Turn east here to follow the south side of a larger valley and the next chain of ponds and lakes ahead.

Contour around the south side of **Laguna Jatun Occecocha**, then cross its outflow and continue east to the next unnamed pond and follow its outflow downstream. At 2.4 km from where you turned east into the larger valley, the streambed abruptly runs dry and the water disappears underground. After this unusual **vanishing point**, the next pond is completely dry. Continue east along its south side, up and over an old moraine, to reach **Laguna Toccacocha**, a larger lake 1 km ahead. A further 800 m east along the south shore are a large cairn, seasonally occupied huts, and **camping** possibilities. The area is heavily grazed, and there are floating trout farms in the lake.

From the huts a faint trail runs east and soon begins to climb steeply over a rocky promontory high above the lake. In still weather the water beautifully mirrors the surrounding crags. The trail then drops to a set of deep, narrow valleys at the east end of the lake, a great place to spot vizcachas (see Hopping Stones, Chapter 2). Climb east through the southernmost (rightmost) valley. At the top is a saddle with a large cairn and a faint trail headed for the south shore of **Laguna Wiskanacocha** (Huascaricocha), the most easterly and largest of the lakes in the valley.

At 1.9 km past the huts of Toccacocha, the trail descends to cross a glacial valley with several stone houses and corrals, then contours above the south side of Wiskanacocha to its outflow, 1.2 km ahead. Cross the outflow, **Río Wiskanamayo**, and follow it northeast downstream to a second crossing on a rough stone bridge. Then cross the **Río Susuya** just above from its confluence with the Wiskanamayo and follow the east side of the valley downstream to meet both a wide ancient trail and the gravel **road to Ayapata**, 1.8 km past Laguna Wiskanacocha.

Laguna Toccacocha in the hinterland behind Allin Capac

The trail runs north parallel to the road, between it and the Río Susuya. Descend gradually through the broad valley filled with stone houses, corrals, and herds of grazing llamas. Many of the homes are abandoned, as people have moved to villages and now commute by motorbike to tend their flocks. The area offers numerous **camping** possibilities. In 3.1 km you reach an impressive 50-m-long low **stone bridge** over the Río Susuya, possibly of Inca origin. On the far side of the bridge a trail climbs to Laguna Umajia, and we were told it continues to Laguna Taype. We did not cross the bridge, and instead continued downstream on a combination of trail and road to the friendly village of **Escalera**, 2.4 km ahead. As its name suggests, the ancient road descended over a stairway here, and some nice sections remain intact.

You can end the trek in Escalera and take a van back to Macusani; see Return, below. If you need to resupply in order to continue, you should visit the larger town of Ayapata, 9 km north along the road. Motorcycles provide transport from Escalera to Ayapata or you can walk, but it is an uninspiring stroll, mostly along the vehicle road with a couple of shortcuts near Ayapata. To resume the trek you can either return to Escalera, or road-walk or take sporadic transport from Ayapata to Taype or Cochahuma (9 km most frequent on Sunday).

Route: **Escalera to Ollachea.** If you return to Escalera as we did, take a trail west from the village, down and across the two rivers in the valley floor, 400 m to the hamlet of **Pizarropampa**. From here climb northwest cross-country, zigzagging alongside potato fields for 2.5 km to cross a ridge on **Cerro Painapata**. You pick up a trail near the top and descend 1.4 km west along this stony path toward the outflow at the east end of **Laguna Taype** below. The outflow is spanned by another low stone bridge, interesting to explore, but do not cross it as our trail heads west along the south side of the lake.

Follow the shore, then climb steadily to reach the hamlet of **Chaccone**, where you might ask for permission to camp, 2.3 km from the outflow.

A steep, narrow trail descends for 800 m alongside a small stream from Chaccone to the slightly larger village of **Cochahuma**, crossing the inflow of Laguna Taype on a cement bridge. Cochahuma is the end of the road from Ayapata and the start of a wide signed trail west to Ollachea, our route ahead marked by concrete milestones. Climb gently along the north side of the valley for 900 m to a signed fork: right directly to Ollachea; left via the Pitumarka archaeological site, a detour with more difficult navigation but well worth the extra effort. Follow the left branch, a slightly smaller trail, past an impressive waterfall and climb 1 km west to **Laguna Q'añacota**. This lake is ringed by reedy marshes, and the surrounding hillsides are filled with ancient stone corrals and houses. In the middle of the turquoise water is a single island with mummies, ceramics, and textiles in situ, which can be visited with advance arrangements in Cochahuma.

The trail ahead is difficult to follow. Head south on the west side of Q'añacota, across several streams and stone walls, 1.2 km to the outflow of **Laguna Allpicota**, a very pretty intensely turquoise little lake surrounded by high cliffs. Follow the east shore of Allpicota south to the base of a waterfall that feeds the inflow of the lake. There are good **camping** possibilities nearby. The way forward here is unbelievable; you climb a stone stairway right through the middle of the cascade! Past the end of the stairway, ford the stream from right to left (west to east) and clamber over a low stone wall. Here the stream you have been climbing (outflow of Laguna Quentayane to the south) curiously divides: one branch flows southeast to Q'añacota, the other south to Allpicota. On your left is a trail leading to a curved stone stairway and the archaeological site of **Pitumarka**, strategically located atop a promontory separating Allpicota and Q'añacota. There are many ancient stone structures here, and the 1.5-hectare site receives its share of visitors, judging by the amount of trash. Pitumarka is a pre-Inca World Heritage Site dating from the 12th century AD.

Return the way you came as far as the outflow of Allpicota (about 1 km round-trip) and cross it on a small stone bridge. Head northwest cross-country along the west side of a valley rising north from the lake. It's slow going over stone walls, by corrals and tilled fields, 1 km to a wooden footbridge, where the wide trail from Cochahuma to Ollachea crosses the outflow of the unnamed lake west of Q'añacota. Follow the trail west along the south shore for 650 m to cross another footbridge over the outflow of the next, also unnamed, lake. Follow the trail west as it climbs above the north shore, past the end of the lake and on to cross its inflow 1.7 km past the second bridge. Continue climbing steadily west along the slope of the ridge above *Lagunas* **Negrococha** and **Chillacocha**, to reach **Apacheta Pass** at 4500 m, 2.5 km ahead. Condors may be seen at the pass, and, not surprisingly, it has an *apacheta* (stone cairn).

From the pass follow the trail west down into the deep Tambillo valley, at first through open country with many streams and bogs but enough flat dry ground for adequate **camping**. Great views ahead include the immense glacier of Quelcaya described in Trek 21. After a shallow ford, 1.4 km from the pass, head west along the south side of **Quebrada Tambillo**. As you descend, the vegetation becomes more lush and the trail

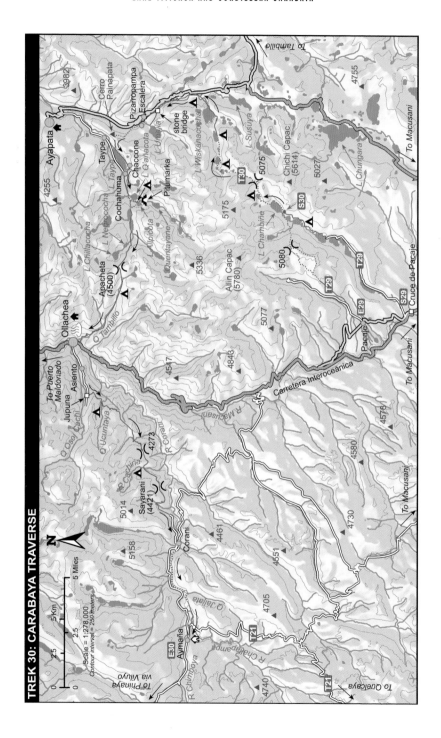

TREK 30: CARABAYA TRAVERSE

Scale = 1:278,000
Contour interval = 250 meters

0   2.5   5 Km
0   2.5   5 Miles

N

narrower and less distinct. In 4.5 km you cross to the north side of the *quebrada* on a rough wooden bridge and move away from the drainage to travel northwest high above it. After 600 m you reach a solitary cross with views to Ollachea in the Río Macusani valley below.

It is another 1.2 km of zigzag descent along forested slope to a concrete footbridge over Quebrada Tambillo, just upstream from its confluence with the **Río Macusani**. After crossing, head down to the shore of the Río Macusani and follow it upstream a short distance to a road and vehicle bridge. The municipal thermal baths are nearby, a welcome sight after many unwashed days on the trail, as well as views of an impressive 50-m-high waterfall. The mining supply town of **Ollachea** is 1 km uphill. You can end the trek here and return to Macusani (see Return, below) or resupply and continue on, but there is not much reason to hang around.

Route: **Ollachea to Aymaña.** From Ollachea climb along the unpaved road to Asiento, 3 km using several shortcuts along the way. The road follows **Quebrada Osoj Cachi**, filled with helter-skelter shacks and machinery used for informal gold mining. The disfigured landscape is a sad sight, and you can't even see all the mercury and cyanide being dumped into the river. Continue along the road past the spread-out hamlet of **Asiento** for 1.6 km to a fork and take the left branch. There are lovely waterfalls at the head of the *quebrada* that have so far escaped the miners. In 1.7 km the road brings you to an uninhabited area called **Jupuna**, with a couple of small stone structures on the right surrounded by potato fields. Ahead the road crosses a small stream and becomes impassable to vehicles. Our route leaves the road before the stream and climbs south to the ridge on the left, which separates Quebrada Osoj Cachi from the Río Corani. Although the trail is wide and clear once it starts to climb, its beginning is hard to find.

Climb steeply along the stony trail to the ridgetop, 850 m past the road. Follow the trail southwest along the ridgeline, crossing a couple of wooden gates before descending to **Quebrada Ucuntaya**, 1.5 km ahead. Ford two branches of this *quebrada* just above their confluence, with good **camping** spots nearby. Look for orange lichen on the rocks here, so bright you could swear they were painted. Take water at Ucuntaya and follow the trail climbing steadily southwest through open country with impressive views of the Río Corani valley on your left. In 2.5 km you cross a fence and metal gate marking the start of an area grazed by cattle, among them fighting bulls. We never saw any but were advised not to tarry between here and the Río Cachiría ahead.

Descend gently southwest along the trail to a small stream and climb again past a few stone buildings and a large cross on the hillside to your left. At 1.6 km from the metal gate you reach a 4273-m-high **pass** marked with an *apacheta*. The next gentle descent brings you to another fence, metal gate, and wooden footbridge over the **Río Cachiría** (Calaverayoc), 1.1 km ahead. This pretty area, with waterfalls upstream and many **camping** possibilities, has unfortunately been earmarked for destruction as mining is planned and a road is being built from Corani.

From Cachiría follow the trail or road, climbing southwest through a broad valley with superb views back to the ridges you have just crossed, all the way to the glaciers of Allin Capac. In 2.1 km you reach **Sayarani Pass** (4421 m) and a fork. Take the right (upper) branch, heading west to meet the road from Corani. Do not descend south to the Río Corani, as it is a long, difficult way down, with no bridge or ford to the south side of the river, and no safe way west along the north shore. It is 11 km from the pass to **Corani**, most of which may be road-walking. Although a district capital, Corani has very few and very basic services. Unless you prefer to finish here and take transport back to Macusani, it is worth continuing on without delay for the final 10 km to Aymaña, a nice gentle finale along impressive ancient road.

From the upper part of Corani, by the plaza, colonial church, and city hall, take a trail climbing northwest 1.4 km to an *apacheta* with views of the **Río Chimboya** below. As you follow the ancient road climbing west above the south side of the Chimboya, note the stairs, paving, and stone bridge by a waterfall along the way. In 4.2 km you reach **Quebrada Jaljata** and a fork; take the right branch, heading west. Climb out of the *quebrada* and pass through an area of *Bosque de Piedra* (rock formations, see Trek 21) for which the area is famous. In 700 m you reach a notch with views of Aymaña in the broad valley below. The trail loses much of its ancient character here, but 1.5 km ahead it still crosses an old stone bridge over the **Río Challapampa**. Pass the cemetery just beyond the bridge and continue 2.1 km to Aymaña.

The flat village of **Aymaña** with its dusty streets and modest tin-roofed houses is not much to look at, but it has a comfortable *tambo*, various shops, and is surrounded by extensive rock formations and caves with rock art, worth taking time to explore; the caves are hard to find, so ask someone to guide you. Aymaña is also the connection to Trek 21 from the Cordillera Vilcanota in Cuzco.

Return. Several vans a day run from Ayapata to Macusani, a 1.5-hour trip, but note that they might be full when they pass Escalera. From Ollachea there is van service to Macusani and Juliaca, as well as to Puerto Maldonado in the jungle. From Aymaña and Corani, see Return in Trek 21.

Opposite: *Sacsarayoc (5991 m) at sunset*

SECTION III

APPENDICES

APPENDIX A: RESOURCES

The following resources are organized by chapter and heading. Under each heading, the printed, online, and on-site resources are listed together in alphabetical order. Peruvian web pages are in Spanish unless otherwise indicated. Links to all resources are provided on www.trekkingperu.org.

CHAPTER 1 TREKKING IN PERU

Explorers and Trekkers

Bingham, Hiram. "Further Exploration in the Land of the Incas." In *National Geographic Magazine*, vol 24, no. 5, May 1916.

——. *Lost City of the Incas* (1948). New York: Atheneum, 1979.

Cieza de León, Pedro. *El Señorío de los Incas, Segunda parte de la Crónica del Perú* (1553). Lima: Instituto de Estudios Peruanos, 1967.

——. *The Discovery and Conquest of Peru* (1553). Translated by Alexandra Parma Cook and Noble David Cook. Durham, NC: Duke University Press, 1999.

Espinosa, Ricardo. *El Perú a Toda Costa*, Lima: Editur, 1997.

——. *La Gran Ruta Inca: El Capaq Ñan* (Spanish and English). Lima: PetroPerú, 2002.

Frost, Peter. *Exploring Cuzco*, 6th ed. Published by the author, www.peterfrost.org. Cuzco, 2017.

Honigsbaum, Mark. *The Fever Trail*. London: Macmillan, 2001.

Hyslop, John. *The Inka Road System*. New York: Academic Press, 1984.

Lee, Vincent R. *Forgotten Vilcabamba*. Published by the author, www.vince-lee.com. Wilson, WY: Sixpac Manco Publications, 2000.

Markham, Clements R. *Travels in Peru and India* (London: John Murray, 1862). Cambridge: Cambridge University Press, 2012.

Raimondi, Antonio. *El Perú: itinerarios de viajes* (1876). Lima: Banco Italiano de Lima, 1929. Accessible online at www.cervantesvirtual.com.

Savoy, Gene. *Antisuyo*. New York: Simon and Shuster, 1970.

Squier, E. George. *Peru Illustrated* (New York: Hurst & Company, 1877). Whitefish, MT: Literary Licensing, 2014.

Varela, Felipe: chaski-rutasdechaski.blogspot.com

von Hagen, Victor W. *Highway of the Sun*. Toronto: Little, Brown and Company, 1955.

von Humboldt, Alexander. *Cosmos* (original in German, 1845, New York: Harper & Brothers, 1858–59). Baltimore: Johns Hopkins University Press, 1997.

Weberbauer, August. *El mundo vegetal de los Andes peruanos*. Lima: Ministerio de Agricultura, 1945.

Weberbauer, August. (1871), and J. Francis Macbride (1892). *Flora of Peru*. Fieldiana Botany, vol 13, no. 1 Chicago: Field Museum of Natural History, 1936. Also see www.sacha.org.

Wright, Ronald. *Cut Stones and Crossroads*. New York: Penguin Books, 1986. Also see www.ronaldwright.com.

Zimmerman, Arthur F. *Francisco de Toledo: Fifth Viceroy of Peru 1566–1881*. Caldwell, ID: The Caxton Printers, Ltd., 1938.

CHAPTER 2 PERU AND ITS PEOPLE

Background Information

Instituto Nacional de Estadística e Informática, vital statistics of Peru:
www.inei.gob.pe/biblioteca-virtual/publicaciones-digitales

Online English newspapers: www.peruthisweek.com and www.peruviantimes.com

Online Peruvian bookshop: www.librosperuanos.com

United Nations human development report about Peru: www.hdr.undp.org

World Bank development indicators for Peru: http://data.worldbank.org/country/peru

Climate

El Niño website: www.climate.gov/enso

Servicio Nacional de Meteorología e Hidrología del Perú (SENAMHI): www.senamhi.gob.pe

Flora and Fauna

Andean Botanical Information System, list of South American flora from the Chicago Field Museum: www.sacha.org (Spanish/English).

Brako, Lois, and James L Zarucchi. *Catalogue of the Flowering Plants and Gymnosperms of Peru.* St. Louis: Missouri Botanical Garden, 1993.

Byers, Clive. *Pocket Photo Guide to the Birds of Peru.* London: Bloomsbury Natural History, 2016.

Cheshire, Gerard, Huw Lloyd, and Barry Walker. *Peruvian Wildlife: A Visitor's Guide to the Central Andes.* UK: Bradt Travel Guides, 2008.

Dean, Robert, illustrator. *Peru Birds* (Laminated Foldout Pocket Field Guide). Camano Island, WA: Rainforest Publications, 2014. In the same series, other Peru bird guides and *Peru Mammals Guide.*

Espinosa, Ricardo. *Areas Naturales Protegidas.* Lima: SERNANP/PROFONANPE, 2010. English edition: https://issuu.com/wendsmz/docs/ilovepdf_merged

Fondo de Promoción de las áreas Naturales Protegidas del Perú, PROFONANPE (Peruvian trust fund for national parks and protected areas): www.profonanpe.org.pe (Spanish/English).

International Union for the Conservation of Nature, red list of endangered species: www.iucnredlist.org.

Kolff, Helen. *Wildflowers of the Cordillera Blanca,* 2nd ed. Lima: The Mountain Institute, 2005.

Ministerio del Ambiente: www.minam.gob.pe

Missouri Botanical Garden database of flora: www.tropicos.org

Pearson, David L., and Les Beletsky. *Travellers' Wildlife Guides Peru,* 4th ed. Boston: Interlink Books, 2014.

Peru Wildlife: www.peruwildlife.info

Schulenberg, Thomas S., et al. *Birds of Peru.* Princeton, NJ: Princeton University Press, 2007, reprinted 2010.

Servicio Nacional de Áreas Naturales Protegidas por el Estado (SERNANP), includes list of national parks and protected areas: www.sernanp.gob.pe

The Plant List (Kew Gardens and Missouri Botanical Garden): www.theplantlist.org

Venero, José L., Alfredo Tupayachi, and Washington Loayza. *Guía de Aves y Flora, Laguna Orurillo.* Municipalidad Distrital de Orurillo, 2012. Available from josvengon@gmail.com.

Walker, Barry. *Field Guide to the Birds of Machu Picchu and the Cusco Region.* Barcelona: Lynx Edicions, 2015.

Conservation

Asociación Ecosistemas Andinos: www.ecoanperu.org (Spanish/English)

Asociación OIKOS: www.oikos.pe

Asociación Peruana para la Conservación de la Naturaleza: www.apeco.org.pe

Conservación Internacional Perú: www.conservation.org/global/peru

Fundación Peruana para la Conservación de la Naturaleza, Pronaturaleza: www.pronaturaleza.org (Spanish/English)

Perú Ecológico: www.peruecologico.com.pe

Sociedad Peruana de Derecho Ambiental (SPDA): www.actualidadambiental.pe

World Wildlife Fund (WWF) Peru: peru.panda.org

Aboriginal Cultures, Archaeology, and History

Achaeological sites: www.ancient-wisdom.com/peru.htm and www.arqueologiadelperu.com.ar

Bauer, Brian S. "Suspension Bridges of the Inca Empire," in *Andean Archaeology*, vol 3, 2006. Helaine Silverman and William H. Isbell, eds. Available from www.academia.edu.

Garcilaso de la Vega, Inca. *Royal Commentaries of the Incas and General History of Peru, Parts I and II* (1609). Translated by H. V. Livermore. Austin: University of Texas Press, 1966.

Guamán Poma de Ayala, Felipe. *Nueva Crónica y Buen Gobierno* (1583–1615). Francisco Carrillo, ed. Lima: Horizonte, 2012.

Hemming, John. *The Conquest of the Incas.* San Diego: Harcourt Brace Jovanovich, 1970.

Hostnig, Rainer. *Carabaya: Paisajes y cultura milenaria.* Cuzco. Published by the author, rainer.hostnig@gmail.com, 2010.

Kendall, Ann. "Terraced Agriculture for Food Security in the Peruvian Andes: Sustainability in the Past and the Present." In *Symposium: Food Economics of Pre-Columbian and Colonial America.* 52nd International Congress of Americanists, Seville, 2006. Available from www.cusichaca.org.

Matos, Ramiro, and Jose Barreiro, eds. *The Great Inka Road: Engineering an Empire.* Washington, DC: Smithsonian Books, 2015.

Ministerio de Cultura, Qhapac Ñan: www.qhapaqnan.cultura.pe

Mosely, Michael E. *The Incas and their Ancestors: The Archaeology of Peru.* New York: Thames and Hudson, 2001.

United Nations World Heritage Convention, information about Peru's twelve heritage sites, including the Capac Ñan: whc.unesco.org

Religion and Fiestas

Peruvian festival calendar: www.peru.travel/what-to-do/festivities-and-events

CHAPTER 3 WHAT TO EXPECT

Peruvian Government Tourist Office
iPerú: phone (01) 574 8000 (24 hours), www.peru.travel

Community Accommodations
Tambos: http://apu.vivienda.gob.pe/tambook

Maps and Navigation
Burns, Bob, and Mike Burns. *Wilderness Navigation*, 3rd ed. Seattle: Mountaineers Books, 2015.

Instituto Geográfico Nacional (IGN): Av Aramburú 1190-1198, Surquillo, Lima, phone (01) 475 9960, comercializacion@ign.gob.pe, www.ign.gob.pe, Monday to Friday 8:15 AM to 4:30 PM.

Maratón, Av de la Cultura 1020, Cuzco, phone (084) 225 387.

Librerías San Francisco, branches at Portal de Flores 138, San Francisco 102-106, and San Francisco 133-135, all in Arequipa.

Lima 2000. www.lima2000.com.pe

Ministerio de Educación, Estadística de la Calidad Educativa (ESCALE): escale.minedu.gob.pe; direct links to download ESCALE maps are found on www.trekkingperu.org.

Österreichischer Alpenverein. www.alpenverein.at

CHAPTER 4 PREPARATIONS

Travel Guidebooks and Tourist Information
Box, Ben. *South American Handbook 2017*, 93rd ed. Bath, UK: Footprint Travel Guides, 2016.

Hornberger, Esteban, and Nancy Hornberger. *Diccionario Trilingüe Quechua de Cusco* (Quechua, English and Spanish), 4th ed. Cuzco: Centro Bartolomé de las Casas, 2013.

iPerú, Peruvian government tourist office. www.peru.travel (multilingual)

Kunstaetter, Robert, Daisy Kunstaetter, and Ben Box. *Footprint Handbook Peru*, 9th ed. Bath, UK: Footprint Travel Guides, 2015.

——. *Peru, Bolivia & Ecuador Handbook.* 5th ed. Bath, UK: Footprint Travel Guides, 2017.

Jenkins, Dilwyn, and Kiki Deere. *The Rough Guide to Peru.* 9th ed. London: Penguin Random House, 2015.

Ministerio de Cultura, includes cultural calendar: www.cultura.gob.pe/en/eventos

Lonely Planet Peru, 9th ed. Melbourne, Australia: Lonely Planet, 2016.

Peru Insight Guides, 8th ed. London: Insight Guides, 2015.

Trekking Guidebooks and Trekking Information
Benson, Sara, et al. *Trekking in Peru*, Melbourne: Lonely Planet, 2008.

Bradt, Hilary, and Kathy Jarvis. *Trekking in Peru.* UK: Bradt Travel Guides, 2014.

Frimer, Jeremy. *Climbs and Treks in the Cordillera Huayhuash of Peru.* Squamish, BC: ELAHO, 2005.

Janecek, William. *Hiking and Biking Peru's Inca Trails.* Milnthorpe, UK: Cicerone Press, 2013.

Pike, Neil, and Harriet Pike. *Peru's Cordilleras Blanca & Huayhuash: The Hiking & Biking Guide.* Hindhead, UK: Trailblazer Guides, 2015.

Stewart, Alexander. *The Inca Trail: Cusco & Machu Picchu,* 5th ed. Hindhead, UK: Trailblazer Publications, 2013.

Trekking Peru—the authors' website for this book: www.trekkingperu.org

Passport and Visas

Ministerio de Relaciones Exteriores, for list of countries that require a visa to enter Peru: www.rree.gob.pe/servicioalciudadano (click on "Requerimento de visa para ciudadanos extranjeros" on right side of page).

Money and Prices

Banco Central de Reserva del Perú (BCRP): www.bcrp.gob.pe

Domestic Airlines

Avianca: www.avianca.com

LATAM: www.latam.com

LC Peru: www.lcperu.pe

Peruvian Airlines: www.peruvianairlines.pe

Star Perú: www.starperu.com

Bus Companies

Cruz del Sur: www.cruzdelsur.com.pe

Móvil Tours: www.moviltours.com.pe

Oltursa: www.oltursa.pe

Ormeño: www.grupo-ormeno.com.pe

CHAPTER 5 AN OUNCE OF PREVENTION

Staying Healthy

Bezruchka, Stephen. *Altitude Illness: Prevention and Treatment,* 2nd ed. Seattle: Mountaineers Books, 2005.

Centers for Disease Control (CDC), USA: www.cdc.gov

Duff, Jim, and Peter Gormly. *Pocket First Aid and Wilderness Medicine,* 11th ed. Cumbria, UK: Cicerone Press, 2013.

Scottish Centre for Infection and Environmental Health (SCIEH). www.fitfortravel.scot.nhs.uk

Weiss, Eric. *Wilderness and Travel Medicine,* 4th ed. Seattle: Mountaineers Books, 2012.

Wilkerson, James A. *Medicine for Mountaineering and Other Wilderness Activities.* 6th ed. Seattle: Mountaineers Books, 2010.

World Health Organization (WHO): www.who.int/ith

CHAPTER 7 Chachapoyas

Trek 1 Gocta

Gocta Andes Lodge, Cocachimba: www.goctalodge.com

CHAPTER 8 Cordillera Blanca

Services and Contacts

Café Andino, Huaraz: www.cafeandino.com

Casa de Guías, Huaraz: Plaza Ginebra, Huaraz, (043) 421 811. Monday to Saturday
9:00 AM to 1:00 PM and 4:00 PM to 6:00 PM

The Lazy Dog Inn, outside Huaraz: www.thelazydoginn.com

Parque Nacional Huascarán, Jr Federico Sal y Rosas 555, by Plazuela Belén, Huaraz, phone (043)
422 086, pnhuascaran@sernanp.gob.pe, Monday–Friday 8:30 AM to 1:00 PM and 2:30 to 5:00 PM

Pony's Expeditions, Caraz: www.ponyexpeditions.com

Refugios Andinos mountain shelters: www.rifugi-omg.org (in Italian)

Trek 10 Pomabamba to Chacas

Andes Lodge Peru: www.andeslodgeperu.com

CHAPTER 9 Central Highlands

Museo de la Memoria ANFASEP: Prolongación Libertad 1229 (cuadra 14), Ayacucho, phone (066)
317 170, Monday to Saturday 9:00 AM to 1:00 PM and 3:00 PM to 6:00 PM.

Trek 13 Llocllapampa to Huarochirí

de Ávila, Francisco. *Dioses y hombres de Huarochirí* (c. 1598–1608). Translated from Quechua to
Spanish by José M. Arguedas. Lima: Instituto de Estudios Peruanos, 1966.

——. *Ritos y tradiciones de Huarochirí* (Quechua–Spanish text). Gerald Taylor, ed. Lima: Instituto de
Estudios Peruanos, Instituto Francés de Estudios Andinos, 2008.

CHAPTER 10 Cuzco

Services and Contacts

Association of Official Tour Guides (AGOTUR), Calle Heladeros 157, office 34-F, Cuzco, phone
(084) 233 457

Trek 18 Huchuy Cuzco

Boleto Turístico de Cuzco (BTC): www.cosituc.gob.pe

Trek 19 Q'eswachaca

The Last Bridge Master, Noonday Films, 2016: www.thelastbridgemaster.com

Trek 21 Vilcanota to Carabaya

Cayetano Crispín, Hostal Tinqui, Tinqui, phone 974 327 538, Cuzco contact (084) 227 768,
ausangate_tour@outlook.com

Trek 22 Choquequirao to Huancacalle

Casa de Salcantay hotel, Cachora: www.salcantay.com

Casa Nostra hotel, Cachora: www.choquequiraotrekk.com

CHAPTER 11 Arequipa

Services and Contacts

Casa de Guías, Pasaje Desaguadero 125, Barrio de San Lázaro, Arequipa.

Colca Canyon: www.colcaperu.gob.pe

Instituto Geofísico del Perú: www.igp.gob.pe

KAT, Calle Jerusalén 524-B, Arequipa, phone (054) 422 479, kuntur.adventure@yahoo.es

Museo Santuarios Andinos, La Merced 110, phone (054) 286-614, ext 105, Monday to Saturday 9:00 AM to 6:00 PM, Sunday 9:00 AM to 3:00 PM.

Trek 24 Cotahuasi Canyon

Purek Tours, Calle Arequipa 103, Cotahuasi, phone (054) 698 081, cotahuasitours@gmail.com

Trek 26 Valley of the Volcanoes to Colca

Grupo GEA: www.grupogea.org.pe

CHAPTER 12 Lake Titicaca and Cordillera Carabaya

Isla Suasi Hotel: www.islasuasi.pe

Richar Cáceres, Jr. Garcilazo de la Vega 506, Macusani, phone 946 680 485

Trek 27 Puente Jipata to Moho: Potatoes for All Seasons

Centro Internacional de la Papa, Lima: http://cipotato.org

APPENDIX B: GLOSSARY

The following are Spanish, Quechua (Q), or Aymara (A) terms used in the text and maps as well as a few other essential words. There are several regional dialects of Quechua, and not all terms listed here are understood in all regions. Names of common plants and animals are found in Chapter 2, foods in Chapter 4, and medical terms in Chapter 5. For a more extensive trekking vocabulary, see www.trekkingperu.org.

abajo	down
abra	mountain pass
acampar	to camp
acequia	irrigation ditch
agua	water
alco (Q, A)	dog
altiplano	high plateau, generally around Lake Titicaca
apacheta (Q)	large cairn, usually marking a mountain pass
apu (Q)	mountain deity
ari (Q)	yes
arriba	up
arriero	muleteer
auto	motor vehicle, shared taxi
auxilio	help, rescue
bodega	general store, shop
bofedal	high-altitude bog
bosque	forest
bravo	fierce, aggressive
burro	donkey
caballo	horse
calamina	metal sheet used for roofing
calaminado	washboarded (road or trail)
caliente	warm, hot
caminata	walk, hike, trek
camino	trail, footpath
camino de herradura	horse trail
camión	truck
camioneta	pickup truck
campesino	rural dweller
canal de riego	irrigation canal
cañón	canyon
capilla	chapel, shrine
carpa	tent
carretera afirmada	unpaved secondary vehicle road

carretera asfaltada	paved vehicle road
carro	motor vehicle, shared taxi
carta topográfica	topographic map
cascada	waterfall
centro poblado	small village, hamlet
cerco	fence
cerro	hill
chaca (Q)	bridge
chaki (Q)	foot
chakitaklla (Q)	foot plow
chicha	fermented corn beverage
chicha morada	purple corn beverage (not fermented)
chiri (Q)	cold
choza	hut, primitive rural dwelling
chullo (Q)	warm wool hat with ear flaps
chullpa (Q)	ancient mausoleum or funeral tower
cobertizo	open-sided animal shelter
cocha (Q)	lake, pond
colca (Q)	ancient storehouse or granary
colectivo	shared taxi
colegio	school
combi	van used for public transport
comida	food
comunero	member of a (usually indigenous) community
cordillera	mountain range
costa	coast
cultivo	crop, worked field
cumbre	summit
derecha	right
empinado	steep
enfermo	sick
escuela	school
estancia	small ranch, rural outpost
este	east
filo	edge, ridge
frío	cold
ganado	cattle
garúa	mist, very fine drizzle
glaciar	glacier
granizo	hail
guía	guide
hacienda	large ranch, landholding
helada	frost
herido	injured

hospedaje	accommodations, guesthouse
hospedaje comunitario	community guesthouse
hospedaje municipal	municipal guesthouse
huayco (Q)	landslide
huchuy (Q)	little
ichik (Q)	little
ichu (Q)	high-altitude straw
inicial	nursery school, kindergarten
izquierda	left
jatun (Q)	big
Jirón (Jr.)	street, used as the abbreviated prefix
kamisaraki (A)	How are you? (universal greeting)
lago	lake
laguna	pond, lake
lliklla (Q)	large colorful cloth used to carry bundles and babies on one's back
locutorio	public phone office, calling center
machay (Q)	cave
maki (Q)	hand
mana (Q)	no
manso	tame, gentle
mapa	map
médico	doctor
mercado	market
micuy (Q)	food
minibus, minivan	van used for public transport
minka	community work project
mirador	scenic overlook, viewpoint
mototaxi	motorized rickshaw taxi
mula	mule
nevado	snow-capped mountain
nieve	snow
norte	north
ñan (Q)	road, path
oeste	west
oroya	cable car
Pachamama (Q)	Mother Earth
páramo	high, wet Andean moorland
pastizal	pasture
peña	cliff
perro	dog
pirca (Q)	stone wall
porteador	porter
posta de salud	basic health center

precipicio	cliff
puente	bridge
puna	high dry Andean plateau
puquial (Q)	spring
qoñi (Q)	warm
quebrada	ravine, gully, valley
queñua	polylepis tree
recarga	cell phone credit
recto	straight ahead
refugio	refuge, trekking shelter
rescate	rescue
río	river
ronda, ronda campesina	community patrol
rumi (Q)	stone, rock
runa (Q)	man, person (usually indigenous)
runa ñan (Q)	people's road, foot trail
saywa (Q)	small devotional cairn placed to propitiate a safe journey
selva	jungle
serrano	highlander
sierra	highlands
su voluntad	it's up to you (referring to the amount of an offered payment or contribution)
sur	south
tambo (Q)	Inca posthouse, contemporary government accommodations (see Community Accommodations, Chapter 3)
tayta (Q)	father, old man
terminal terrestre	large intercity bus terminal
tienda	general store, shop
tinku (Q)	confluence of two rivers
tormenta	storm
toro	bull
trocha carrozable	rough vehicle track
turismo comunitario, turismo vivencial	community tourism
uno (Q)	water
vaca	cow
valle	valley
viento	wind
volcán	volcano
waliki (A)	(I am) well (reply to Aymara greeting)
warmi (Q)	woman
wayra (Q)	wind
yacu (Q)	water

APPENDIX C: UNIT CONVERSION TABLE

METRIC	ENGLISH
1 meter (m)	3.28 feet
1 kilometer (km)	0.62 miles
1 centimeter (cm)	0.39 inches
1 hectare (ha)	2.47 acres
1 square kilometer (km²)	0.39 square miles
1 kilogram (kg)	2.21 pounds
1 gram (gr)	0.035 ounces
1 liter (l)	1.06 quarts
degrees Celcius (°C)	(°F - 32) x 5/9

ENGLISH	METRIC
1 foot (ft)	0.31 meters
1 mile (mi)	1.61 kilometers
1 inch (in)	2.54 centimeters
1 acre (ac)	0.41 hectares
1 square mile (sq mi)	2.56 square kilometers
1 pound (lb)	0.45 kilograms
1 ounce (oz)	28.35 grams
1 quart (qt)	0.95 liters
degrees Fahrenheit (°F)	(°C x 9/5) + 32

INDEX

ABOUT THE AUTHORS

Robert and Daisy Kunstaetter have trekked in Peru since 1987, but Daisy had begun hiking in the Andes of her native Ecuador long before, at age five when she promptly fell into a *quebrada*. Little did she know how many more *quebradas* lay ahead.

Daisy's trail eventually led her to Montreal, Canada, for university, where she met Robert and his idea of traveling for "a year or so." Their training in medicine and occupational therapy had prepared them for a different set of challenges, so they continued their education at the National Outdoor Leadership School (NOLS), in Wyoming, USA, before hitting the road. The year proved to be elastic, and they have since traveled and trekked throughout Latin America, gradually acquiring the profession of travel writing along the way.

Since 1994 Robert and Daisy have been correspondents for annual editions of the *South American Handbook* and subsequently authors and cartographers of numerous travel guidebooks about Peru, Bolivia, and Ecuador. They are also authors of *Trekking in Ecuador* (Mountaineers Books).

Notoriously leisurely on the trail, they might be found enjoying an after-lunch siesta in the sun or chatting with *campesinos* along the way. When asked "Who is your guide?", they usually point to one another.

MOUNTAINEERS BOOKS is a leading publisher of mountaineering literature and guides—including our flagship title, *Mountaineering: The Freedom of the Hills*—as well as adventure narratives, natural history, and general outdoor recreation. Through our two imprints, Skipstone and Braided River, we also publish titles on sustainability and conservation. We are committed to supporting the environmental and educational goals of our organization by providing expert information on human-powered adventure, sustainable practices at home and on the trail, and preservation of wilderness.

The Mountaineers, founded in 1906, is a 501(c)(3) nonprofit outdoor recreation and conservation organization whose mission is to enrich lives and communities by helping people "explore, conserve, learn about, and enjoy the lands and waters of the Pacific Northwest and beyond." One of the largest such organizations in the United States, it sponsors classes and year-round outdoor activities throughout the Pacific Northwest, including climbing, hiking, backcountry skiing, snowshoeing, camping, kayaking, sailing, and more. The Mountaineers also supports its mission through its publishing division, Mountaineers Books, and promotes environmental education and citizen engagement. For more information, visit The Mountaineers Program Center, 7700 Sand Point Way NE, Seattle, WA 98115-3996; phone 206-521-6001; www.mountaineers.org; or email info@mountaineers.org.

Our publications are made possible through the generosity of donors and through sales of more than 600 titles on outdoor recreation, sustainable lifestyle, and conservation. To donate, purchase books, or learn more, visit us online:

MOUNTAINEERS BOOKS
1001 SW Klickitat Way, • Suite 201 Seattle, WA 98134
800-553-4453 • mbooks@mountaineersbooks.org • www.mountaineersbooks.org

Mountaineers Books is proud to be a corporate sponsor of The Leave No Trace Center for Outdoor Ethics, whose mission is to promote and inspire responsible outdoor recreation through education, research, and partnerships • The Leave No Trace program is focused specifically on human-powered (nonmotorized) recreation • Leave No Trace strives to educate visitors about the nature of their recreational impacts and offers techniques to prevent and minimize such impacts • Leave No Trace is best understood as an educational and ethical program, not as a set of rules and regulations • For more information, visit www.lnt.org, or call 800-332-4100.

OTHER TITLES YOU MIGHT ENJOY FROM MOUNTAINEERS BOOKS

Trekking in Eucador
Robert & Daisy Kunstaetter
Well researched and accessibly written, *Trekking in Ecuador* includes 29 trekking adventures from easy afternoons to remote excursions.

Costa Rica: National Parks and Preserves, 3rd edition
Joseph Franke
Get off the beaten path with this guide to all 46 of Costa Rica's natural areas and preserves.

The Galapagos Islands and Ecuador, 3rd edition
Marylee Stephenson
"Marylee Stephenson is brilliantly equipped to act as both armchair and practical guide to the Galapagos Islands . . . this book is required reading."
—Margaret Atwood

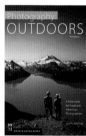

Photography Outdoors, 3rd edition
James Martin
Award-winning photographer shares his tips for getting stunning photographs in exotic settings.

Don't Get Sick, 2nd edition
Buck Tilton and Rick Bennett
A little book that's jam-packed with information on how to avoid health dangers while on the trail

---

www.mountaineersbooks.org